Waterways World
Burton-on-Trent

Published by Waterways World Ltd,
The Well House, High Street, Burton-on-Trent,
Staffordshire DE14 1JQ, England

© Graham Booth 2000

Based on original material by Andy Burnett, and published as the New Inland Boat
Owner's Book in 1995 by Waterway Productions Ltd

This edition first published 2000

British Library Cataloguing In Publication Data
A catalogue record for this book is available from the British Library

ISBN 1 870002 86 5

Design and typesetting by Steve Bellaby
Sketches and diagrams by Andy Burnett and Graham Booth
Colour origination, Derbyshire Colour Services, Alfreton, Derbyshire
Printed and bound in the United Kingdom by Arkle Print Ltd

Inland Boat Owner's Book

WELCOME

Boating for pleasure on Britain's inland waterways has a long tradition, although its tremendous increase over the last forty years is mostly due to the renaissance of the country's narrow canal network. The relaxing effect of canal cruising is legendary. It is so seductive that, after their first hire boat holiday, many new enthusiasts yearn only to acquire their own boat. Then they discover the world of inland boat ownership – long holidays discovering Britain by its back door. . . lazy weekends on a quiet home mooring. . . the conviviality of like-minded owners at boat clubs.

Many find that it takes them over completely, so they abandon the parts of their lives they can no longer stand – their house and sometimes their jobs – to live on the inland waterways. Some then move on to different types of craft – down-sizing to trailable cruisers or taking on enormous Dutch barges; retiring to remote Pennine canals or escaping under continental sunshine. To all of you, *Waterways World* offers the *Inland Boat Owner's Book* – 3rd Edition.

The first *IBOB*, written by Andy Burnett, was published in 1989 and sold out quickly, allowing *WW* to introduce a revised, enlarged and full-colour version in 1995. Like its predecessor, this was serialised in monthly chapters in the magazine, then published in book form. The third edition has been planned, from the outset, as a book. This has enabled me to re-arrange the information in a more logical order than the six, equally sized supplements previously allowed. It is now in five sections, each containing separate chapters.

The first section provides general information about the canal systems of Great Britain, Ireland and the Continent. As well as giving a description of each waterway, it also includes the navigation authority and maximum craft dimensions. It goes on to describe the many different types of inland craft, both steel and glass fibre. Then the running costs of owning a boat, from the licence to annual maintenance, are examined. Finally, it deals with three specific types of boat ownership – shared ownership, residential and trail boating.

The second and third sections cover the purchase of new and secondhand boats. Section two has chapters on the current regulations, the anatomy of a narrowboat shell, engines, electrical systems and cabin equipment. It also has a list of boatbuilders and fitters. Section three tells you what to look for in a secondhand boat and how to go about buying one. Section four deals with the maintenance necessary to protect your investment.

The last section contains appendices including lists of boatbuilders and engines, lists of names and telephone numbers of companies providing useful products and services, a glossary of commonly used waterways terms and a list of licence plate numbers and dates.

Inland Boat Owner's Book

CONTENTS

CHAPTER 1

WHERE THE WATERWAYS ARE

For many *Waterways World* readers, the term 'inland waterway' is likely to conjure up the image of a narrow canal, probably somewhere in the network roughly contained within the London-Manchester-Bristol triangle.

This canal system was a product of the Industrial Revolution of the late eighteenth and early nineteenth centuries. It played a significant role in changing Britain from a mainly agricultural nation into an industrial one. With the arrival of railways, the canal system entered into a gradual commercial decline that resulted in the closure of many artificial navigations. Today, commercial carrying narrowboats make up only a notional part of canal traffic.

The boatable canal system owes much of its survival to epic campaigning by the Inland Waterways Association and to sheer physical labour by associated volunteer bodies over the last forty or so years. By contrast, British Waterways (navigation authority for much of the country's inland waterways) and its Government masters showed remarkably little enthusiasm for maintaining the canal system until the boating boom of the late seventies caused them to realise that this awkward liability might become a decided asset to tourism, leisure and general amenity. Now tourism is so important to the national economy that BW, the Government – and even the European Union – are encouraging the restoration of derelict canals.

However, many of Britain's inland waterways are outside this Midlands-centred network of narrow canals. Boating is established on over 1,000 more miles of UK rivers and canals, offering wide variations of scale, landscape and boating practices (see map on page 2). For the canal-jaded and for newcomers alike, we offer a lightning tour of Britain's inland waterways – conveniently packaged into ten groups:

The 'narrow' system

. . . is made up of some 20 canals, totalling over 900 miles in length and broken up by only slightly fewer locks. While this means that boating can involve almost as much time locking as cruising, the spread of locks is by no means even. Many are concentrated into flights, while several pounds (lengths of canal between locks) are over twenty miles long. Some of the locks are not even narrow but narrow-beam craft – canal cruisers and narrowboats – are almost the only types of craft to be found on these navigations. This part of the system is not just narrow – it is intimate in scale. Visitors from continental waterways marvel at the frequency of small country villages and at the concentrated variation of landscape to be found in both rural and urban settings. Daily progress on these canals may be slow if measured in miles but its effect in mentally unwinding those who travel on them is legendary.

The four major navigations that form (effectively) the dual spinal column of the central system are the Grand Union, Oxford, Shropshire Union and Trent & Mersey canals. Four other canals, although still starting from this narrow system, are untypical in travelling into dramatic hilly settings.

Cropredy on the Oxford Canal.

These are the Macclesfield, Peak Forest and Caldon which creep into the Derbyshire Peaks; and (perhaps more popular than any other) the Llangollen which ventures across the Welsh border into a dramatic mountain setting. Comfortable maximum craft dimensions: 70ft x 6ft 10in. Navigation authority: mainly British Waterways.

The Birmingham Canal Navigations

Virtually a separate system within the 'narrow canal' network, it forms the pelvis of the north-south spinal canals and is the cultural heartland of narrowboat building. While most other canals were built to link existing industrial centres, the Black Country's industry was partly constructed around a unique tangle of main line canals,

The BCN is rich in industrial archaeology.

canal loops, branches and spurs. Much of it has disappeared but over 100 miles remain, connecting an intriguing mix of industrial archaeology, re-insurgent countryside and some dramatic civic rebuilding. Comfortable maximum craft dimensions: 70ft x 6ft 10in. Navigation Authority: British Waterways.

1

Britain's inland waterways

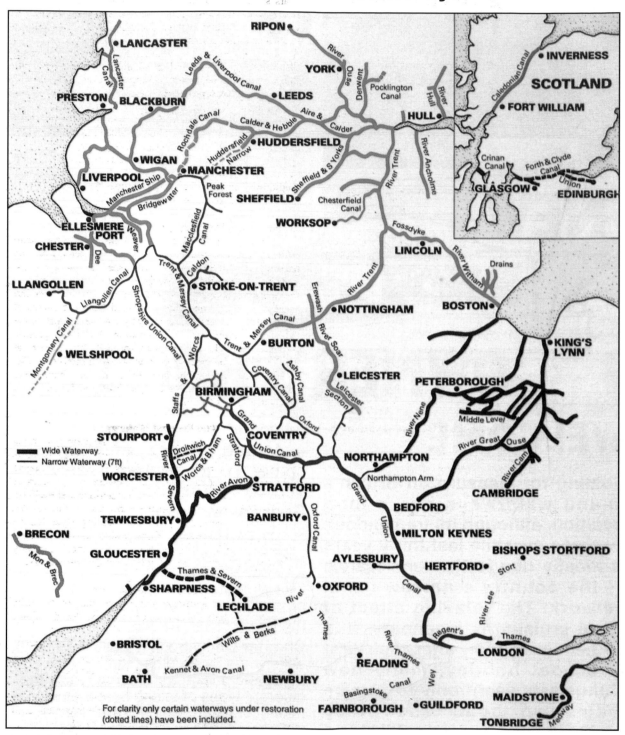

For clarity only certain waterways under restoration (dotted lines) have been included.

Waterways of the East Midlands and North

. . . make up a system of 500 miles and 250 locks that allows wide-beam craft to travel from Market Harborough to York and from Boston to Liverpool. It connects with the narrow system via the river Trent in the east and via the Bridgwater Canal in the west. The 500 miles presently consist of 13 navigations which are widely disparate although most are wider and deeper than canals of the central system. Those in the East Midlands and East Yorkshire include a high percentage of rivers on which glass-fibre craft, generally with better hull performance, rival narrowboats for popularity. Although they too are accessible to wide-beam craft, the Pennine waterways appear to have been largely taken over by narrowboats (see also 'Forthcoming Features' below). Terrain in this system varies from the flatlands of the lower Trent to the rolling

A variety of boats at Knottingley on the Aire & Calder.

grandeur of the Yorkshire Dales. Comfortable maximum craft dimensions: 60ft x 14ft (to pass through Leeds & Liverpool Canal), 57ft 6in x 14ft (to pass through Calder & Hebble Navigation). Navigation authority: mainly British Waterways.

Southern waterways

The rivers Thames, Wey, Lee & Stort, the Basingstoke Canal, and the Kennet & Avon Canal can be identified as a loose network totalling 300 navigable miles. The Thames (124 non-tidal miles, 44 locks) is the country's most famous river. It is very posh towards its lower end where expensive multi-storey seagoing craft, ungainly forward-steering hire cruisers and varnished launches figure

Henley-on-Thames.

strongly among the huge variety of craft to be seen. Here, narrowboats are sometimes viewed with apprehension for the damage they might inflict on those immaculate hulls. However, towards its upper reaches and along the rivers that join it, boating is on a more comfortable scale. There, narrowboats are on the increase but outboard-powered glass-fibre canal cruisers are particularly popular because they deliver boaty lines at budget prices.

The Wey, heading southwards into Surrey, and the rivers Lee and Stort, northwards into Essex, add a further 60 miles and 50 locks. The Basingstoke Canal, entered from the river Wey, adds a further 32 miles and 29 locks.

After completing its forty-year restoration in 1990, the Kennet & Avon Canal runs from the River Thames at Reading for 86 miles, through 104 locks, to Bristol. Through navigation has not always been easy in the years since restoration – but is improving. On its way to Bristol's exotic waterfront, the K&A passes through a variety of attractive settings, including the rolling Vale of Pewsey and dramatic hillsides near Bath.

Access to the Thames from the central canal system is by Oxford and London. For wide-beam craft stable enough to cope with the upper reaches of the Bristol Channel, the K&A provides access to the River Severn via the Gloucester & Sharpness Canal. That passage is not recommended for narrowboats without a pilot and appropriate equipment. Comfortable maximum craft dimensions: 72ft x 13ft 10in (inc Basingstoke).

Navigation authorities: Environment Agency (Thames), National Trust (Wey), Basingstoke Canal Authority, (Basingstoke Canal), British Waterways (rivers Lee and Stort, Kennet & Avon Canal).

The rivers Severn and Avon

. . . offer together 100 miles of wide-beam cruising with just 24 locks. the Severn is entered from the narrow canals at Stourport or Worcester and runs vigorous, wide and high-sided to Gloucester where it is canalised to the sea lock at Sharpness. The Avon, a smaller river but volatile in flood conditions, is joined from the canals at Stratford. It was restored, entirely by volunteer effort, in the fifties and sixties and the navigation now winds prettily through the Vale of Evesham to meet the Severn at Tewkesbury. Comfortable maximum craft dimensions: 70ft x 13ft 6in. Navigation authorities: British Waterways (Severn), Upper Avon Navigation Trust and Lower Avon Navigation Trust (Avon)

The Fenland Waterways

. . . can only be entered from the main system via the river Nene near Northampton. The boat population of its 250 wide-beam miles and 60 locks is relatively sparse although its associated rivers have several scenic sections beyond Northampton and towards Cambridge and Bedford. The Fens themselves are to the north-east of this region. Their vast flatness and the local building style lend a slightly Dutch character. Comfortable maximum craft dimensions: 70ft x 10ft 6in. Navigation authority: mainly Environment Agency and Middle Level Commissioners.

Forthcoming attractions

Three significant canals are due to be fully re-opened to the main network in the first decade of this century.

Part of the Rochdale Canal's 33 miles has already been reconnected to the Yorkshire waterways. Craft will be able to climb into wonderful Pennine landscapes – but not descend to the Manchester end for several more years. When fully re-opened the 92-lock Rochdale will create one of three new Pennine circuits. Comfortable maximum craft dimensions: 57ft 6in x 14ft (dictated by the adjoining Calder & Hebble Navigation). The other canals from which the circuits will be permutated are the existing Leeds & Liverpool, and the 20 mile/74 lock Huddersfield Narrow Canal – which also ends in Manchester, and is due for re-opening in the spring of 2001. HNC's comfortable maximum craft dimensions: 70ft x 6ft 10ins.

Ten isolated miles of the Montgomery Canal are now open to trailable boats and narrowboats can venture from Welsh Frankton to Queen's Head. When fully re-opened, it will connect the Llangollen Canal to Newtown in mid-Wales, nearly 50 miles distant. Comfortable maximum craft dimensions: 70ft x 6ft 10ins.

Detached canals

For uncongested boating through stunning landscapes, the Monmouthshire & Brecon Canal is unbeatable. It winds narrow and shallow for 33 miles with a flight of 6 locks, often clinging to the flanks of the Brecon Beacons. Comfortable maximum craft dimensions: 44ft 3ins x 8ft 6in. Navigation authority: British Waterways.

The Lancaster Canal wanders northwards from Preston, with the M6 motorway shadowing it from a distance until it actually cuts it off at its present terminus near Carnforth. Before amputation, the canal reached right to Kendal in the Lake District. However its remaining 45 miles still take in the city of Lancaster and a three mile spur drops via the canal's only 7 locks to the coast at Glasson Dock. Comfortable maximum craft dimensions: 72ft x 14ft 6in. Navigation authority: British Waterways.

The Broads

Of the waterways that are not connected to the central canal system, the Broads form the largest group. The 'broads' themselves are man-made lagoons, frequently of sailable size, connected by winding rivers. For Broads motor cruising, the choice ranges between wide hire-style cruisers (usually with forward or centre cockpits), pseudo-coastal craft and budget-priced canal cruisers. The most significant restriction is height – many large Broads cruisers are specially designed to pass under a number of awkwardly low bridges. Like the Thames (and the canals for that

Cruising on the Norfolk Broads.

matter), the most popular parts of the Broads can be congested in high season. However, few of the summer visitors penetrate all of the system's 127 picturesque and lock-free miles. Navigation authority: Broads Authority.

The Caledonian Canal

Scotland's principal inland waterway (and probably Britain's most awesome) is the Caledonian Canal. Its 60 miles, 29 locks and numerous swing bridges take craft of small ship size from the west coast to the east. For much of the distance, it has the Scottish Highlands for a backdrop and it takes in the lochs Ness (22 miles long), Oich and Lochy. Navigation authority: British Waterways.

Majestic scenery on the Caledonian Canal.

Ireland's waterways

Ireland offers four impressive waterways – and a new link. The Grand Canal traverses the country from east to west. The river Barrow spurs off from it to the south. The River Shannon wanders north from the west coast, in and out of loughs in a decidedly Irish fashion. Lough Erne lies on the border with Northern Ireland and was connected with the Shannon by the new Shannon-Erne Waterway in 1994.

European waterways

The ambition of many experienced inland boaters is to sample European waterways – for a holiday, for a season's cruising, or perhaps for retirement under the continental sun. A slipway in northern France is, after all, now only a decent morning's drive from London with a trailable boat. Streethay Wharf's Ray Bowern (see Appendix 4) specialises in transporting narrowboats by road to Euro waterways and back. The UK canal industry's simple construction techniques adapt readily to building inexpensive wide barges as floating gîtes.

The connected network of European waterways extends from Poland and from the Black Sea to the south of France. The most readily accessible parts (in bureaucratic as well as geographic terms) are in Holland, Belgium and France.

The Dutch have an enviable inland boating tradition, based on a large mileage of wide canals and lakes and on barges, variously elegant and chubby, and trim steel cruisers. France's network of waterways is extensive and blessed with fine landscapes, wines and food. Surprisingly, leisure boating in France has been popular for less than twenty years. The Belgian waterways? They connect France and Holland.

European countries have individual craft licensing and navigational conditions. Depending on the size and speed of boat they may demand a certificate of competence in boat handling. They may also require sight of ship's registration papers on its temporary importation. The Royal Yachting Association (see Appendix 4) publishes notes for foreign-going boaters, runs internationally recognised handling courses, and can advise on detailed questions – particularly if you join the RYA.

Narrowboats should not attempt even the shortest Channel crossing. Wide-beam inland craft may be suitable for calm-sea crossings, subject to assessment by a marine surveyor.

The French waterways.

How wide, how long, how deep, how high?

The comfortable maximum craft dimensions quoted for each area of waterway is the figure that allows navigation anywhere. However, some parts of those areas may allow larger craft. The Grand Union Canal (part of the 'narrow' system) was built to take boats up to 14ft 6in wide, although British Waterways does not encourage other than narrow-beam boats.

'Narrow-beam' conventionally means 6ft 10in wide, although traditional working boats were built to a beam of 7ft and those remaining afloat today manage to squeeze through almost, but not all narrow locks. Problems are likely to occur first on the Staffs & Worcs, Llangollen and southern Stratford canals. But all these are accessible if your ageing boat has not spread beyond an exact 7ft.

Even if your length and beam fit the maxima listed, do not blithely assume that your boat can navigate a particular waterway. The river Stort, for instance, accepts 85ft length x 13ft 3in beam – but limits headroom to 5ft 9in, less than the minimum height of any Dutch barge. Few conventional narrowboats stand more than 6ft above water, with full water tanks. The norm is around 5ft 8in, which should allow passage (just about) everywhere.

The question of underwater draught still arouses the ire of traditionalists. They suggest that resorting to shallow draughts (say less than 2ft 0in on a flat-bottomed narrowboat) causes shallow canal sections to silt from a channel to a saucer shape. They also make the more doubtful point that reducing draughts encourages British Waterways to economise in its dredging operations, setting up a process of continually diminishing draughts. The draught of the average leisure narrowboat has been established at around 1ft 10in for the last thirty years – and

does not look set to reduce any. This is the figure that has proved to be consistent with the propeller diameter of popular engines, with stability and with allowing comfortable accommodation proportions. All else being equal, vee-bottomed craft can draw slightly more because their keels make only point contact with obstructions and their chines are relatively shallow for coming alongside banks in shelving water.

'Full-length' on the main canal network is conventionally taken as 70ft – this can be argued up to 71ft 6in (including fenders). Looking beyond the narrow system, the most significant length limits are those of the Leeds & Liverpool Canal and the Calder & Hebble Navigation (60ft and 57ft 6in). These roughly coincide with the popular maximum length for narrowboats (around 60ft – the number built longer than that is relatively small). Given the certain popularity of the restored Pennine canals and associated circuits in less than ten years from the date of writing, your narrowboat may have limited market appeal then if it does not fit.

More detailed information on dimensions (including maximum draughts and heights) can be found from:

• *Inland Waterways of Great Britain* by Jane Cumberlidge.

• Cruising guides for individual waterways (mainly published by *Waterways World* and by *Nicholsons*).

• and, for reliable up-to-date figures, local waterways authority personnel. (Addresses of regional offices are shown in *Waterways World's Canalmanac* – published as part of the new *Waterways World Annual*, every January).

CHAPTER 2

TYPES OF INLAND BOATS

Britain's varied waterways and buyers' tastes and pockets are suited by a range of different boat types. Of these, it is the narrowboat that tends to come into the mind first – although it is an ungainly craft on all but narrow canals and its value-for-money reputation is only relative to other types of boat – a reasonable quality, young, medium-length narrowboat can cost as much as two new family cars. So, if your priority isn't regular long-distance canal cruising, or your budget is restricted, the merits of other craft deserve consideration. But first: narrowboats.

Narrowboats

A narrowboat (note that this special type is defined by a single word and that it is only a 'long boat' in the river Severn area and definitely not a 'barge' anywhere) might be more comprehensively named a tall-narrow-shallow-boat. It is designed to fit the minimum dimensions of the locks on the narrow canal system snugly, in order to provide maximum accommodation.

Consequently, it is characteristically a boxy vessel both in appearance and hull performance. The bottom is usually flat and hull sides are approximately (but seldom completely) perpendicular. Cabin sides have slightly more tumblehome (lean-in) to avoid catching on bridge holes without compromising internal airiness. The

benefits their second-hand values. This is not to say that steel is always trouble-free. Any hull over, say, five years old may be liable to severe corrosion below the waterline, if not correctly fitted-out and maintained.

What makes narrowboats so popular? They are extremely sturdy, basically durable, competitively priced compared to other large craft types – and extremely comfortable. The interior of a large modern private craft, with permanent double bed, armchairs and solid fuel stove, is more akin to a slow-moving cottage than a real boat.

Despite their size and weight (between seven and seventeen tons for the most popular 35ft to 60ft length range), narrowboats are surprisingly easy to handle. The tiller is simple and direct and the steerer has a commanding view of his/her vessel's progress into the tightest spots. Handling is usually predictable – all that weight and square water-gripping hull sides create considerable inertia. This also means that stopping is slower than in other craft. Misjudged arrivals rarely cause any damage to heavily protected narrowboats, although it does promote a "No, after you" politeness from glass-fibre boat owners at locks.

Narrowboats fall into two basic styles – cruiser and traditional. The former is functional and unpretentious, with engine under an open aft cockpit well of six to nine feet in length. Traditional style at its crudest simply means

A traditional style narrowboat.

A cruiser style narrowboat has a longer rear deck.

average example has decks at bow and stern, is steered by tiller rather than wheel and is propelled at a modest but dignified speed by an inboard diesel engine.

Although many working narrowboats were constructed of timber and/or riveted iron, the modern leisure version is built of welded mild steel. In the seventies, builders combined steel hulls with various types of superstructure – traditional masonite (a sort of oil-tempered hardboard), ply, aluminium on ply, glass-fibre on ply, moulded glass-fibre – and steel. Today almost every narrowboat is built of steel, with a tendency to make every external detail – door skins, hatch slides, locker lids – in that material. While the number of ply and glass-fibre-topped narrowboats available second-hand should provide several more years of service, the maintenance of steel superstructures is regarded as less complicated and this

a shorter aft deck so that the steerer stands inside the aft cabin door. Enhancements include a rise in the deck-line towards the bow and stern (matched by a lift along the aft cabin), raised cants (upstands) around forward and aft decks, solid (rather than raised) handrail along the cabin edge and a triangular cratchboard with 'canvas' cover over the forward cockpit. The accoutrements of true trad-style are based on a rigid convention – not least in the painted livery and decorative details that are applied. Some enthusiasts include in their accommodation a faithful copy of the thirteen feet of original boatman's cabin and engine room – although this does not always make the most space-effective use of the available length.

Fitting a cabin over what would be the hold in a working boat detracts from the traditional elevation. Some feel that building on trad tug lines (many of which had long forward cabins) overcomes this. Replica tugs normally carry portholes rather than windows on their cabin sides which makes them a better bet against vandalism and their low deck lines (the originals had to be deep draughted to swing very big props for best towing power) are seen as particularly stylish. However, long forward 'tug' decks also reduce space-effectiveness.

Other than keeping the steerer's feet warm and turning the engine compartment into a useful utility room,

The rear deck of a semi-traditional narrowboat.

ordinary trad-style has no undisputable advantages over cruiser-style. Nevertheless it is more popular and therefore tends to fare better in terms of resale depreciation. Those who prefer a party-sized aft well might consider a semi-traditional stern where, in elevation, the boat has all the attributes of true trad but, in plan, its rear deck can be seen to extend forward inside the cabin sides.

Inspection launches & barges
Several narrowboat builders have attempted to offer their customers a more imaginative product by copying the style of inspection launches. The originals were built, on the lines of elegant Thames launches, to carry senior canal company officials around their watery domains in comfort. Replicas have varied from mildly modified narrowboats to the all-steel masterpieces created by Sagar Marine. Balliol Fowden of Anglo-European Marine followed a different track by altering Dutch barge proportions to create a narrow beamer with narrowboat standards of accommodation and stylish, shiplike lines – which include all-weather wheelhouse steering.

Ex-working boats
If you need much introduction to ex-working boats, you should probably steer clear of them – they are not for the

An inspection launch.

A narrow beam boat with the lines of a Dutch barge.

inexperienced buyer, particularly if he/she is tempted by the idea of a large boat for little money. For a more detailed look at the various types of working boats, see Chapter 16.

Compared to their smoothly developed bows and sterns and, occasionally, rounded chines, even the best modern hulls are crudely made. At correct canal speeds this isn't too important but the mountainous waves and deep troughs created by a modern narrowboat on rivers at maximum six or so miles an hour contrast sadly with the cleaner wakes of older working boats.

Many working craft have been converted to leisure use, with original boatmans cabin and engine room extended the full length of the hold. Not a few of these conversions were done in the sixties and seventies and are

Ex-working boats are very attractive but require a lot of maintenance.

themselves showing their age. Most are fitted with contemporary engines – large, slow-revving and indestructible. Although the converted working boat was seen, until fairly recently, as a cheap way to get afloat, many are being acquired by committed traditionalists. This type of owner is generally handy at even heavy maintenance tasks or has the funds available to pay for the boat to be kept in cherished condition. He/she tends to remove cabin conversions and restore the craft back to its original condition.

If you are adamant that you, as a first-timer, want to start with the real thing, one or two companies may be able to find craft to renovate and convert to a 'new' standard. Suitable unconverted boats are now in short supply and these boatyards are now reluctant to tamper further with history by putting cabins on craft with

This replica working boat has a closed, 'tug' style front deck.

Narrow beam glass fibre cruisers are equally at home on rivers and canals.

recognised ancestry. They prefer to convert anonymous craft (like those used as 'day boats' around Birmingham) or to redo existing conversions. And, increasingly, the real specialists will build new, very close replicas.

Mini-narrowboats

Springer Engineering invented the mini-narrowboat with its 20ft Water Bug in the mid-eighties. This model, and a 23ft version, were built in large numbers, so are readily available secondhand as starter boats. The Water Bug, not presently produced, had a pronounced vee bottom and most examples were outboard-powered. Consequently it tended to roll, and all-steel construction made it heavier than glass-fibre competitors – thus less easy to tow by road, and harder for the relatively small outboard to push through water. Steel mini-narrowboats are still built by other manufacturers but most are inboard powered and flat-bottomed.

Mini-narrowboats offer enjoyable boating and some are towable.

In the early nineties, Sea Otter started to produce a similar sized boat but built in aluminium. It now builds in two lengths – 26ft and 30ft. The boats are trailable by 4 x 4 off-roaders and use canal water as ballast, releasing it as they are recovered on the trailer. Both boats offer a remarkable amount of internal space for their length and are powered by inboard diesel engines.

Canal cruisers

The term 'canal cruiser' is given to any craft that can simply do that – cruise canals – but is not a narrowboat. Most are of glass-fibre construction with wheel steering from aft, centre or forward cockpits. Unlike most narrowboats, these cockpits are civilised by a drop-down wheelhouse shelter and/or folding pram canopy. Even so, totally enclosed cruising in wet weather is seldom possible because of the lack of windscreen wipers. Propulsion is by outboard motor,

inboard diesel engine or – much less desirably – by inboard petrol engine (the numbers of the last gradually dwindle as a few blow up each year).

These days the name 'canal cruiser' may be a misnomer when applied to many new glass-fibre versions. Most are not styled primarily for the rough-and-tumble of bridge and lock work. Several builders have developed designs from the seventies into pocket motor cruisers for river cruising – the 6ft 10in beam remains as a residual benefit.

However, second-hand glass-fibre canal cruisers, from which the shine has been removed from both hull finish and resale value, fill an important canal market gap. With slab sides and good headroom, they often provide enough space and equipment for extended canal cruises and their prices fall well below those of the cheapest narrowboats. You can pick up a middle-aged but basically sound 25ft/four-berth glass-fibre canal cruiser for as little as £5,000.

Owners of better protected canal cruisers may argue that polishing out scratches and tar marks is less onerous than having to repaint narrowboat hulls bi-annually; that a 25-footer weighs half as much as a comparable narrowboat so is easier to manhandle; that vulnerability to wind is balanced by increased manoeuvrability; that an undercover helm is more comfortable than a tiller in bad weather; and that narrowboats don't look like real boats anyway …

Narrowboaters will counter with many arguments, the most telling of which is that, in a collision between a glass-fibre boat and a steel one, only the latter will emerge unscathed. And, ultimately, glass-fibre is not maintenance-free; hulls (particularly those moulded in less than perfect conditions) are liable over many years to be gradually afflicted with osmosis, a sort of acne that can eventually destroy the glass-fibre surface, if not treated. However, early osmosis is easily identified and not difficult to halt.

Until a few years ago standard cabin specifications were basic but hot & cold water systems, showers, fridges and space heating are not unusual in younger canal cruisers. The majority of glass-fibre canal cruisers are powered by four-stroke outboard motors – chosen because they are less temperamental and more economical than two-strokes at canal speeds.

Another notable benefit of this type of engine is its lack of noise. In many cruiser applications, it is the quietest form of propulsion available – as quiet as some electric installations. For many years, inland owners have had to chose from three Honda and one Yamaha four-stroke models. Nowadays, there are more manufacturers of four-stroke outboards than there are of canal cruisers.

Petrol-powered outboards have two disadvantages. Until 1999, the Boat Safety Scheme did not allow gas fridges to be used on boats with inboard or outboard petrol engines (after that date, conventionally flued gas fridges were effectively banned on all new boats by British Standard 5482 Part 3). Outboards also lack the electric power output of alternator-equipped inboard engines. For these reasons, inboard diesel engines (though noisier and more expensive to buy) are generally considered more desirable. The favoured inboard installation of the seventies used a steerable outdrive leg. Spares for the two most popular outdrives are still available, and this type of drive may well return to popularity, as one, the Enfield outdrive, is now in the hands of a canal-oriented company (Bob Knowles Plant Services) and the latest generation of tiny Japanese diesels are well suited to canal cruisers. Unless it is an essential element in a vintage boat, *IBOB* can find nothing to recommend any inboard petrol engine.

Wide-beam cruisers

Although the majority of inland waterways are not 'narrow', few of the wide ones are heavily populated with boats. The two that are are the Thames and Broads. The variety of craft throughout the latter is relatively limited by low bridges but the Thames is inhabited by almost every type of craft imaginable. Some owners regard river cruising as a substitute for sea-going. Not a few flybridge cruisers with aggressive lines and powerful twin engines can be seen as far up as Oxford but they are not at their most comfortable when moving sedately in confined waters.

The current model most readily identified as pure river cruiser is Viking's 26, which is budget-priced by Thames standards and conservatively styled by comparison with most off-shore aspirants. It is primarily designed for propulsion by outboard motor and is available in 20, 22 and 24-foot lengths. Viking has now been joined in this market by the 21ft Shetland Four plus Two. Current inboard river cruisers with shaft driven propellers and responsive rudder steering include the Capriole 740 and 900, the Shetland 27 and the Shadow 26.

A wide beam cruiser.

The secondhand river market yields plenty of elderly Seamaster, Madeira/Elysian, and Freeman glass fibre cruisers – all with good keels and rudder steering. With suitable engines and equipment, these can be suitable for coast hopping but are really happiest on rivers. Of the three defunct makes, Freeman is most associated with the Thames. Its conservative lines and walnut veneered, heavily chromed interiors were styled as floating limousines.

Further down-market but still in production – and more genuine inland and coastal all-rounders – are Hardy motor cruisers. Although models as short as 18ft are built, none are narrow beam. However, several are moulded with good keels and all have handsome workmanlike lines and sturdy detailing – even to a rope fender encircling the hull.

The Thames has its own traditional type – the launch. Almost all are of varnished timber and are expensive both to buy and maintain. Narrow-beam inspection launches are described under 'Narrowboats' but several companies now offer glass fibre hulled launches, with traditionally clean swimming lines.

The Broads industry produces an awesome variety of inland cruisers – too many to describe. Almost all are geared to the hire industry. Many tend to aggressive styling but combine that with excellent low speed handling and low-wash hulls. Styles range from forward steerers (with an inherent tail-wags-dog tendency when seen from the stern) to luxury cruisers with dual steering stations.

Broads cruisers generally do not tend to be floating cottages in the way that 'wide-beam narrowboats' (with full insulation and solid fuel stoves) can be. This all-steel seeming paradox has most of the virtues of the conventional canal narrowboat and it balances the disadvantage of not being able to pass through narrow locks with a staggering increase in flat-floored space. Widening beam from 6ft 10in by say 50% to 10ft 6in increases inside space by a much greater proportion – from 5ft 8in to 9ft 4in between cabin sides. If you are looking for a cottage in the Yorkshire Dales, near Stratford, Bath or Lancaster, even a new wide-beamer is competitively priced and its tiller, although open to the weather, allows better handling than any forward steerer. Wide narrowboats are on record as having made channel crossings to reach continental waterways. For that purpose the shell needs beefed-up framing, gussets between bottom and hull side frames and, preferably, a vee-shaped (rather than flat) bottom with decently deep keelson. If more than a one-time crossing is planned, the craft should be redesigned as a coastal vessel rather than a modified narrowboat.

The Dutch offer two useful types of wide beam boat – both metal-built. Dutch steel cruisers tend to be built of welded steel and follow a conservative line in styling. Traditional Dutch working barges were built in several styles. The round-cheeked tjalk is basically not as spacious as the luxemotor – the style most often imported into this country. Where the wide-beam narrowboat's increased girth worsens its boxiness, the average luxemotor or steilsteven is a superb craft with its powerful straight stem, elegant re-entrant counter, curving deckline and ship's wheelhouse. Although all are incredibly old by our narrowboat standards (sixty years is common), Dutch barges seem to survive well. Apart from timber fold-down wheelhouses, their

A small Dutch barge used as a residential boat.

British short, wide barge.

superstructures are steel and their hulls (frequently of riveted iron or steel) are flat-bottomed with rounded chines (the joint between bottom and side). However, in the most attractive size range (50ft to 80ft x 11ft to 14ft), availability is now dwindling and prices rising. Potential buys also need careful inspection because of their age and (for us) unusual construction. Although, in competent hands, they are safe for calm North Sea crossings, luxemotors are not sea-kindly craft.

Finally, there is yet another paradox (in addition to the narrow-beam Dutch barge, and the wide-beam narrowboat) – the British Dutch barge. Purpose-built versions can be more convenient and space-effective by altering deck heights (and thus window eye-line) and by shifting and/or reducing the engine room. The mini-Dutch barge (say 45ft x 10ft) also becomes possible. However, as in modern narrowboats, the result is unlikely to be as subtle as the originals, either above or below the waterline.

The interiors of inland boats vary as much as their exteriors.

CHAPTER 3

THE COSTS OF OWNERSHIP

What will boat ownership cost you? Just finding the right craft could involve you in spending several hundred pounds – then there are the running costs. This chapter looks at them in detail.

The buying process

A few lucky owners are clear in their mind about who will build their next boat but most, particularly first timers, are faced by a bewildering list of names. Our 'Who's Who' feature in Chapter 9 may help a little, our list of builders and fitters-out in Appendix 1 should shorten your list. You might also avoid some wasted miles by inspecting the different makes on display at major inland boat shows. Ultimately, there is no substitute for driving to different boat yards. Only this first-hand experience will quickly teach you as much about the boat as you can realistically expect.

The problem is compounded, with secondhand craft, by the names of builders from the past and by the additional variables of condition and age. Brokers, increasingly, try to bring boats together so that potential buyers can view a selection in their yards. But it's the private ads from remote canals that yield 'one nervous owner, never been through a lock' boats. So, the first cost of buying could be around 500 miles in your car. At, say, 25 pence per mile, that's £125.

If the boat is to be a new one, you may be involved with a similar mileage cost in keeping an eye on the builder during construction. If buying secondhand, you will almost certainly incur survey costs. Only the most knowledgeable or careless buyer does not employ a specialised inland waterways surveyor to inspect the proposed purchase in and out of water. A typical survey cost is £250 plus about £100 for pulling the boat out. This survey, incidentally, is not the same as an inspection for British Waterways/Environment Agency Boat Safety Certificate or a condition report for obtaining a marine mortgage. Neither of those is nearly so detailed as a full survey for purchase.

Surveyors are adept at finding sufficient faults to reduce the sale price by more than their fees but, equally, the survey may report so many faults or so low a value that you are frightened from the purchase. You have to put that £350 down to experience and prepare yourself to spend the same amount in seeking the next boat. . . and perhaps the one after that. When you do agree to buy that secondhand boat, you will almost certainly follow the surveyor's good advice to re-black the hull, replace sacrificial anodes – even grit blast the underwater steelwork.

And you probably will not stop there. Many owners, fired with initial enthusiasm, undertake refurbishments and improvements that they would not bother to contemplate a few months later. Perhaps this should be budgeted for as a fair and proper cost, to compensate for the inadequate maintenance that a large proportion of boats suffer when their owners lose interest (typically in years two and three, before selling in year four to indulge their new passion for. . . something else).

The indirect costs of buying are likely to total at least £450, or, with some allowance for post-purchase flights of enthusiasm, probably nearer £1,000.

Depreciation

Once you have bought your boat, what will happen to the value of your investment? As a basic rule, the higher the price of the boat, the more it will depreciate. A new £85,000 narrowboat could lose 25% of its value in the first year (almost anyone with that sort of budget will only settle for a boat that meets their exact needs so is not likely to accept a second-hand craft built to someone else's specification).

At the other end of the market, an elderly £2,500 Dawncraft Dandy is not likely to depreciate much further. In the mid-range – youngish 45ft to 55ft narrowboats between £20,000 and £30,000 – depreciation depends on market conditions. The second-hand market took off in the 'boom & bust' late eighties and these boats gained value, in real terms. The late nineties and early 2000s also saw a sellers' market but the greater number of presentable boats on the system ensured that prices stayed more level.

Running costs

Arguably the more you use your boat, the less it costs to keep. An unvisited boat is likely to attract mustiness and damp and steel hulls seem to corrode faster when tied up than under way! Many hire narrowboats are not fitted with sacrificial anodes as they seem to corrode less than private craft, presumably because they spend so much time on the move.

A large proportion of running costs are indirect – they have to be met whether the boat is used or not. The five identifiable cost groups are:

● Licence: most inland owners have to license their boats with British Waterways or with the Environment Agency, even when the craft is just tied up afloat (as during winter).

● Insurance: your boat must be covered by third party insurance, against the risk of damage to others, and, given the time it is left exposed alone to the elements and vandals, it really needs comprehensive cover.

● Moorings: probably the largest single item of cost – and the most variable. You might pay £200 a year to drive your narrowboat's mooring stakes into a farmer's field; or £3,000 for a berth in London's dockland. More typically, a 50ft narrowboat would cost about £1,000 to £1,250 to moor in a Midlands marina.

● Maintenance: hauling out of water every two or three years, repainting, engine services – those are just some of the scheduled maintenance items. You must also budget over, say, three years for unexpected costs, like a failed alternator, water pump or cooker. And boats are inspected for a Boat Safety Certificate every four years, often involving gas system update, some rewiring, new flexible fuel lines ... Maintenance is discussed in detail in Chapter 22.

● Fuel: surprisingly little for inboard diesel engines and small four-stroke petrol outboards. Unusually, manufacturers' brochure figures are likely to be more pessimistic that those you achieve, probably because inland engines rarely work hard.

Licences

Not unreasonably, the various navigation authorities that run Britain's inland waterways ask boat owners to make a contribution to their upkeep in the form of a licence. There are several dozen authorities but the vast majority of craft on the country's connected waterway system will be licensed with one of two: British Waterways (most rivers and canals including the 'narrow' canal network) and the Environment Agency (covering the non-tidal Thames, Fenland and associated waterways).

British Waterways issues private craft licences for canal & river use and for river use only. Opting for river use saves about 40%. Licences are also issued for categories other than private cruising such as houseboats, hire/trip/hotel boats, commercial carrying craft, and 'multi-user' boats (as in shared ownership). Licences for houseboats used to be higher than for pleasure boats but 3 years of inflation-plus-10% rises for pleasure craft licences mean they are now the same. The other categories, like multi-user and hire boats, are charged at a higher rate. BW has proposed a high-intensity cruising licence for continuously cruising private boaters but, as yet, has not managed to implement it.

A range of discounts is offered in most categories. One, 10% for payment before the licence starts, applies widely. Then there is 25% for battery-powered boats and 10% for accepted historic boats. If you managed to qualify for all three, they would reduce a £240 licence to £145.80.

Short term licences are also available – for seven days and for one month – which are mainly taken up by visitors from waterways of other authorities. Boaters wanting to make more substantial use of both BW and EA waters can now obtain a 'Gold' licence. This costs about 25% more than the standard BW licence with the prompt payment discount.

Several popular cruising routes involve passage through the waterways of yet other authorities. The Bridgewater Canal (owned by the Manchester Ship Canal Company) links BW's Leeds & Liverpool Canal with its Trent & Mersey Canal. BW-licensed craft can remain on the Bridgewater for up to seven days without charge.

Cruising the Cheshire Ring takes in a single mile and nine locks in Manchester owned by the Rochdale Canal Company which makes a charge for the passage through. The Avon Ring involves the Warwickshire Avon – rescued and thus administered by the Lower Avon and Upper Avon navigation trusts, who also make their own joint visitor's charge.

Insurance

The investment in your boat – usually a higher figure than for a car, and sometimes as much as for a small house – needs protection. One of the attractions of inland waterways cruising is that it is not hazardous. But even this tranquil pastime has its risks. Craft sink (even a sinking in 3ft of water can cost thousands of pounds to repair), are broken into, catch fire, suffer damage by storm, frost or collision. Then crew slip, vandals hurl, rodents gnaw, cowboys bodge. . . The further worry is that this valuable asset lies far away, unchecked for weeks at a time. The protection and reassurance you need is provided by sound insurance.

The company that insures your car or house may be the same that covers your boat. But if you approach that company direct, it will probably be unable to assess the risk,

To visit this lively rally at Evesham on the river Avon, BW licence holders would need one, or possibly two, additional licences.

and consequent premium. The risk needs to be appraised by a specialist underwriter. For every underwriter concerned with inland waterways craft, there are approximately ten who deal mainly with the yacht business. If you seek cover from the latter, they may well offer an inappropriate and needlessly expensive policy.

I recently decided to test the market when re-insuring *Rome*, the subject of the *Narrowboat Builder's Book* 3rd Edition which is the companion volume to this book. I approached my existing insurer plus nine others listed in Appendix 4. The following paragraphs contain some observations on the marine insurance business in general and specific comments on some of the companies I approached.

Valuation. Unlike car insurance, most marine policies will pay out the full 'agreed' value of the craft in the event of a total loss. For this reason, it is important that the sum reasonably reflects the value of the boat.

If the boat is new or has been recently bought second hand, the value is the amount you paid. Boats that are bought as shells or sailaways and fitted out by their owners are insured using special policies in which the amount insured increases as the work proceeds. If you already own the boat and want to change insurers, things are not quite so straight forward.

Some of the companies I approached were happy to accept the present insured value of my boat but, when I queried the point, others wanted it confirmed by a surveyor's valuation even though this was not mentioned in the quotation. A valuation can cost anything from £50 to £150 which is bearable if you intend staying with the new insurer for a long time but is a strong disincentive to switching companies too frequently.

Once a value has been agreed, it is not normal for the insurer to ask for it to be changed as the years roll by. In times of low inflation and where no improvements to the boat are carried out, this works in the owner's favour but, if

Disaster can strike boats of all sizes.

the reverse conditions apply, it could be advantageous to have the boat revalued periodically.

Total losses are, thankfully, rare but, if the worst should happen and the cost of repairing the boat is greater than the agreed value, the insurer pays out that sum and takes what is left of the boat. It is then up to the owner whether he 'buys back' the boat from the insurer and tries to get the work done more cheaply or goes off and buys another boat. The cost of salvaging is not normally deducted from the agreed value.

Drewe Insurance is unusual in using the 'market' value when dealing with a claim. In the event of a total loss, an assessor values the boat at that time, regardless of the amount for which it is insured. In this case, the insurer did not insist on a valuation but advised me to consider having one done to avoid paying premiums based on too high an amount.

Incidentally, another way in which marine and car policies differ is that there is no 'period of grace' for boats so make sure you pay up before the old policy expires.

No-Claim Bonus. Most companies allow you a no-claim bonus (NCB) which is generally 5% a year up to a maximum of between 20% and 40%. It is possible to transfer your existing NCB provided you have a renewal notice to prove how much you have earned. Michael Stimpson offers the highest maximum NCB to existing clients but proposed to start me at 25%. He is the only one to offer a protected NCB whereby a single claim pushes you two years down the scale rather than taking you right back to the start. Newton Crum does not offer an NCB but said that my previous clean record had been taken into account when calculating the premium (which compared well with those that were discounted). One advantage of this arrangement is that, since you don't have an NCB, you can't lose it.

Third party claims. British Waterways requires boaters to hold a minimum of £1M third party cover but some insurers feel that this is insufficient and have increased their cover to £2M. In order to make comparisons easier, I asked all companies to quote on this basis.

Voluntary excess. This is the amount you agree to pay towards the cost of each claim and is meant to dissuade you from making claims for trivial amounts. As an incentive to accept a higher excess (or as a sweetener if it is compulsory), insurers offer a lower premium. The 2 companies that quoted on both my excess options wanted £30 to £35 more for a policy with a £50 excess than one with £100.

Personal effects. I have never had personal effects cover, assuming that any such items that I took on holiday were covered by the All Risks section of my house contents insurance. A call to my house contents insurer, the Halifax, confirmed that this was so but only up to 30 days at a time. With my work commitments, this is no problem for the time being but, if I ever wanted to do any extended cruising, I might have to think again so, out of curiosity, I asked the boat insurers how much it would be to have £5,000 personal effects cover.

Some companies simply added the £5,000 to the value of the boat meaning that, if the total premium was £200, the personal effects part was being charged at about

£18. Newton Crum wanted an additional premium of £17.50 if the boat was fitted with a burglar alarm and £50 if it was not. Single items over £100 to £200 in value (depending on the insurer) normally have to be listed.

The situation is rather different with residential craft where the owner keeps a much larger number of possessions on board all year round. What is needed here is more akin to the contents policy for a house and two companies which specialise in these are Michael Stimpson and Collidge & Partners.

Personal accident cover. Although I did not request it, several companies included 'free' personal accident cover, presumably in the hope that I would accept their quotation in preference to a similarly priced one that did not.

Legal protection cover. Another option I did not request – this pays for legal expenses (up to a stated value) if you are involved in an accident or dispute. One or two companies included this in the price but most offered it as an extra. One offered 2 levels of cover depending on the complexity of the dispute.

Emergency Support. St Margarets Insurance offered marine emergency support which, as I discovered on reading the small print, includes the main inland waterways of England Wales and Holland. For an additional annual premium of £20, the insurer will contact main dealers or chandlers to arrange assistance for you. If a repairer is required, £65 (including VAT) will be paid towards the cost of the call-out provided the insurer agrees to the visit first. You don't get a lot of call-out time for £65 these days but St Margarets reports that some canal users have taken it up.

GJW offered cover from Marine Support Services in conjunction with the RAC but this is really aimed at sea-going vessels.

Cruising range. Most of the insurers accepted my proposed range without question. Michael Stimpson was happy for me to cruise from Brentford to Teddington or Limehouse but would require an additional premium for more hazardous journeys such as those across the Wash or from Sharpness to Bristol. He also recommends that trips on tidal waters are made with another boat as, no matter how good the emergency services are, a boat travelling in convoy will always get to you more quickly if your engine fails.

Mooring

The rent on a berth for your boat is usually the most expensive item in your indirect costs. It may be just a bankside, but the moorings owner has to pay a commercial rate to the local authority, and probably an access fee to the waterway's navigation authority before he/she begins to invest in amenities. Your priorities for a permanent leisure (as against residential) mooring will probably be permutated from the following:

Security for boat and for parked cars: The boat will be unattended for 90% of its life and, for the other 10%, your car may be unattended on the empty mooring. Owners of apparently secure moorings will probably not want to tell you about a spate of recent break-ins so ask around – particularly of existing moorers. Yards that look secure, but lack staff or moorers permanently on-site, allow thieves to break defences down at their leisure.

If you cannot depend on site security, you may have to construct your own defences. All-steel narrowboats (particularly with steel hatches and door skins) can be fitted with steel window shutters (or you can specify smaller portholes instead of windows for your new narrowboat). Deck and cratch covers may keep the weather out but they also conceal intruders while they attack your doors. Even if door skins are of steel, check the way they are fitted. When you accidentally leave keys inside the cabin, you will be surprised how easily the boatyard can break into your boat by unscrewing hinges, lifting hinges off pintles, working internal bolts free. . .

After fitting shutters, you can install a burglar alarm ranging from single dry-cell-powered passive infra-red sensors linked to an external siren (price around £100), to sophisticated marine systems (available from major chandlers) that protect many points of the boat at a cost of around £400. If the mooring is so isolated that even a loud siren is out of earshot, you could consider a burglar alarm with radio link. A system featured by *WW* in January 2000 alerts a distant receiver which sets off an alarm or sends a telephone alarm call to a keyholder. Three models are available ranging in price from £1,057 to £1,762 depending on the type of transmission required. ADL Communications (01460 55655) markets the system.

Thieves may be disconcerted by security lights. If the mooring lacks a 230-volt supply, you can fit a solar-powered light, which has sufficient capacity in its rechargeable battery to switch on for over a hundred one-minute cycles before needing a spell of daylight recharging.

Accessible and safe environment: Your chosen mooring may be close enough to allow you to visit it on summer evenings. Whatever season of the year you first see the berth, it may yield nasty surprises at other times. A rural bankside could turn to axle-deep mire after rain. Your boat might not be able to come close to the bank after drought – if rise and fall between wet and dry conditions is 9in, the point where your (typical) narrowboat's stern comes alongside will need approximately 2ft 9in of water before levels start to drop. Is the berth in a marina, laid out so densely that you cannot enter or leave easily, particularly in strong winds? If it is canalside, how far must you travel to a winding hole where you can turn your boat round?

Is it a river mooring, vulnerable to several feet of rise and fall? If so, is it on a floating pontoon, or fitted with sliding mooring rings – or will it dump your boat on (or worse, half-on) the bank after floods? Is the site exposed to gales, putting your canopy or mooring lines at risk? Does the local water have a reputation for accelerating corrosion? – a particular possibility in industrial areas.

Dog owners are notorious for regarding towpaths as canine loos. This thoughtlessness can turn your towpath mooring into a nightmare, especially if you bring young children to the boat. Marinas and boat clubs are usually stricter on dog hygiene.

Ready access to your preferred cruising routes: Although owners buy with the intention of a series of epic cruises, they often scale ambition down to a weekly run to the local waterside pub. While a picturesque mooring may be enchanting initially, it could become a disincentive if it lies towards the terminus of a remote canal, so that you have several days of familiar scenery before you can find fresh cruising.

Conviviality: If you prefer the company of other boaters, boat clubs are usually convivial and so are some small working boatyards. Some large marinas are more impersonal, although more than one has an active club based within it.

Creature comforts on site for you and your crew: The largest and most modern marinas contain a provisions shop, clubhouse/restaurant, showers and laundrette. Braunston Marina even has a coin-in-the-slot wc pump-out machine. More than one marina is developing a 'village' of independent small businesses to encourage special services like craft shops, fender makers, and upholsterers/canopy repairers.

Service support for your boat: Large marinas make sure full service support is available for your boat. Occasionally though, this is franchised exclusively to a few contractors, and you are not permitted to bring others in. If you are planning major DIY work, check the marina's attitude. Some allocate particular mooring bays and yard space to DIY fitters-out. Smaller working yards tend to be more pragmatic, although a few are run by idiosyncratic escapees from the rat race (remember Basil Fawlty?).

Good relationship with staff and a sound contract with the moorings owner: Interested and sympathetic yard staff are a decided asset. They may, for instance, notice that your boat is sitting an inch or two deeper than it should – before the bilge pump finally gives up and lets it sink.

You need a moorings contract to establish exactly who you are dealing with, how much is to be paid, what notice of leaving is needed. And what terms apply: Is your berth location fixed? Can the owner put other boats in it while you are away? Are you required to pay the owner a percentage of the price if you sell your boat from the moorings. . ?

Marinas The emphasis in many boatyards is on building, repair or hire, with moorings as a subsidiary source of income. In marinas it is the other way round. There, moorings are usually in a purpose-dug basin and, as suggested above, the largest and most modern marinas are more like leisure centres.

Typical mooring charges in a marina (in 2000) are between £15 and £25 per foot length of boat per year, compared to between £9 and £16 per foot on a linear boatyard mooring.

A purpose built marina in tranquil surroundings.

A coming variation on renting in inland marinas is 'berth lease', where a long-term lease agreement secures a massive savings over rental. Typically a payment of £16,500 secures a 52ft berth in an up-market marina for 35 years. The agreement involves solicitors and the Land Registry; but the lessee (boat owner) can sell the lease on to others.

The magnificent club house and moorings built by members of the Stafford Boat Club.

Clubs The most sophisticated boat clubs match almost all the facilities of large marinas. Others may exist to provide simple but secure moorings in a rural setting. A few are co-operatives with some emphasis on residential moorings. All, because they are non-commercial, can charge lower mooring rates than marinas and most boatyards. However, members are generally expected to contribute some time and physical labour – to site maintenance, improvements, helping to pull other members' boats out of water, etc. The members of Stafford Boat Club have built themselves a splendid clubhouse overlooking an arm in which they have constructed mooring jetties. Club social life can be so developed that some members don't actually bother with any boating.

Coombeswood Canal Trust on the Birmingham Canal Navigations has been run as a charitable trust for many years. On-site security rivals Fort Knox, the site has a number of residential berths, economically priced diesel fuel, a heavy slipway and most facilities – including a machine shop where qualified members can operate milling machines for modifying stern gear.

Nearly 100 clubs (including Coombeswood Canal Trust) are linked through the Association of Waterway Cruising Clubs. Members can apply for temporary moorings at other associated clubs. This provides considerable peace of mind when 'weekending' round the waterways, as the boat is sure of secure between-weekend moorings at reasonable cost. AWCC also has an informal rescue service. If members break down far from home, they can telephone the nearest associated club for advice or even practical assistance. If club boating sounds right for you, the Association can direct you to the nearest. Contact: the Secretary, AWCC, 126 Cudham Lane North, Cudham Common, Sevenoaks TN14 7QS. Tel: 01689 862046.

BW moorings British Waterways currently operates 517 sites. Typically these are linear moorings in villages, at locks or near major canal junctions but they can be in town or city basins or even purpose built marinas. Facilities and character of the sites vary widely. In January 1995, BW introduced a new matrix system to assess mooring rates according to a multitude of cross-referenced factors. Sites are given a 'bollard' score, reflecting facilities like car parking, access and security. They are then assessed for location and given a letter from A to J depending on how popular the area is and how much is charged at nearby private mooring sites. From these factors, fourteen different mooring rates are computed, ranging from £17.87 to £95.20 per metre per year in 2000. Residential sites and a few 'premium' sites in central London are to be charged on a different scale. Local British Waterways management offices can provide details of available moorings.

Ends of garden & farmers' fields If a canal under British Waterways' authority runs along the end of your garden, you are required to pay BW for access. The charge is set at 50% of the basic rate for a similar BW moorings in that vicinity. So it only varies according to factors like condition of the canal, and property values in the neighbourhood.

The same levy applies to moorings at the edge of farmers' fields. Except, of course, that the farmer must charge you more than that to make the transaction worthwhile to him/her.

On line moorings on the Shropshire Union Canal.

CHAPTER 4

SHARED OWNERSHIP

To indulge a passion for narrow-boating you must either buy a boat or hire one. In the first case you would be lucky to find a sound new craft at under £35,000, or a secondhand one for less than £20,000. Nor will you be left with much change from £1,750 a year in running costs. Coincidentally, if you hire, the typical price for a mid-season fortnight is also about £1,750. But, in the nineties, a third option appeared – shared ownership. Against those figures, it can look very attractive. Most schemes slash the cost of purchase to a level that the average man-in-the-street might afford – around the price of a secondhand car. And they reduce running costs by the same factor – usually well below the cost of a week's hire.

The theory of shared ownership is sound and, over the years, many informal groups – from families to clubs – have made it work. The concept only started to take off commercially in 1990, but hit a rich vein when hundreds of inland waterways enthusiasts saw a concept that met their aspirations and that they could afford. In the initial years, some operators were aggressively competitive towards each other but they now differ so much in size and type of scheme that they co-exist more amicably.

The advantages of commercial schemes are that you do not have to find other sharers yourself and that, to differing extents, you may escape responsibility for maintenance and administration. None of the schemes is time share (where participants only purchase a lease for a number of years). Instead, shared owners buy a share in perpetuity – when the boat is eventually sold they receive a part of the proceeds in proportion to their share.

Sharing does mean that you cannot go to your narrowboat every week or weekend of the year but acres of dusty narrowboats in marinas testify that many private owners only use their boats on high days and holidays.

Other disadvantages are that operators are in it for a living, so no scheme will be quite as cheap as, for instance, a private group that buys a secondhand boat and maintains it themselves. Also, of course, you have to share your vessel with strangers. Will they bring smelly dogs, cigarettes, chip pans aboard? Operators say not. Because: a) buying even a part of a narrowboat fosters pride of ownership so that sharers take much greater care of their boat than most hirers do and: b) sharers do not enter the arrangement as friends, so they are less inhibited about complaining to the operator, who (in most cases) will act as an intermediary, dealing tactfully with conflicts.

Several operators report that sharers have indeed proved to be a special breed. The idea seems to appeal to a more rational and motivated section of the public than does hiring – or even buying outright. Among the downside niggles: most sharers have to clean their boat scrupulously and remove all personal possessions at every handover – which can take up to a valuable day out of the holiday. And, several operators and sharers are concerned that the success of shared ownership could produce its own problem – some shared boats are used so intensively (more than any hire boat) that their operational lives may be much shorter than planned.

In the mid-nineties, when the last *Inland Boat Owner's Book* was produced, the popularity of shared ownership seemed to know no bounds and everyone was jumping on the bandwagon. By the end of the decade, the number of these operators still actively promoting schemes had reduced to three with the others either continuing only as demand arose or having withdrawn completely. In the meantime, other builders have dabbled with shared ownership but most have given up because of the healthy demand for solely owned boats which require far less publicity and administrative effort.

OwnerShips

Narrowboat shared ownership is dominated by OwnerShips. It was launched in 1990 by Allen Matthews, whose talent for administrative detail is one of the reasons for its success. OwnerShips is now so large that it can enjoy some unusual fruits of scale: its bank manager is a sharer and some sharers have gone native to the extent of joining the company. Matthews' enthusiasm for the operation appears to be undimmed.

ABOVE AND BELOW: The standard of fit out of this OwnerShips boat rivals many good quality, privately owned boats.

The way that shares are allocated is always one of the most contentious aspects of any shared ownership scheme. OwnerShips' system reflects an almost anguished concern for probity – it is certainly the most complicated one on offer. In year 1, under its 'Three Tier Rotating Priority', one Owner (sic) is given first choice of the basic three weeks, another given second choice, another third choice. . . and so on. The next year every Owner moves up the list two places. After the annual booking process, Owners may book any unbagged weeks on a two-months-ahead basis – but the booking priority for these is reversed – so he/she who came last in the three weeks stakes gets first choice here. In addition, unbooked weeks or weekends can be grabbed at short notice on a first-come, first-served basis. Got all that? Well for some Owners, some of it doesn't entirely apply. They pay an extra 25% into the maintenance fund for the privilege of three main weeks guaranteed in school holidays. Each boat is only allowed a maximum of three 'priority sharers'.

Most of OwnerShips' 60 boat fleet has been built by Pat Buckle, whose development has (of necessity) matched that of the operation. His original narrowboat product was relatively unsophisticated but has benefited from extensive feedback and has been altered by more up-market material and equipment specs. Fit-outs are in pleasant cottage style, with plenty of pine scrolls. More recent boats have been fitted out by John Milburn and others on shells built by Graham Reeves. OwnerShips does not earn revenue from building its own craft but prices do not appear to contain a large profit margin.

When *WW* once queried whether OwnerShips' preferred Mitsubishi 1.4 litre diesels might be small for its typical 58ft long boats, it was rebuked by sharers as much as by the company – reflecting the scheme's 'club' spirit. Nevertheless, CB Marine BMC 1.8 engines are now nearly always fitted. Equipment specs on larger boats are opulent, and include microwave oven, large corner bath, colour TV, CD player – even a mobile phone for incoming and breakdown calls.

After they have purchased their boat, each group of OwnerShips sharers is free to operate and dispose of it as they collectively wish. However, they are offered the company's management service free-of-charge in the first year and all have retained that in subsequent years. Given the company's administrative experience and track record, and the scope of the service provided, this is not surprising – even though the management service is the most expensive of the narrowboat shared ownership operators. OwnerShips organises a small army of maintenance engineers and arranges regular sharer meetings when individual groups can discuss the company's overhaul

Adventurous colour scheme on an OwnerShips Dutch barge.

recommendations, projected maintenance budgets – and their own future cruising plans.

Should a sharer wish to sell his/her share, OwnerShips undertakes to handle the sale for a nominal commission. If the sharer prefers to transfer to another boat, the company guarantees to buy the share at a fair market price.

OwnerShips' centre of operations is Blue Lias Marina close to Braunston, the 'hub' of the South Midland waterways but sharers are free to choose other bases. Boats currently operate from eight other strategically-placed bases across the system.

In 1999, OwnerShips started to add wide beam Dutch barge style boats which are to be based on the Thames, in Ireland and in France. As well as being a new boat type, the Dutch barges come with a new, more flexible ownership agreement. Owners can choose to switch their summer holiday to a boat based on one of the other waterways to give them fresh cruising possibilities. They can also opt not to use the boat at all for one year in which case their main holiday costs (about £600) will be refunded and the boat let to another Owner.

OwnerShips, 39 Westminster Drive, London N13 4NT. Tel/Fax: 020 8888 5555.

Boats like this will operate on the Thames, in Ireland and in France.

Challenger Syndicateships

Ed & Gill Rimmer ran narrowboat hire fleets from 1976 to 1992, finally with a small specialised operation for up-market hirers. This was almost a natural precursor to shared ownership which the company has been marketing with characteristic ebullience. Barely a boat show or festival takes place without a Challenger stand. The company also promotes shared ownership of Broads, Thames and France based boats as well as sea-going cruisers in the Mediterranean – with the enticing possibility of informal holiday swaps between narrowboat and gin palace sharers.

The company runs yet another variation on share allocation: the sharers draw lots for a week in each season – spring, summer, autumn and winter, although each year different sharers get first chance at booking the four most popular weeks.

The fleet is notable for its high standard of fitting-out. The work was done exclusively by Blue Haven Marine, one of the canals' most experienced and accomplished narrowboat fitters but is now shared with another quality fitter, Nimbus Narrowboats. Demand dictates that shells are 80% semi-trad with the rest comprising some very meaty, Josher style tugs. Cabin equipment includes a solid fuel stove and independent on-board 230-volt electrics.

The Rimmers have considerable administrative experience (they have been in the hotel business too). The company's management service covers all usual running costs – but can include the arrangement of cabin cleaning. Its estimate of maintenance costs even contains a contingency item for breakdowns. Turn-round and maintenance work is mainly sub-contracted. Overhauls are done at the yard where the boats are based. Challenger's narrowboats are based at twelve sites around the system including Blue Haven's Rugby yard, Nantwich, Skipton, Worcester and Devizes.

***Arthur's* traditional engine room and boatman's cabin.**

Traditional Challenger tug in the foreground and the popular semi-trad style narrowboat moored alongside.

The interior of Challenger's tug *Arthur* has many attractive features.

Black Prince

Of the other 4 schemes described in the last *Inland Boat Owner's Book*, only one company, Black Prince, is still selling shares but only as and when demand occurs. Terms and conditions are basically similar to the other schemes with the yearly management fee set at £235 plus inflation after the first free year. Boats are similar to those in the hire fleet but painted in 'private' colours.

Black Prince Holidays Ltd, Stoke Prior, Bromsgrove, Worcs B60 4LA. Tel: 01527 575115, fax: 01527 575116.

The company has now gone full circle and is about to add to the fleet similarly specified boats which can be hired. These will give anyone thinking of joining the shared ownership scheme a taster before they make a commitment.

Challenger Syndicateships, Hampton Park Farmhouse, Red Lane, Hampton, Evesham, Worcs, WR11 6RF. Tel: 01386 421281.

JD Boat Services

J D Boat Services, run by Jim Matthias, started life as a boatfitting company but is now also associated with Canal Craft – the shell builder – and operates a hire fleet under franchise. JD's workmanship is notable for its immaculately installed systems – gas, electric, water, engine – and joinery held together by a profusion of aligned brass screws. The company launched its shared ownership scheme in 1993 and currently has seven narrowboats in operation with two more planned for 2000. As the company builds its own boats, its prices do not include a mark-up other than a small amount to cover the extra publicity that selling a shared ownership boat requires.

Each boat is sold in eight or twelve shares – none retained by JD Boat Services. Eight or twelve sharers buy six or four weeks, half of which are in-season and fixed in perpetuity (the weeks have been chosen on a surprisingly successful mixture of first-come-first-served and informal negotiation). The remaining weeks are booked out of season by agreement with the other owners. JD Boat Services offers to manage the consortium but makes no administration charge in the first year.

The boats are in semi-trad style, originally based on the shells of Gary Gorton but now built by Canal Craft. They are generally fitted with Yanmar or Vetus engines, 230-volt electrics and free-standing furniture. Boats presently start from the company's hire base on the Staffordshire & Worcester Canal, convenient for several Midland routes; and, by road, just half a mile from the M6 motorway.

JD Boat Services Gailey Ltd, The Wharf, Watling Street, Gailey, Staffs ST19 5PR. Tel: 01902 791811.

Recent schemes

A recent survey for the *Waterways World* Annual 2000 identified 4 new shared ownership schemes. All offer only narrowboats and are based solely in the United Kingdom. The operators are –

Bath Narrowboats, Sydney Wharf, Bathwick Hill, Bath BA2 4EL. Tel: 01225 447276.

Coronet Canal Carrying Company Ltd, 36 High Street, West Haddon, Northants NN6 7AP. Tel: 01788 510410.

Owners Afloat, Braunston Marina, The Wharf, Braunston, Northants NN11 7HJ. Tel: 01788 891727.

Shepley Bridge Marina, Huddersfield Road, Mirfield, West Yorks WF14 9HR. Tel: 01924 491872.

Timeshare

Shared ownership is sometimes confused with, but is not the same as, timeshare. The main difference is that, with timeshare, participants buy the right to use any boat (or villa or hotel) in the scheme for a certain number of weeks a year for a certain number of years, rather than an actual share in one particular boat in perpetuity. If they wish to leave the timeshare scheme, they can recoup some of the initial purchase price by selling the remainder of their entitlement. Timeshare schemes are gradually losing their initial poor image and becoming more popular. They appeal more to people who want to try the canals as just one of a number of different types of holiday.

Operators identified in the *WW Annual 2000* are –

Canaltime Heritage – Bath, Sydney Wharf, Bathwick Hill, Bath BA2 4EL. Tel: 01225 447276.

The Watertime Club, Merchant's House, North Wapping Road, Bristol BS1 4RW. Tel: 0117 921 0673.

CHAPTER 5

LIVING AFLOAT

Attitudes to residential boating on England's canals have changed markedly over the last few years. In the eighties, many boaters lived surreptitiously on the cut. British Waterways, the navigation authority, issued only 200 residential licences (or 'houseboat certificates', as they are officially known), although the number of residential craft was many times that number.

Then BW decided to regularise the unauthorised live-aboards – and generate some extra income from them. Almost at the same time, a new breed of residential boaters hit the canals in the wake of the eighties. Burnt-out fast-trackers, early retirers, golden redundancy recipients all decided to redirect their lives with sabbaticals – or longer – afloat.

Apart from this influx, the profile of residential boaters is no less varied than the general population. It is not unusual to come across commuters who return from nine-to-five jobs to a home on the cut. A large proportion of residential boats is in the London area where the high cost of housing makes life afloat look particularly attractive (especially as the price of new immobile houseboats – those without engine or steering gear – is not liable to VAT). The immediate financial advantages are romantically coloured by the idea of living in the ambience of traditional working boatmen, free of the pettiness of life ashore. This vision frequently obscures the considerable real difficulties of living without the comforts that house dwellers take for granted (like mains water and sewage drainage) in the long, bitter depths of winter and of being permanently caged up with another person in a confined space.

A surprising number embark on life afloat with no previous boating experience. Quite a few quit after a few squalid months. At the other extreme, some find that canal life takes them over – a substantial number go native, and gradually abandon links with Real Life. While hire boats are not representative of residential narrowboats, a couple of weeks on one out-of-season will give you some idea of the limitations of living afloat. Better still would be a season or two in a shared ownership scheme where the narrowboats are generally larger and more similar in specification to residential craft. Talking to residential boaters (or, better still, staying with them) can also reveal aspects of the lifestyle that might not have occurred to you.

Where do you moor?

Once the decision has been made, the biggest problem for many residential boaters is finding a suitable mooring. A purchaser may be assured by the seller of a boat that its mooring is residential, only to find the moorings owner non-committal about its future use. Many landlords who allow residential craft are reluctant to strike up any formal contract. So the insecurity of mooring without a lease is a fact of life that a large number of boat dwellers learn to accept.

This risk can be reduced by discreet research. Is the landlord really the landlord? Does the site have planning permission for residential berths? Planning permission is needed but local authorities vary considerably in their attitudes. Some are simply too busy to concern themselves with the occasional and ephemeral boat unless someone complains about it. They have to prove that you are living aboard full-time and are likely to be more concerned if you alter the bankside or vehicle access. Local authorities' attitudes to residential moorings are not necessarily the same as the navigation authorities'.

If you can persuade your landlord to sign a written residential mooring agreement, make sure that it clearly names both parties, the exact mooring location, rights of access, responsibilities for maintaining the mooring, the amount of mooring fees and charges for additional services (like power supply), whether the boat can be sold on this residential berth, terms for giving notice of leaving or eviction.

Alternatively you can seek advice on agreements from the Residential Boat Owners' Association. The RBOA, which was founded in 1963, seeks to protect the rights of live-aboard boaters; and has helped on questions of taxation, rates, voting census records, and harassment. It is also a social organisation, with a regular newsletter.

Residential Boat Owners Association, PO Box 46, Grays RM18 8DZ. Tel: 0370 785869.

Many of the canals' working wharves and basins have been transformed into residential moorings – Bull's Bridge, Rickmansworth, Uxbridge, in London; Hockley Port, Gas Street Basin in Birmingham are examples. Most sites looked unkempt until authorities' grudging acceptance changed to realisation that colourful narrowboats are an asset to urban landscapes – and gentrified their moorings. Despite BW's relaxation towards residential boats, it is not likely to grant many new houseboat licences in these urban areas. Consequently, if a boat that is legitimately residential in BW's London waters is offered on the open market the chances are that its asking price is over the odds. BW residential licences now apply to the boat rather than the owner so that, if the boat is sold, the new owner can live on it. If he then wishes to dispose of the boat, he must sell it as a pleasure boat and cannot bring a new boat onto the mooring if there were other people on the waiting list for that site when he bought the first boat.

Houseboats on London's tidal Thames come under the Port of London Authority. Few boats provide unofficial accommodation because the tidal section has no casual moorings between which craft can flit. And as expensive new building developments spread along the waterfront, many existing residential moorings become priced out of the average reach (if you will pardon the pun).

The non-tidal Thames (ie above Teddington Lock) is regulated by the Environment Agency whose patrols diligently check that boats do not squat on casual moorings. The value of property adjoining the river is so high and the likelihood of ructions from local planning authorities so great as to severely limit opportunities for new residential moorings against private land. In fact, the number of residential craft on the non-tidal Thames is decreasing so here too houseboats change hands for very high prices.

Many residential craft avoid transgression by mooring in private marinas or old basins outside the jurisdiction of navigation authorities. New marina developments are probably the easiest place to find residential berths. These are generally negotiated at the marinas' planning stage with navigation and local authorities, and supported by good facilities. Other boatyard or towpath moorings often include isolated residential berths to improve security. Several off-line urban basins are populated by cohesive communities of residential craft. A notable example is the co-operative run by the London Narrow Boat Association in Battlebridge Basin on the Regents Canal behind Kings Cross Station.

When they arrive at some crossroads in their lives, a surprising number of people decide to sell up and take to the water for a sabbatical year or two. Just take a look at a map of England and work out how little of its interesting parts you will realistically be able to explore in your three-score-and-ten years unless you do something positive. A Grand Tour by narrowboat is a comfortable, but not total, solution to this dilemma, if properly planned. As, in practice, three-score-and-ten is more likely to be four-score-and-then-some, the crossroads for many extended cruisers is retirement from work. For others, it is a modern version of hitching up the wagons and rolling towards the Wild West to see what turns up.

Extended cruising does not require a residential licence although BW has attempted to introduce a 'high intensity' licence for continuous cruisers. Boats with cruising licences are normally allowed to be occupied for a fortnight in one place but BW accepts that, during winter months, navigation maintenance work and frost or flood prevent movement.

There are two distinct possibilities for living afloat outside the UK inland waterways. Many residential boaters simply want to be afloat and may not be too concerned whether their bit of sheltered water is attached to a canal or the sea. Often craft on tidal waters do not have to be licensed by a navigation authority. The river Medway, in particular, has been identified as a haven for residential boats, with about a hundred in boatyards around Rochester. Communities within commuting distance of London can also be found in inlets along Suffolk, Essex and Sussex coasts and in the Solent.

Increasing numbers of UK inland boaters retire to European waterways, where the sun is more constant, and food, drink and life are more exotic. Narrowboats fit (in fact get lost in) continental waterways and can be ferried across there for less than £2,000. Many owners buy Dutch barges – or have wide-beam craft built in this country.

Simple wide-beam steel cruisers can be very competitive in price, even compared (on tonnage) to narrowboats. The latter need special built-in furniture to be space-effective while a 50ft x 12ft cruiser can have almost as much space as a small bungalow and could be largely fitted with inexpensive free-standing furniture. A not-too-expensive builder should be able supply a simple wide-beam 'narrowboat' of this order of size for not much more than £40,000. That price would not get you a boat sturdy enough to tackle Channel crossings though – it would have to travel by ferry.

You could fit-out a wide-beam steel shell in this country and live on it here until you are ready to move abroad. As Chapter 1 points out, the UK waterways include areas of several hundred miles where wide-beam craft can cruise although they cannot traverse the Midlands 'narrow' system.

The least attractive category of residential boat is that which is dumped against a towpath just to provide nightly shelter for its city-obsessed occupants. It pays no mooring fee, nor does it carry any licence – cruising or residential. The maintenance it receives is minimal and sometimes dangerously makeshift.

That's the instant image conveyed by the word but even the most committed extended cruiser must plan for periods of inactivity. After several months of continual boating, anyone would need to tie up for week or two's rest. Then, as your resolution to stay on the canals outreaches your finances, you could easily slip from respectable extended cruiser to squatter. The licence runs out but you let renewal slip for a month, then another . . . You find it cheaper to stay where you are – local waterways officials' attempts to move you on are half-hearted. Material that you originally stacked neatly on board, now sprawls along the hedgerow. You don't care – canal life has made you that laid back. You too are a squatter.

Planning a residential boat

A quick poll of residential boaters produced four priorities for life afloat:

1. Tolerance: The limited space in most boats, particularly narrowboats, offers little escape from other occupants. You must be able to tolerate their irritating little habits, and they, your saintliness. The traditional boatmans cabin really comes into its own as a den where one of you can go to cool off.

2. Discipline: When you move from house to boat, you will be appalled by the items you have to abandon. Then when living afloat, you will have to keep to new standards of discipline, tidying things away immediately after use. (Good news though; cleaning and tidying a narrowboat cabin takes much less time than a house or flat).

1 Saloon   2 Galley   3 Bathroom   4 Bedroom   5 Engine   6 Back cabin

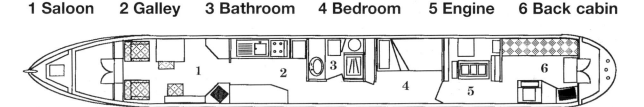

Plan of a residential narrowboat.

The saloon and galley of a residential boat.

Storage and neatness have a high priority.

3. Storage: However tidy you are, you will need much more storage space than in your holiday boat. In particular, you will need masses of utility storage space – for vacuum cleaner, washing machine, refuse bin, ironing board, food mixer, freezer, folding bikes, generator, computer, sewing machine, folding workbench, power tools, hand tools, coal & logs......

4. Health: Many residential boaters move aboard in their forties and fifties, when they are in perfect health. Only a few years later they may suffer a minor health problem – typically a bad back – that would be merely irritating in a house but which makes boating impossible. Although it is not reasonable to expect to stay afloat for the rest of your days, the number of residential boaters who have not made contingency plans for coming ashore is surprising.

Chapter 14 deals with cabin systems and appliances but the particular considerations for a residential boat are outlined here:

The average length of modern 'holiday' narrowboats has increased over the last fifteen years, so that many are quite long enough for living in. A couple could be comfortable in a 55ft boat with permanent double bedroom, toilet compartment and large galley/saloon. Likewise a live-alone narrowboater should be comfortable in 45ft and might find any boat longer than 45ft a handful (even then he/she would need special design details to help in working through locks and lift/swing-bridges – like extra grab handles, a midships rope ring, cabin-top ladder, even a bow thruster). However, always go for the biggest boat

you – and your finances – can manage. You will always appreciate that extra few feet of space and it is much more expensive to add it later.

Accommodating four (all adults or two plus two children) needs at least 60ft overall length – preferably 70ft. Adapting the conventional orientation (permanent double bedroom aft, galley/saloon forward) to provide privacy for the extra berths might involve fitting upper & lower bunks in a private side cabin, or by shifting the galley/saloon to the middle of the boat with sleeping and toilet compartments either side of it. More extreme solutions might be a traditional-style forecabin, forward of a cratch-covered cockpit, or a traditional aft boatman's cabin.

Fit-out for living

365-day residential use is, not surprisingly, harder on a boat than holidays and weekends. Hire fleets who fit-out, or fitters-out for hire fleets, have the experience to build durable interiors.

Spray foam insulation is particularly desirable on a residential boat.

The insulation of residential craft needs to be much better than that of hire boats though. It has to keep the occupants warm through weeks of frost (not difficult), without creating pools of condensation to stain linings or gradually saturate the aft cabin bilge (more difficult). Sprayed foam is by far the best insulation in this situation.

Double glazed windows are readily available for narrowboats but not often fitted to holiday boats. However, wet windows and soggy curtains from October to March may become more than irritating so the extra cost could be justified. It is not unusual to come across residential boats with perspex panels jammed into the side doors, to increase light without draught. You could arrive at a more elegant solution (like double side doors – outer steel shutters, inner glazed panels), when planning side doors in a new boat. A cratch cover over the forward well deck is almost a necessity on a residential narrowboat, to create a utility/dog washing porch.

Many boats can simply plug into a land 230-volt supply but there are others where the engine's daily function is just to charge batteries and to provide cabin hot water via a calorifier. Most propulsion diesels are too large for this duty and, unless worked harder, are likely to suffer expensive long term lubrication problems. Power generation is a particular problem for residential craft, so here is a summary of options:

An extension lead from a mains supply on the bank (protected by a Residual Current Device) to a consumer unit (distribution board) on board is perhaps the simplest and least mobile arrangement. More frequently cruised boats and those with no supporting services available on their moorings need a self contained system.

A sophisticated 230-volt engine-driven alternator can stabilise AC to 50Hz frequency whatever the engine speed.

Very quiet, 1kW Honda generator.

Electrolux Travelpower unit when fitted on a Beta engine, as the entire package is approved and covered by Beta's warranty). 230-volt alternators are often fitted in conjunction with combined inverter/chargers – when power is generated, they charge the batteries very efficiently and 230-volt power is then available from the inverter for minor loads without starting the engine.

Typically, a residential boater will run the 230-volt alternator to power a washing machine/tumble dryer, charging batteries at the same time, and using hot water

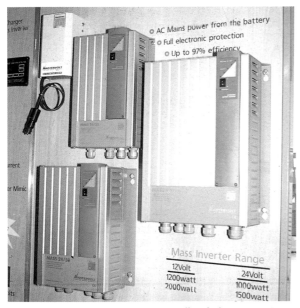

Inverters provide 230-volt power silently but cannot produce it.

A diesel powered generator is the ultimate answer to mains-voltage power.

A conventional 12 (or 24-volt) alternator may be fitted with battery management system (also known as alternator controllers) to improve charging efficiency. The power is stored in the battery bank and fed through an inverter when 230-volt power is needed.

Inverters (stepping up from 12 volts or 24 volts to 230 volts) are not a means of power generation – you still have to charge batteries to run the inverters to provide 230-volts. Engine-driven 230-volt alternators are an improvement on conventional 12-volt or 24-volt alternators (even with alternator controllers) because they make the engine work harder and for shorter periods. However, the engine is still not running within its recommended regime if used only for power generation (not a problem with the

from the engine's cooling system to heat the cabin calorifier via one of its heating coils. This operation happens every two or three days and, when it does, the combined duty ensures that the engine is under reasonable load.

A portable generator costs a fraction of the price of built-in generating equipment so can be very cost-effective – as long as you can find somewhere safe, convenient and not anti-social to run it in all weathers and seasons. Any narrowboat builder out to score brownie points with potential customers should be able to come up with a built-in store for a portable generator – one that is convenient to use, acoustically discreet, well-ventilated (but sealed from the cabin), and secure.

The ultimately desirable source of on-board power is a built-in diesel generator that can be operated from a remote control panel in the cabin, with the cocooned generator installed in the engine room (not permissible with a portable petrol generator). Its diesel engine can be much smaller than the propulsion unit so is never running under-loaded. However, built-in generators are quite expensive – typically between £4,000 and £6,000.

The need for on-board power will become so emphasised over the next decade that propulsion may become a subsidiary function of power generation – the generator will run an electric motor on the propshaft to propel the boat, making the main engine redundant. A number of factors make this concept attractive, and it is discussed further in Chapter Thirteen.

The attractive alternative for conservation-minded boaters is to rely entirely on 12 or 24 volts, eking out special low-consumption electric lights with atmospheric paraffin lamps. The only other electric equipment absolutely necessary for existence afloat is a pressure pump for the water system and an evacuation pump for the shower (although the latter could be replaced by a hand pump). An economical electric system might just be supported by solar panel charging (which becomes more efficient and cost-effective by the year) and/or a wind-driven generator. However these sources trickle charge at best, and will not fully support relatively high consumption appliances like an electric fridge.

In residential use, it is more important than ever that the boat's batteries are of the type that tolerate deep discharge rather than the 'heavy-duty' automotive ones that discount suppliers try to palm off. Those that do qualify are variously described as traction, semi-traction, or leisure.

Increasing numbers of boaters are concerned about the safety of gas but improvements in gas appliances have made them virtually risk-free. Alde gas boilers are now fitted with balanced flues and new gas cookers must have flame failure devices to all burners. However, gas cabin heating is expensive and inconvenient (bottles need frequent changing), in year-round use. Year-round boaters use propane (in red bottles), rather than butane (blue) as the latter freezes. The popular bottle size for narrowboats is 13kg, often with two bottles hooked up through an automatic changeover valve, and a third carried as spare. If the gas locker will carry 19kg bottles upright, gas capacity is effectively increased by 50% and its cost per kg reduced.

Most boat dwellers agree that the single greatest contribution to dry, warm, year-round boating is a solid fuel stove. A small stove, just ticking over, will keep a saloon snug in arctic conditions. A slightly larger one with back boiler will maintain large bore central heating pipes and a final radiator so that even a 55ft cabin can be comfortable through the winter. A few boaters even run the heating pipe through a calorifier to provide hot cabin water but trying to achieve both central heating and water heating from a back boiler is not always successful. Solid fuel stoves are economical – bought fuel can be eked out with driftwood and fallen branches; and most have a flat top for simmering kettles or casseroles.

Diesel heating – drawing on the engine's fuel tank – is undoubtedly the most convenient in year-round use. If your boat has good electric power resources it can run a compact forced-combustion type – like Eberspacher, Mikuni, Webasto, Ardic. These are available in warm air or radiator versions. The latter is usually installed in narrow-

Natural draught diesel stoves give controllable heat without the need to carry coal.

boats, not least because it also serves to heat cabin water.

Natural draught diesel stoves and boilers were the success story of the nineties. They run without attention for weeks or even months, almost silently, and require no electric support. Stoves can be in a saloon fireplace, providing radiant heat and/or running radiators. Boilers sit discreetly in airing cupboards or engine rooms to heat radiators and a calorifier. Leading names are Kabola stoves and boilers, Bubble stoves, Taylors stoves, Refleks stoves, Lockgate stoves. Seven-day timers are available for both forced combustion and natural draught heaters. The main cause of breakdowns in diesel stoves is empty fuel tanks. If ordering a new boat with diesel heating, specify a larger capacity than the average 35 gallons tank.

Options for residential water heating are mainly based on a calorifier – particularly the type with twin coils that can be heated by the engine when cruising and by boiler (gas, diesel, solid fuel) when tied up. A 230-volt immersion heater by-passes these if you have access to a landline of sufficient power, or provides useful load for the engine via a 230-volt alternator. The simplest, cheapest and instant source of hot water is an instantaneous gas heater but, at the time of writing, none has a balanced flue and so cannot be fitted on new boats or replaced in existing ones.

Gas cookers are still hard to beat for convenience, speed, and price. Diesel cookers are available; small solid fuel ranges are often fitted (as much for character as for use), larger ones only occasionally. All apart from gas cookers and microwave ovens could make the galley uncomfortably hot in summer unless side doors or a 'Houdini' hatch are fitted.

Other desirable residential appliances are freezers and washing machines. Economical, low-voltage freezers are available in all sizes. A few modern marinas provide laundrettes, otherwise you should look for a compact 230-volt washer/dryer, not just because it takes up less space but because it probably uses less water than full-size domestic types. It may, however use more power because most have only a cold feed so the water has to be heated by electricity in the machine. You can run a small washing machine from a 1.8kW inverter or a 230-volt alternator but you cannot run a washer/dryer from an inverter or smaller portable generators.

Microwave oven, conventional oven and washing machine in two feet of boat length.

The other services that house dwellers take for granted are water supply and sewage and refuse disposal. Few residential boaters can connect into the mains water supply. If you can, then safeguards are needed – like a warning device and automatic cut-off in case water begins to flood the hull. For most who stay tied up, the hope is to be within a hosepipe's distance of a water point. Refilling is a real chore so water tank capacity should be a consideration when choosing a boat to live on (try measuring the size roughly: 1 cu ft contains 6.25 gallons). The average under-front deck tank holds about 150 gallons; larger narrowboats can carry up to 300 gallons. An on-board washing machine consumes disproportionate quantities of water.

A boat water tank that is in constant use will stay sweeter than that of an intermittently inhabited boat. If it does become contaminated the consequences, if no alternative supply is available, could be dire. Most chandlers sell sterilising tablets for periodic flushing through. You can also fit a bacteriological filter in-line to a drinking water tap.

When moving aboard, the hardest part to come to terms with may be toilet technology. Many residential boaters stop using their flush water WCs with holding tanks because year-round pump-outs can be difficult to find and expensive. Many resort to the portable plastic Porta-Potti, often keeping a spare holding cartridge handy. The died-in-the-wool boater settles for the simple bucket-and-chuck-it Elsan. This has no parts to go wrong, is easily kept hygienic and is light enough when full to carry to an acceptable emptying point.

Upright and chest freezers are available in 12-volt form.

Living afloat does not mean you have to abandon modern conveniences.

CHAPTER 6

TRAIL BOATING

Trail boating adds a whole new dimension to inland boating. Many parts of the waterways system are exotically remote to narrowboat owners but, by road trailer, your boat can be afloat on the Mon & Brec, Leeds & Liverpool, or Montgomery canals, the Broads, English Lakes, or even the Caledonian Canal in a matter of hours.

Perhaps the pioneering spirit of inland boating now rests (ironically) with the road-borne cruiser. While the average narrowboater, pampered by microwave oven and central heating, chuffs through a couple of locks for the weekend, the trail boat owner actually goes to these canals – and plans his/her summer expedition to the Canal du Nivernais. Best of all, trail boating can make a virtue out of necessity – the boat will probably be fairly small so why not keep it on a trailer and save on mooring costs?

Unbraked trailers are limited to a gross weight of 750kg (1,650lb) or half the weight of the unladen car – whichever is less. A Ford Fiesta (or similar) could therefore tow a 400kg (900lb) unbraked boat/trailer combination – equivalent to a 16ft boat with small cabin shelter and simple tiller-steered outboard motor.

A conventional 17ft long canal cruiser, equipped with cooker, toilet, pram canopy, (but no water heater, shower or fridge), and weighing less than 800kg (1,750lb) on its braked trailer, can be towed by the likes of a Vauxhall Astra 1.4. Move up to a Ford Mondeo 2.0 (or similar) and you can consider an all-up weight of 1,000kg (2,200lb), which could mean a 20ft boat with more (but not full) headroom, better internal linings (to resist condensation) and, conceivably, some real mod cons. The upper limit of comfortable towability for large cars (like a Volvo 940) seems to be about 1315kg (2,900lb).

The three last examples are based on 85% of the towing vehicle's unladen weight. This percentage invariably amounts to less than the maximum towing weight quoted by car manufacturers but it is the established gauge for caravanners and the towing industry, who generally regard manufacturers' figures as optimistic for regular towing. The ability to cope with side-winds on caravans' slab sides has something to do with this, but if you are at all mechanically sympathetic to engine, clutch and gearbox – particularly when retrieving your boat on steep slipways – you should adhere to the 85% figure.

The exception to this is four-wheel drive vehicles. Until recently they were cumbersome, uncomfortable, uneconomical and slow so were owned only by the most committed of trail boaters. The most significant development in trail boating in the nineties has been the boom in civilised and affordable four-wheel drive vehicles like the Ford Maverick and Vauxhall Frontera. Diesel versions are little more expensive to buy than two-litre petrol-engined Mondeos and Vectras, and rival them for economy. However four-wheel drive and the ability to switch between high ratio and low ratio sets of gears, mean that these vehicles can realistically tow much heavier craft – 2,800kg (6,200lb) in the Maverick's case.

The legal weight limit for trailers with conventional 'over-run' braking systems is 3,500kg (7,700lb). A few larger four-wheel drive vehicles – like the Nissan Patrol and Toyota Land Cruiser are approved to tow that weight, and are still quite civilised. Land Rovers may look tempting but the older ones, especially the leaf-sprung Series 2, are not suitable although the long wheel base, coil-sprung County and Defender models are acceptable. Older Discoverys have suspension which is designed for limited off-roading combined with comfortable motorway performance which makes them wallow when towing at speed. More recent models have been radically revised and are better.

Sea Otter's aluminium narrowboat is available in 26 and 30ft lengths.

With 3,500kg capacity, you could consider a 'mini-narrowboat'. This species of all-steel craft became popular in the mid-eighties, mainly as a starter boat, and some lighter examples may just be towable by substantial four-wheel drive vehicles. Also in this category are Sea Otter's more recently introduced, and lighter, range of aluminium narrowboats.

Towing and launching a Sea Otter boat requires a 4x4 off-roader or the company will arrange to have it moved for you.

Non-commercial vehicles can only haul trailer chassis lengths up to 7m (23ft). However, in addition to the nominal 7m, the trailer's drawbar (that portion of it forward of the boat's bow) is allowed and so are items overhanging the stern – such as an outboard motor – subject to appropriate marker boards and lighting. Width is not such a problem with narrow-beam craft. Trailers can be 2.3m (7ft 6in) wide, with an overhang of 0.3m (1ft) on either side. There are no legal limits for height but it can be a real practical problem – the pram canopy of a towed boat routinely stands high enough to catch branches, telephone wires and projecting roof eaves. You may also have to use the lorry bay instead of the car bay on the cross channel ferry and this is a lot more expensive.

Specialised practicalities of boat trailers

A four-wheel trailer tends to be more stable on the road and allows a lower loading height but has greater rolling resistance than two wheels – and is less easy to manhandle. Rear-wheel drive cars invariably provide better traction than front-wheel drive on slipways – particularly if the trailer download on the hitch is heavy. Reversing is more difficult to describe than to do but, if you have ever been infuriated by the refusal of a small trailer to steer backwards, take heart – the longer the trailer, the easier it is to reverse.

Consider the shape as well as the weight of your boat when specifying a new trailer. If the boat has a keel or keels (most Dawncraft have two) its weight must be evenly transmitted through it/them. Side supports should only stabilise the boat from rolling over – not carry loads. As the vee-hull of many canal cruisers is fairly flat and the cabins stand relatively high, they can be prone to slipping sideways off a poorly designed trailer at the crucial point of pulling out of water. Removable guide posts fitted to mudguard supports help to line the boat up in muddied water. A well-serviced winch is often invaluable for pulling the boat on to the semi-immersed trailer, rather than drifting it vaguely to a position where you hope the fully-immersed trailer will pick it up.

Because they are regularly immersed, boat trailer bearings need frequent lubrication, if possible, with special boat trailer bearing grease like Aqualube. Spring-loaded bearing caps are available to keep the bearings pressure-fed with grease – reducing the opportunity for water to enter. Indespension offers a PTFE inner bearing seal to restrain the pressurised grease from forcing out the other side on to brakes. It is a good plan, in any case, to keep a spare set of wheel bearings.

Car rear springs sometimes need to be fitted with assisters to cope with the trailer's nose weight. Weight on the hitch should usually be between 50kg (110lbs) and 100kg (220lb) – set up initially by adjusting the trailer axle to the boat, then by adjusting the winch post position, finally by moving contents within the boat). If the download is much less than this, it may encourage the trailer to weave on the road. If it is more, it can affect the car's steering (although each manufacturer specifies a maximum hitch weight). If the trailer does not sit level when hitched up, the tow ball height should be adjusted. This is particularly important if using a twin axle trailer. Caravanners use a stabilising arm to damp down the caravan's tendency to weave. These are rare on other types of trailer and should not, in any case, be fitted to overcome a poor set-up.

Wilderness boats are towed backwards to prevent damage to the outboard and to make launching easier.

Until a few years ago, boats were secured to trailers by ropes. Today strong nylon straps, equipped with ratchet tighteners, really do make loads secure. Folding wheelhouses and windscreens need tying down separately. A flat cockpit cover allows pram-type canopies to be left folded – cutting wind resistance and prolonging canopy life.

Outboard legs and outdrives are required by law to be covered against impact – ideally by mounting the trailer lighting board on telescopic arms aft of the prop. The Wilderness range goes one better by towing stern first to meet this requirement and to keep the outboard safe in the event of a shunt.

Light sets are required to repeat all the lights on the back of your car (apart from reversing lights). Wiring up a socket from car electrics (and fitting a towbar, for that matter) is often a DIY job (unless (a): the car has computerised electrics or, (b): the fuel tank needs removing).

Boats on trailers (even just the trailers alone) are a great temptation to the light-fingered. They are often left by remote watersides where thieves can labour undisturbed for hours to overcome security devices. Insurance companies may not look kindly on claims where flimsy locks are used but might be more impressed by substantial wheel clamps and sophisticated hitch locks. Indespension's Triplelock is one but, as suggested by the name, it requires three hands to use it.

Many boat trailers are bought secondhand, often as a package with the boat. Any that do not carry professional builders' specification plates, showing nett and gross weights, should be regarded with extreme doubt. It is almost impossible to gauge the safe weight limit of a DIY-built trailer. Indespension sells trailer frames in kits – which can be identified from the manual. Older ones were often fitted with secondhand bearings, wheels, tyres and brakes from various types of vehicle, which may affect weight capacity (but, since 1989, it has not been permissible to fit brakes salvaged from a car to a trailer).

If contemplating a secondhand trailer, you should check for corrosion beyond surface rust, particularly if the trailer has been in salt water. Factory-galvanised trailers are much more durable than painted ones. Heavily corroded clamp bolts are likely to sheer if they need adjustment to fit your hull. Wheel rims and tyres have to be examined for damage, corrosion and wear. The trailer should be jacked up

All ready for a day's cruising.

to test wheel bearings, which must rotate freely, without pronounced rumble and with barely detectable play at the wheel rim. Check for adequate and even suspension movement, and for brake operation.

Establish tyre ratings carefully – original tyres could have been replaced by lower specification types which reduce weight capacity by as much as 33%. Boat trailer and caravan tyres are called upon to operate much closer to their design limits and tend to balloon with age. They should be replaced if over 5 years old regardless of the amount of tread remaining. Winch, winch cable, tie-down straps and lighting board should all be examined for chafing and seen to be working adequately.

The definitive inland trail boat

Many production glass-fibre motor cruisers around 20ft long are light and narrow enough to be considered road-towable but the activity calls for its own specialised style: a stable, flat-bottomed craft, with spacious cabin and canal-friendly tiller steering. Steel mini-narrowboats are too heavy for comfortable handling in and out of water (and, because their weight requires more propulsion power, they are much noisier too). The Mallard 23, a glass-fibre narrowboat, ceased production in 1995. All existing examples are inboard-powered and are rumoured to weigh close to $3^{1}/_{2}$ tonnes.

The ultimate builder of trailable inland cruisers is Wilderness Boats, which has dominated this specialised

market for over thirty years. The two largest craft in its three-boat range (17ft 6in, 19ft 6in and 23ft long) can provide comparable accommodation to a 28ft narrowboat. All three may be fitted with shower, fridge and, even, central heating. They are tiller-steered, delightfully manoeuvrable and very quiet on canals, with outboard motor purring gently at the steerer's ankle. They can be recovered from water quickly on special trailers. However, all are substantially built, so that the 17ft 6in Beaver Cub needs a medium/large car as a towing vehicle, while the 23ft Beaver requires a four-wheel drive vehicle.

Indespension's indispensable trailer manual

Several companies build road trailers suitable for inland waterways cruisers. The most common names include Snipe, Bramber, Rapide, SBS and Hallmark. The last is a trade-name of Indespension, which stands apart because of its remarkable trailer manual. This started life as a glorified brochure for parts and trailer kits but the advice content increased over the years. It was completely re-written in 1994 as a comprehensive reference manual. Its 150 pages include indispensable items on towing law, the towing limits of individual vehicles, guidance on steering a car/trailer combination, towing in Europe, trailer servicing, and trailer electrics. It lists Indespension's own products – but also spare parts for several other trailer makes. The manual is available from Indespension, Belmont Road, Bolton, Lancs BL1 7AQ.

CHAPTER 7

LEGISLATION

British Waterways' first bye-law concerning the design of boats dates back to 1954. A set of Boat Safety Standards were introduced in the seventies and these were made compulsory for hire craft in 1979. The application of mandatory boat standards to private craft can only be described as erratic. Several introduction dates were announced and abandoned and the scheme was finally introduced in 1997. Their introduction caused a furore among boat owners, mainly because of their complexity and the cost of bringing older vessels up to standard.

They are referred to as Harmonised Standards because they were published jointly by British Waterways, the National Rivers Authority (now the Environment Agency) and the Broads Authority. The NRA's requirement for boats on its waterways (the river Thames and Anglian waterways) to meet minimum safety standards pre-dates the BSS by some years. All boats on BW waters have now to comply. The EA had a phased introduction of the BSS from 1997 to 2000. After its initial involvement, the Broads Authority opted out of implementation for a while but now plans to make all boats comply by 2005.

The Standards for new craft were drawn up to reflect the anticipated technical requirements of the Recreational Craft Directive (see below) so that, if a boat complied with one, it should comply with the other too. Unfortunately, since there has been a delay in harmonising British and European standards, this aim has not been achieved.

After inspection, a Boat Safety Certificate is issued and is valid for four years (providing relevant parts of the boat have not been altered during that time). To cope with the additional workload when the scheme became mandatory, BW introduced a new class of 'examiners' who were often, but not always, people with some waterways experience like boatyard staff. The training ensures adequate coverage of all parts of the Standards and consistent interpretation. Surveyors were originally allowed some discretion in interpreting the Standards. Although most applied this wisely, it raised the danger of inconsistencies so this discretion was curtailed, causing the surveyors to complain about bureaucratic inflexibility.

BW's on-off policy did mean that mandatory introduction was less traumatic than it might originally have been as many boats on its waterways had voluntarily obtained a 'Certificate of Compliance', or 'Boat Safety Certificate' as it is now called. In fact, not having a CofC (or BSC) was an impediment to credibility when selling a secondhand boat. The following looks at points which cause particular problems to existing boats. The Boat Standards go into much more detail so, before you set out to find a new or secondhand inland boat, you should obtain a copy (from local British Waterways offices or telephone 01923 201278).

Fuel system requirements, which apply broadly to all boats, cover inboard fuel filler, tank and fuel piping in detail. They require, for instance, an approved flame-proof tank vent. Flexible fuel piping, where used, should meet a specific British Standard. Fuel supply pipes must be fitted with a cut-off tap and excess diesel fuel return pipes must be metal rather than plastic.

The part covering electric systems demands a covered, ventilated battery box decently away from parts of the gas and fuel system. Wiring has to be of adequate capacity and adequately secured. A master switch is required to cut off all power – although circuits for automatic bilge pumps and burglar alarms may by-pass it.

Exposed engine exhausts must be lagged.

The PVC insulation coating on wire must not be in contact with the polystyrene thermal insulation behind linings – although that had been common practice for many years. Interaction between the two plastics has been found to make the PVC brittle, reducing its insulation properties. In practice, surveyors will measure the insulation resistance of circuits in existing PVC/polystyrene boats and only require (expensive) replacement when faults are indicated. Typically, main trunking and spurs to lights are carried in conduits.

The Standards set out detailed requirements for fire extinguishers. Each extinguisher is now rated according to its ability to deal with two different types of fire – A: of solids (such as wood and textiles) and B: of flammable liquids.

Length of vessel	Min no extgshrs	Min rating of each	Min comb rating
Up to 23ft	2	5A/34B	10A/68B
23ft-36ft	2	5A/34B	13A/89B
Over 36ft	3	5A/34B	21A/144B

New boats (built after the introduction of mandatory standards) will have to use upholstery and polystyrene insulation that meets British Standards (or Euro equivalents) for flame resistance and toxicity. Boats built after 1993 must have two directions of escape from accommodation.

Fire extinguishers must be the right size and type.

The main gas shut-off valve must be marked and accessible.

Gas is, statistically, the greatest threat to safety in canal boats – more so than the waterway itself. Many surveyors are, and all examiners will be, trained in marine gas installation. Many secondhand boats have DIY gas systems and most have gas faults.

Broadly, gas bottles must be kept in approved lockers, supply piping has to be of copper, adequately sized,

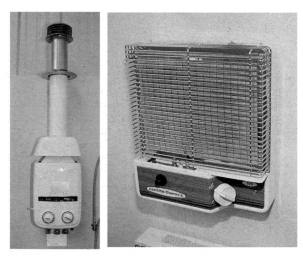

Instantaneous gas water heaters and catalytic space heaters cannot be installed in new boats or replaced in existing ones.

properly supported, and with compression (not soldered!) joints. It has to avoid electric wiring, the engine compartment, and solid fuel stove. It must run well above floor level and be fitted with a cut-off tap before entering each appliance. Any flexible piping must be as short as possible and of approved armoured type. The gas locker lid must not be locked while the boat is being used

The Alde gas boiler has a balanced flue and so satisfies BS5482.

so that the main valve can be reached quickly in an emergency. Systems must be fitted with an approved gas test point.

The Standards have recently been revised to reflect BS 5482 part 3. This requires all new gas appliances, other than the cooker, to be room sealed and all burners and pilot lights to have flame failure devices. However, the new requirements do not apply to existing, non-room sealed appliances as long as they remain in serviceable condition. Only when owners need to replace defective appliances or add new ones do they have to comply with the new standards.

Portable generators are regarded as fuel burning appliances – so petrol-powered ones (and spare petrol cans) are required to be stored in an enclosure similar to a gas bottle locker.

Ventilation requirements are largely based on the number of fuel-burning appliances carried. The following examples show individual needs:

Appliance	Approx input (kW)	Min ventilation needed – sq in	
		Unflued	Flued
Two burner cooker & grill	7.5	22.5	n/a
Two burners, grill & oven	8.4	28.7	n/a
Four burners grill & oven	15	51	n/a
Tor Gem solid fuel stove	2.5	n/a	1.75
Kabola diesel boiler	5.8	n/a	4.1

Permanent low-level ventilation is needed.

To calculate the needs of an appliance not listed, multiply the input rating in kW by 3.4 if it is unflued, or by 0.7 if flued to give the ventilation requirement in square inches.

In addition an allowance of 1 sq in should be made for each crew member; and each compartment must have a minimum of 6 sq in fixed ventilation. So a calculation for a typical narrowboat mig

Galley/saloon

Vanette cooker	51 sq in
Tor Gem stove	1.75 sq in
Six seated crew	6 sq in
(although only two sleep here)	
Total	**58.75 sq in**

Aft cabin

Alde boiler	3.5 sq in
Two berths	2 sq in
Total (minimum)	**6.5 sq in**

Centre cabin

Two berths	2 sq in
Total (minimum)	**6.5 sq in**

The ventilation should be divided equally between high and low level. Three 4in diameter cabin top vents would satisfy the galley/saloon's high level need for 29.4 sq in. While 8in x 2in vents as low as possible in aft and forward cabin bulkheads, with 1/2 in gap under any intermediate doors, would satisfy the low level requirements. Most owners would, understandably, be horrified at an 8in x 2in draught screaming through the cabin and some surveyors appear to compromise by, for instance, reasoning that the cooker is unlikely to be running at maximum output for long.

The Recreational Craft Directive

In the late nineteen eighties, Britain's boat building industry, one of the largest in Europe, foresaw that it might be disadvantaged in valuable export markets as individual countries adopt their own national standards or that it might have other countries' priorities forced upon it as Europe-wide standards are introduced. So the UK has played a major role in formulating the Recreational Craft Directive which became law in Britain in June 1996. After that date, builders could choose whether or not to apply the Directive for the next 2 years. From June 1998 onwards, it was mandatory for all new craft. The Directive is 'policed' by local Trading Standards Officers and the ultimate authority in this country is the Department of Trade & Industry.

The Directive's technical requirements do not differ substantially from those of the UK Harmonised Boat Safety Standards but there are additional sections on hull construction, buoyancy and stability. However, whereas the BSS is written in fairly precise terms, telling builders what they should and should not do, the RCD gives a number of Essential Safety Requirements and leaves the builder to decide how he will comply with them. This approach places a much greater onus on professional boat builders but they are allowed to use the BSS for any parts of the boat to which

it applies. While some builders of coastal craft will have to submit them to a Notified Body for examination, inland waterways builders will be able to 'self-certify' their products. They will be required keep documentation proving that their boats conform for at least ten years after production.

Owners know that their boats conform to the RCD by the 'CE' mark it has to display and by the builder's declaration of conformity in the boat's manual. This enables the owner to license the boat for the first four years, after which it is required to pass an inspection every four years to

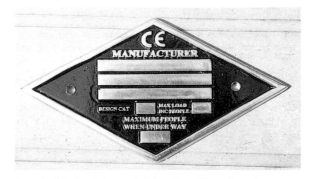

New builder's plate containing the CE mark and space for information about the boat.

ensure that it has been maintained to the specification in the declaration or complies with the BSS. Some confusion/conflict is possible when the first CE marked boats are inspected but, once standards are harmonised throughout Europe, the process should be much more straightforward.

If you buy a shell from one company and then take it to another for the fit out, you may find that you are deemed to be the 'project manager' and have to take responsibility for CE marking the boat and the Recreational Craft Directive documentation. Most boat fitters out would probably offer to do this for you but you can avoid the risk altogether by commissioning the fitter to supply the whole boat, specifying that he procures the shell from the shell builder of your choice.

One phrase in the RCD is particularly relevant to DIY narrowboat fitters – "Craft built for own use shall be excluded from the scope of the Directive, provided they are not subsequently placed on the Community market for a period of five years". The British Marine Industries Federation (which has fought Britain's corner in formulating the RCD) and British Waterways are reasonably confident that, provided DIY boats pass a Boat Safety Standards inspection, they will not be tangled in this restriction. So far, so good but there is no agreement about when the 5 year period starts or what happens if, for personal reasons, the boat has to be sold during that period. The situation will only be resolved completely when it has been tested in court. There is also a possibility that, in a few years time, boats without full RCD documentation that are offered for sale will be at the same disadvantage as boats without a BSC were in the mid nineties.

In any case, all the major parts that are professionally supplied to a DIY fitter (the shell, for instance), will have to conform to the RCD, and be marked and declared as such by their suppliers. BMIF is campaigning for 'kit boats' to be allowed 'Post Completion Certification' to regularise them and their market completely with the Directive.

CHAPTER 8

THE SHELL AND LININGS

Chapter 1 discusses the lengths, widths, heights and depths that will fit into Britain's main canal system but, when ordering a new boat, you need to consider how you can make best use of the dimensions that meet these restrictions.

Height from base plate to cabin top is based on depth of bilge and linings thickness (the two typically totalling 6in to 8in) plus cabin headroom (usually 6ft 2in to

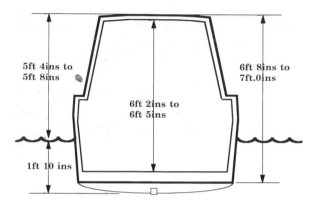

5ft 4ins to 5ft 8ins

6ft 8ins to 7ft.0ins

6ft 2ins to 6ft 5ins

1ft 10 ins

6ft 5in). Within those constraints, the actual height of shell is mainly conditioned by the standard plate sizes that shell builders like to use without trimming, but is usually between 6ft 8in and 7ft 0in. Subtract the height above water that is convenient for most canals (5ft 4in to 5ft 8in), allow for approximately 6in stern-down trim – and the average narrowboat draught of 1ft 10in is arrived at by simple ergonomics.

That dimension is about ideal for the 17in diameter propeller specified for the typical higher-revving diesel engine – it leaves reasonable clearance between blade tip and the steelwork above and below. In this context, 1ft 10in draught means a stern post – that through which the prop shaft sticks – of about 1ft 8in height. The other 2in allows for protrusion of skeg below the bottom plate, and for the counter to be slightly immersed. When underway, the stern will sit deeper, increasing draught by another couple of inches. Like humans, boats put on weight with age – so, if you specify a 1ft 8in stern post, your stern could well scrape a 2ft 2in underwater obstruction in ten years time.

Draught is a contentious matter with traditionalists who are concerned that hulls of average or less draught tend to reduce the cruisability of canals and with waterways politicians who argue that, given an excuse to save costs, British Waterways will not dredge canals as deep as required by statute. Working boats, which commonly drew 3ft or more, used to create a definite channel. Modern narrowboats promote a vaguer saucer-shaped section across which they tend to wander with increased likelihood of going aground.

A traditional slow-revving diesel is the ultimate ambition of many narrowboaters but, even with the help of modern propeller technology, the typical 1,000rpm engine requires a static draught in excess of 2ft 3in.

A small band of boatbuilders offers an opposing argument: narrowboats should be no deeper than absolutely necessary – 1ft 6in is possible without compromising headroom and height above water. Heavy displacement hulls, they argue, are slow (particularly on rivers), unresponsive and more likely to create an anti-social wash. Using artificial ballast to pull a boat down in the water, they go on, is an offence against good design – especially in this energy-conscious era. Shallower draughts need less engine power, requiring smaller propellers – which will fit shallower stern posts. However low displacement hulls can be tender (prone to roll from side to side), and vulnerable to drift in side winds.

The swims (the part of the underwater hull that tapers from full width to the stem post forward, or to stern post aft) should be as long as practicable. Short, abrupt swims contribute to excessive wash and to poor handling. The aft swim is often a foot or two longer than the forward one. Narrowboats of 60ft or 70ft length can carry swims of 15ft length with advantage but a 40 footer could not, without compromising accommodation and, perhaps, stability. In practice, a 9ft or 10ft aft swim is average (but less than ideal) in middle market shells. The aft swim should curve gently from full section to a sharp-edged (as against flat-faced) stern post.

Builders of true working boat replicas go to lengths to construct graceful bows and sterns. The typical replica is based on a 'Josher' with long bow fabricated of

This very abrupt swim on a short, modern boat is, fortunately, not typical.

The fine lines and faired skeg of a traditional working boat ensure that it swims well.

Replica double curved bow fabricated from steel strips.

steel strips to emulate the double curvature of the original construction. The aft underwater swim sometimes follows a fine S shape (seen from above) and 'Grand Union' replicas are given swims which, when seen from end-on, are narrower at the bottom than the top. These shapes are more expensive to build and seldom seen but the closer the shape is to those of original working boats, the better the hull will swim.

Most flat-bottomed narrowboats are based on a two-metre (6ft 6in) wide bottom plate. This requires the hull sides to lean out as they rise to make the overall beam of 6ft 10in at top rubbing strake level. A few builders around Birmingham keep hull sides absolutely perpendicular and sit them on a 6ft 10in wide bottom plate. One or two elsewhere fold the hull sides in near the bottom so that they will sit on a 6ft wide bottom plate, thus reducing cross section area and resistance under water.

Side deck height and width: Although the overall height of shell averages, as noted above, about 6ft 10in, side deck height varies according to stylistic preference. Higher side decks allow better accommodation (particularly when planning beds across the cabin as in a traditional boatmans cabin); lower side decks look better and permit deeper windows. Stepped side decks, which solve the accommodation/window depth conflict, were once common on hire boats but were never popular with private owners.

Dropped gunwales and deeper windows are popular with hirers but not with private owners.

The common width for side decks is 4in – anything less denies a safe foothold. If hulls do not lean in at the top, the dimension saved can be used to make side decks wider – or to increase cabin width.

Excessively wide side decks and/or cabin sides that lean in too much make for claustrophobic interiors. Cabin sides that do not lean in enough look ungainly and are liable to catch bridges. An angle of 1 in 7 seems about average, as does a camber of 3in across the cabin top.

The cumulative gain in internal width in a well-planned narrowboat can be considerable – as much as 3in below side deck height and 6in at eye level. About half of those gains depend on the exact profile of the shell section.

Plating

The conventional shorthand for describing the thickness of narrowboat shell plating is 10/6/4 (or 6/5/3, or

Two hulls taking shape in a modern workshop.

12/6/5). The figures are the thicknesses in millimetres of bottom plate, hull sides and superstructure.

Typical bottom plate thicknesses increased from 6mm to 10mm in the eighties. The change was instigated by upmanship among builders rather than by urgent structural necessity. However, the extra thickness does provide more protection against wear from below and corrosion from inside (particularly where the cabin bilge is not kept dry and ventilated). It also makes compact ballast – the extra 4mm of 10/6/4 over 6/6/4 weighs $^3/_4$ ton more for a 50ft shell; and 25/6/4 would add a further $2^3/_4$ tons eliminating the need for added ballast in almost any depth of hull (however, concrete slab or brick ballast is less expensive and can be adjusted for trim). On most flat bottomed narrowboats, the bottom plate stands proud of the hull sides by about 3/4in to guard against wear on the join so extra thickness provides valuable resistance there.

The bottom plates of vee-sectioned hulls tend to be the same thickness as hull sides – the builder might argue that the width of unfolded plate is smaller, wear is less (except on the keel and chine), and corroding moisture does not stand on the plate. A slightly thicker plate is better though.

In the seventies, hull sides were commonly of 5mm plate; today almost all are 6mm. As corrosion is most common on the waterline, the extra 1mm resists thinning for several extra years before overplating becomes necessary (assuming it does – good maintenance can prevent corrosion indefinitely).

As well as leaning out from the bottom to the top rubbing strakes, most hull sides (apart from the straight-sided Birmingham ones) come back in about 1in as they rise from the rubbing strake to the side deck. This is termed hull 'tumblehome'. Folds in the plating stiffen it – not so much against impact as against distortion during hull assembly. Hull welds rarely leak. The ones that do are usually in tricky details like fuel tanks, water tanks, skin cooling tanks and weedhatches.

Conventional thickness for cabin tops has increased from 3mm to 4mm over the years, to reduce waviness, and weld marks where internal framing is attached. A few builders use 5mm plate on the cabin sides for straightness, and 4mm on the cabin roof– so their plating specs take on four numbers: like 10/6/5/4.

Seen out of water in the workshop, hull imperfections tend to catch the eye; while superstructure waviness, above eye level and camouflaged by dust, passes unnoticed. Afloat and gloss-painted, it is very much the other way round. So note those builders who make special efforts to achieve straight cabin sides – like using the longest possible plates to avoid welded joints.

The generally accepted material for narrowboat shells is 43A plate, described as general shipbuilding steel. The classification deals more with the rolling process than the actual composition of the steel. If you need confirmation of the grade, ask your builder to obtain a certificate when your batch is supplied by the rolling mill.

Welding standards

Narrowboat shell builders use either CO_2 ('MIG') or arc ('stick') welding. Either is accepted if carried out properly. The equipment for CO_2 welding needs more setting up; arc welds need careful cleaning to remove porous slag. Fancy techniques, like plasma cutting (which gives a precise cut, free from distortion), are only used by a few builders, and then generally on detail work or relatively thin plate.

Weld preparation is particularly important. Edges of butting plates are often chamfered to ensure weld penetration. Plating below waterline should be welded on both sides – which means that the entire bottom plate has to be turned over. The intense local heat involved in welding distorts steel plate. Builders minimise this in highly visible (but less vulnerable) areas by welding on one side only and, occasionally, by bracing the joining plates (on the inside) with a 'butt strap'.

While plating thicknesses increased in the eighties, steelwork finish is clearly where builders concentrated on improvement in the nineties. Lumpy welds, uneven grinding-off are not acceptable, except at the extreme budget end of the market. Emphasis on steel finish will become even greater as really glossy sprayed paint schemes finally take over the market for new narrowboats.

Framing

Flat steel plate has little structural strength and increasing plate thickness has negligible structural benefit. Forming angled sections in the steelwork (as at the joint between hull bottom and sides, and at side decks and cabin top) provides basic rigidity, as do steel bulkheads.

Internal framing also strengthens but it is just as important for providing mountings (usually via intermediate timber noggins) for cabin linings. Standard steel sections are almost always used. Abbreviations for the different types are: RSA (Rolled steel angle), RSC (Rolled steel channel) and RHS (Rectangular hollow section).

The bottom plate is braced by transverse frames, usually at 2ft centres to coincide with standard 8ft x 4ft timber floor panels. The frames are invariably of 'L' section and stand between 2in and 5in high. They must be cut away at either end to allow any water in the bilge to run back to the aft bulkhead or engine compartment bilge. Longitudinal frames (keelsons) are sometimes used although they only have a real structural function in wide-beam craft.

Hull side framing is more variable. Typically it consists of one or two longitudinal L-sections (stringers) with verticals (knees) at 4ft or 8ft centres. Depth of framing from the hull side is typically between 2in and $2\frac{1}{2}$in.

Cabin side framing is likely to be of 1in or $1\frac{1}{4}$in square tube, running longitudinally to clear window apertures by about 1in and framing windows and door apertures vertically with the same clearance. Several years ago, a number of builders dispensed with framing on the cabin sides because the weld fixings marks show on the outside paint scheme. Most of these have given way to prevailing demand and fit cabin side framing.

Cabin tops are framed in similar sections but transversely at 1ft 4in or 2ft centres. With a decent cabin top camber (about 3in) these will prevent the roof from flexing when crew jump down from a lock side.

Internal framing is generally stitched rather than continuously welded to the shell (although some builders fix hull side frames more robustly to provide greater impact resistance). Where frames meet, they must be cut away to avoid building in weld stresses and to prevent water traps which would eventually show up as stains through the cabin linings.

Rubbing strakes are just that, and not really external frames. The majority used to be continuously welded along top edges and stitched along the bottom but, increasingly, builders are welding along the top and bottom. This is particularly important where strakes descend under water to avoid corrosion traps. Nevertheless, a few budget builders stitch along the top and fill the intermittent gap with mastic.

Steelwork items

The basic narrowboat shell is only a part of what must be of steel. Other items should be steel and some others could well be. The integral hardware must include rudder assembly (almost always with industrial-type bearing where it emerges through the aft deck), two mooring cleats aft, one forward, eyes for bow, stern and side fenders, cabin-top ring for midships handling rope, gas bottle locker and lid, weedhatch, engine beds, skin cooling

Steel is ideal for small external details and lasts well.

tank or large mud strainer (assuming a raw water-cooled engine), cabin top handrails. Front and rear decks are almost always of steel and self-draining. Engine fuel tanks are usually integral – built into the hull counter, set either side of the engine beds or under a boatmans cabin.

There are good reasons for specifying every possible external detail in steel. It makes honest use of the material – and shell builders usually charge less than joiners for these jobs. Hatches, door skins, pigeon boxes, seat lockers, instrument consoles, taffrails, pole/plank racks, cratch frames, will all survive better and need less maintenance in steel than in timber. Some builders excel at crafting these items in steel; all should be able to make presentable versions.

Other uses for steel include bridgeguards (as fitted to some hire boats), cabin-top vents (instead of brass), vent ducts, window security shutters, engine silencer, cooling header tank, internal bulkheads (as between engine room and cabin), frames for other bulkheads, hearth for solid fuel stove, shower tray sump.

Three items sometimes built into the shell are better in other materials. Integral water tanks, with inspection access through the cockpit deck, have been common but are vulnerable to pollution if the hatch seal is imperfect. Integral WC holding tanks are liable to corrosion (better in stainless steel or polypropylene). Finally, large engine access panels are safer in chequer-plate aluminium than steel (which is dangerous if dropped on hand or foot – unless hinged and supported by a gas strut).

Between shell & lining

Even a bare shell is not supplied as bare steel. Typically it is coated inside and out with a coat or two of primer (like zinc phosphate) with the external hull sides from base plate to top rubbing strake in some form of bitumen paint.

Before the builder applies his standard protection, you should consider grit blasting the external steelwork. For around £700, a mobile grit blasting service will remove rust

Grit blasting is well worth the effort and expense.

and mill scale (which is initially invisible) creating a microscopically irregular surface as an efficient key for primer. The blasted plate should be coated immediately with epoxy primer to establish tough well-bonded protection. The benefits of grit blasting – as one means of resisting hull corrosion and to make a durable base for your expensive cabin-side painted livery – may take several years to yield. Magnesium sacrificial hull anodes are additional, not alternative, means of protection. The cabin

Engineering brick ballast is very dense and easier to adjust than concrete slabs.

bilge – most vulnerable part of the internal steelwork – is sometimes coated with primer, sometimes with bitumen paint, but best with Waxoyl which is self-healing if damaged.

The space under the cabin floor is where almost all ballast is carried. Most common ballast material is concrete slabs – engineering bricks (more dense and resistant to moisture) are better. Steel ballast in large sections is acceptable but not at small, moisture-retaining consistency. Materials like poured concrete (difficult to adjust) and gravel ballast (also moisture-retaining) should be resisted. Slabs, plate and bricks are often laid on bitumen felt but, if you are unlucky enough to have a flood, this can trap water and prolong the drying out period. Slabs sometimes stand on tiny wooden or plastic blocks to make an air gap between them and the bottom plate.

Insulation

Thermal insulation is applied inside the hull sides, cabin sides, deckhead and end bulkheads of a narrowboat shell. Some owners fix it to the underside of cabin floors but this is probably counter-productive. Heat loss downwards is not great and the space taken up by insulation and ballast leaves little for airing the bilge.

Expanded polystyrene sheet is the most popular insulation material. Typically it is applied 2in thick below sidedecks and 1in above. Polystyrene is easy to cut and apply. However, the material reacts adversely with the PVC coating round low-voltage wiring – the latter becomes brittle and breaks, losing its insulation value. So wiring must be kept apart from the polystyrene – by a barrier sheet, or by routing in conduits. The other popular materials, glass wool and rock wool, do not react with PVC, but are less easy to handle and, unlike polystyrene, can be made soggily ineffective by damp.

The most effective, but costly, insulation material is sprayed polyurethane foam. This has higher insulation values than the other materials and creeps into awkward crevices. It also acts as a vapour barrier – preventing water vapour from reaching the steel plate where it can condense. All these qualities are particularly important where use is intensive – as in residential boats. Modern blown foam is free of cfc gas (the one held to blame for eroding the ozone layer). If the job is done by an operator used to the priorities of narrowboats, you (or your fitter-out) should save on several tedious days of shaving off extraneous foam, to allow linings to fit up to noggins.

Sprayed-on foam insulation is superior to pre-formed but has to be trimmed back.

Interior of a budget class boat from a respected builder – complete with bird cage!

Noggins? Cabin linings are usually attached to the shell's steel frames via intermediate timber noggins. These making the fixing job easier and prevent cold from striking straight through from the steel. A few fitters-out use hardwood noggins while some others use softwood noggins treated with preservative – commonly, roofing battens. Noggins under cabin floors and adjacent to windows are at most risk of rot.

Cabin floors are typically of 18mm ply or resin-bonded chipboard (ordinary chipboard should not be used for linings or furniture except were owners fit or accept bought-in kitchen units). Hull side, cabin side and deckhead linings are mainly ply-backed, or of tongued & grooved boards. Bulkheads and furniture are usually of ply (12mm, 15mm or 18mm thick) or blockboard; although MDF (medium density fibreboard), a mainstay of the pub refurbishment industry, is becoming more common, particularly at the budget end of the market.

For a decade or so, leisure narrowboats had varnished cabins – based on plain ply, t&g knotty pine boards and modest amounts of mahogany cappings. The result was brown and dull but very durable. The natural extension of this is oak-faced ply which is just as durable but several shades lighter.

Today's budget narrowboat is typically lined in carpet-faced ply to side deck level, then with oak-faced ply or pine t&g boards above. Furniture is oak-faced with simple square section cappings. Pay a few thousands more and you get meatier cappings, routed into decorative sections and set off by leaded glass-fronted cupboards and turned pillars.

The aim typically is to recreate the character of a country cottage, perhaps flavoured with features from a traditional boatman's cabin. Flamboyant mid-market interiors owe rather more to theme pub than cottage in style. Good quality fit-outs are generally more restrained with emphasis on detail workmanship (cabinet-making rather than joinery) and materials.

Some owners still prefer the rich glow of mahogany but there is a general movement towards lighter temperate hardwoods in fitting-out. Timber merchants have an increasing range of these – mostly grown in the USA – to promote. While some of the lesser known types can look bland, compared to the strong grain patterns of oak and ash, several are already established. Maple is a tough timber, suited to floors and worktops. Cherry is rich, fairly dark,

A more up-market interior from the same builder.

Bird's eye maple with sapele framing meets ash T&G with red oak trim.

Imaginative use of stains and thin washes produces a very atmospheric interior.

with unusual hues in its grain, and could be a politically correct alternative to mahogany. Elm has narrowboat associations (timber boat bottoms were made from it) but is so subtle as to need sensitive schemes to bring out its colour and grain.

Softwood does not necessarily mean knotty pine. Quality softwoods include southern yellow pine (very light and strong grained), parana pine (which matures to a deep honey glow but has a tendency to twist), and red cedar (darker, strong grained and, not surprisingly, with reddish tint).

Popular finishes, like ash, can be given new character by staining. Plain softwoods can provide a base for painted timber finishes – like 'scumbling' to copy oak, and artificial marbling. These techniques are particularly relevant to narrowboats as they are extensions of those traditionally used in a boatman's cabin.

Tiles are frequently used for worktops and fireplaces. Quarry tiles and slate tiles are sometimes used on cabin floors, although any unusual floor surface needs checking against slipperiness when wet. On the other hand, light coloured carpets that compel you to ask guests to remove their shoes before entering are equally unsuitable. During serious cruising, rapid entry from outside to loo or galley is unavoidable and the cabin floor should be able to survive that sort of duty. Carpet tiles (the worn or soiled ones can be changed) are probably the most functional floor covering, with vinyl in galley and toilet areas.

Windows

In a glass-fibre production boat you have to settle for the manufacturer's standard windows. Most steel boats are individual designs and you should be able to specify any type of window you desire. However, 95% of narrowboats are fitted with 36in x 21in windows with rounded bottom corners and drop back top vents. The style appears to be based on secondhand vehicle windows fitted to early narrowboat conversions yet window makers are able and willing to tackle new shapes.

Almost all windows are aluminium-framed, although stainless steel versions are still available and you can order uPVC types from domestic double glazing suppliers. Those two less usual materials can only be made with all right-angled corners which can look slightly stark on a cabin-side. However, rectangular frames in aluminium could be colour-keyed to a traditional cabin-side livery as several manufacturers offer bright powder coated colours in addition to the popular natural and 'brass' finishes.

Other shapes you might consider in aluminium include four rounded corners (for a more sophisticated elevation), arched top (as popularised by Dutch barge conversions) and large round portholes.

Drop back top vents provide ventilation in almost any weather but are so small as to avoid a security risk when left open. Full-height drop back vents can usually be taken right out to let in more air in hot conditions – but are less secure. Sliding panels set below drop back top vents in a single window unit increase the options for fresh air and create a communications- or even escape-hatch. Louvre windows (more often framed in stainless steel) have been popular in hire craft because the louvre glazing is easily replaced. Most private owners are less impressed – the louvres tend to be draughty, leak at the corners and the blades project out over the side deck when open. Note that all windows should be glazed in toughened glass.

Portholes offer security and privacy and do not make the interior as dark as you might think.

Typical narrowboat window with square top corners and rounded bottom ones.

Arch topped windows are often used on Dutch barges but can add interest to the elevation of a narrowboat.

Some owners prefer an elevation with only portholes for their greater security, privacy and traditional authenticity. However, these, and tinted windows, may not solve the privacy issue entirely. Owners report that towpath walkers are liable to peer in, unaware that the boat is occupied. Engraved or painted glass could attract its own problem – it makes a tempting target for vandals. Leaded patterns, increasingly popular, can be applied by the manufacturer, or you can buy a DIY kit for existing windows.

Narrowboat window makers offer double-glazed units and these are becoming increasingly popular. They are specified not so much for added insulation but to prevent condensation. This works on the glass but tends to produce even more condensation on the frame which, being so slender, cannot be made with a thermal break like windows in buildings. The usual answer is to incorporate a channel around the inside to catch the condensation and direct it outside.

Further reading: *The Narrowboat Builder's Book* – 3rd edition, published by *Waterways World*, is a guide to fitting-out narrowboats. If you plan to fit-out a shell or part-complete boat, that book is essential reading. If you are ordering a complete boat, its information is no less useful.

CHAPTER 9

WHO'S WHO IN BOATBUILDING

Anyone new to the boatbuilding scene is faced with a myriad of builders all claiming to be the best and often rubbishing the opposition mercilessly. How do you tell the value-for-money bargain from the cheap and nasty or the quality in depth from the 'all fur coat and no knickers'?

There is no real substitute for experience gained by looking at as many boats and talking to as many people as possible. There is also no single 'best narrowboat builder'. One company might be recognised for its replicas of working narrowboats, another for its ability to do innovative details in steel, another for basic, economically-priced boats.

The following list is divided into specialisations, with commentary on some of the names to help newcomers to the canals to work out just who is who.

Replica builders

The small group of builders who create close replicas of working craft has grown out of repairers of working boats in response to a shortage of craft to convert and reluctance to desecrate historic boats by turning them into floating cottages. While real replica builders rate very highly with narrowboat enthusiasts, the term 'replica' has been loosely applied by less skilful builders. Replica builders tend to be unassuming, down-to-earth characters, and generally show remarkable lack of competitiveness towards each other.

The **Warwickshire Fly Boat Company** has operated, repaired and sold working boats at Stockton for many years. Ex WFBC personnel Steve Priest and Rex Wain together with Rex's brother, Simon, have now set up

Unusual shell, modelled on a harbour launch, by Five Towns Boat Building.

Perhaps the most prolific replica builder so far is **Five Towns Boat Building**, better known by the name of its principal Roger Fuller. As well as producing replica narrowboats, Roger is well known for river tugs and narrowbeam Dutch barges. Roger's brother Martin coined the evocative term 'washer joshers' for replicas (steel washers are used to form dummy rivets).

BCN builders

The Black Country has a long tradition of narrowboat building. Several builders around Birmingham build in a distinctive and pleasing style which is clearly traditional but

Replica Josher bow by the Warwickshire Fly Boat Company.

Brinklow Boat Services at Stretton under Fosse. **Ian Kemp** is held in very high regard but is particularly self-effacing and mainly concerns himself with restoring. He is now based at Stourbridge in a yard which he shares with well respected BCN boatbuilder, **David Harris,** and boat painter, Phil Speight. Richard Hurley, who trained with Ian, is based at Oldbury Boat Services but is no longer building new boats. Keith Ball, trading as **Industry Narrowboats** is at Stretton on the Shropshire Union.

Solid, BCN character from Canal Transport Services.

does not exactly replicate particular builders of the past. Their craft also tend to be very robust in their details.

The doyen of BCN builders was Les Allen & Sons, not least because, before the company closed its doors in 1998, it was the country's only surviving builder of working narrowboats boasting a century-long association with canals. Ex-employee John Horton continues to build in similar style at **Oldbury Boat Services** yard. **Canal Transport Services**, the company of Denis Cooper, has been building and restoring traditional boats for thirty

Well-proportioned, traditional shell by Limekiln Narrowboats.

The unassuming but attractive lines of a Colecraft.

years. Graham Edgson, trading as **Norton Canes Boatbuilders,** produces an exceptional standard of steelwork. In recent years, he has veered towards being a replica builder. **CanalCraft** (not to be confused with the brokerage company) was started by Graham Parker but he has since retired. It is now run by Neil Butlin and operates in association with JD Boat Services at Gailey. Other BCN names include **Orion Narrowboats** (long, low tugs),

Arcrite Engineering has been building quietly-styled narrowboats, many of them for hire fleets, for more than two decades. **John South's** output, similarly discreet, mainly goes to hire boat operator, Starline Narrowboats. **Liverpool Boats** – a major shell builder that started at the budget end but is now edging towards middle-of-the-market – is one of the most experienced of this group. **John White** is a Liverpudlian neighbour and competitor, producing well proportioned, simply detailed shells.

Characteristic bow from Steve Hudson.

Traditional references on this bow by Liverpool Boats.

Limekiln Narrowboats (similar lines to Les Allen) and **Phil Jones** (meaty but elegant boats).

In addition to these are two builders who, although they are not located around the Black Country, draw their inspiration from it. **Steve Hudson** builds in Josher style with chunky, no-nonsense detail and, preferably, a vintage engine. Hudson is Leicestershire born but is now based at Glascote. Burton-on-Trent based **Tony Francis** owned boats by David Harris and their influence is evident in the boats he now produces.

Leading production builders

Some builders have concentrated on serving the market with a reliable product – well finished, on (or near) time – with pleasant lines if not such ambitious styling as the replica and BCN builders.

Colecraft, one of the canal's most prolific current builders, celebrated its 25th anniversary in 1999. Its original output – with chubby bow surmounted by double-stepped deck cants – was a trademark although it now offers a Josher-inspired alternative. Recently, Colecraft has faced competition from ex-employee, Graham Reeves. **G & J Reeves** has developed a style of its own and shells are increasingly sought after by the fitting out trade.

One of Liverpool Boats' other competitors, in terms of volume and price, is **R&D Marine**. The company is run by Ray Denton who started his career with Hancock & Lane. Some R&D boats have a special slipper swim designed to reduce wash. **South West Durham Steelcraft** is based in Durham, and attracts many of its narrowboat orders from the Leeds & Liverpool Canal. **Heron Boatbuilders** started fitting out bought in shells for shared ownership in 1996 but now build their own shells and fit them out for the sole-owner market.

Hire operators

Hire fleets have the experience to fit-out durably and some have developed to be as much recognised for their boatbuilding as their hire holidays. **Alvechurch Boat Centres** specialise in chunky-looking steelwork and wash-reducing Eco hulls. **C T Fox** has individual ideas on narrowboat building. Stem posts are topped by an unmistakable dorsal fin, intended to stop them catching under lock gates.

Other hire-proven companies building and fitting out for the private market are **Bettisfield Pleasure Boats, Club Line, Severn Valley Boat Centre, Snaygill Boats** and **Starline Narrowboats**

The bulbous bow of an Eco hull by Alvechurch Boat Centres.

Narrow beam Dutch barge by Dave Thomas.

Specialist builders

Sagar Marine is a leading builder of inspection launches. The company has exceptional expertise in fabricating complicated shapes in steel – which its be-columned launches show off well. **Peter Nicholls'** launches are less decorative. Both builders have also tackled barge styles – Peter Nicholls' barges are aimed up-market and some of them are designed for sail. The Nicholls reputation also benefits from his ability to maintain good relationships with customers – a notable virtue in the canal industry. Sagar's neighbour **Tayberg Boats** has built a not un-Sagar-like launch.

is equally at home producing sea-going yachts, narrowbeam Dutch barges and narrowboats.

Wide beam Dutch barge built by French and Peel.

The Shropshire Union line

Shropshire Union Cruisers' pioneering Cutlass narrowboat of the early sixties begat a large family of independent builders who share in common a broad-bladed stempost and generally pleasant lines – even from the most modest of them. However, as a group, they are often reluctant to admit common styling influence.

The style was originally disseminated by Seamus Walsh and by David Piper, now trading as **Piper Boatbuilding** who has built up a strong following (including an owners' club) for his thoughtfully engineered boats. The influence passed to **Stoke-on-Trent Boat Building**, which has specialised in up-market craft, via Phil Trotter who is now at **R W Davies & Son**.

Elegant inspection launch by Sagar Marine.

The concept of British-built Dutch barges was introduced by Balliol Fowden in the mid-eighties. He managed to translate the style to narrow-beam with great subtlety. 'Balliol's barges', both wide and narrow, are built by ex-employees **Dave Thomas** and Roger Farrington (**Ivybridge Marine**). Conventional narrowboats built by these individuals are also good-looking and well built.
Heritage Boat Builders is an enterprising company based at Evesham (its output has included a futuristic narrowboat and a short wheelhouse barge). **Branson Boats** willingly undertakes unusual projects. Its output so far includes a variety of traditional-style launches, and a huge trawler-style barge.
French & Peel, which has ship-building background, can tackle a wide variety of inland and coastal shell designs.
R&D Marine, already mentioned as a production builder, does value-for-money Dutch barges and even better value wide-beam narrowboats. Pennine-based **Pickwell & Arnold** produces similarly spacious barges. **Sirius Yachts**

This David Piper boat has slightly untypical, arch-topped windows – most have long horizontal ones.

The Northwich Trader class, which recreates working boat proportions and details, is built by Phil Trotter, now at R W Davis & Son.

Mike Heywood, also ex-David Piper, is a pivotal figure in the industry. He built several hundred shells in this common style – all so low priced as to influence pricing widely. Heywood is now employed by **Evans & Son**, who continue to build pleasant shells at competitive prices. Despite his budget identity, Heywood has brought forth several impressive builders. Not least of these is his

Mike Heywood is another ex-Piper employee who influenced many builders in his turn.

nephew, **Jonathan Wilson**, whose flamboyant shells have been used by more than one prize-winning fitter-out. Erstwhile Wilson partner, **Gary Gorton**, offers neat finishes as do **GT Narrowboats** (also ex-Heywood).

Midland Canal Centre's lines were inherited via Jonathan Wilson.

Wilson stayed long enough at **Midland Canal Centre** to provide it with a strong visual identity. MCC has good facilities and management resource, is building in quantity, and has won the IWA's 'Best Value Boatbuilder' award. Back at Shropshire Union Cruisers, the inheritor of that company, **Falcon**, still builds in the broad-bladed stem style.

Unclassified

Several builders do not fit into any of the categories listed so far. **Stowe Hill Marine** specialises in traditional tug-style (low-slung) boats, usually fully-fitted in exuberant style. **Mel Davis** rejoices in introducing

Stowe Hill Marine is well known for its low-slung tugs.

sweeping curves into his shells. **Measham Boats** was started by two coded welders and is becoming popular with the trade. **Cotswold Narrowboat Co** can produce boats of meaty, working boat proportions as well as more conventional types. Jim Sparks and Richard Fee both learned their trade around the Stourport area and now run their own companies – **Alexander Boatbuilders** and **Ledgard Bridge Boat Co**. Finally, **John Pinder** has built just about every kind of boat from broad beam Dutch barges to narrowboats and from trans-Atlantic yachts to a narrowbeam frigate for Royal Navy recruitment.

Budget builders

Several builders, like Stoke on Trent Boat Building, and Midland Canal Centre (see above) have introduced budget class starter boats alongside their standard ranges.

A number of other companies who concentrate their activities solely at this end of the market have come and gone in recent years. In this category, the old saying 'you get what you pay for' is particularly relevant. Buyers should pay close attention to the build quality of the boat and the financial soundness of the company.

Budget class boat from Stoke-on-Trent Boat Building.

The curvaceous desk in this Warble interior ingeniously conceals the PropGen power unit.

Fitters-out

Shell builders are readily identifiable because of the scale of their activities. Fitters out vary from large, nationally known companies to one-man-bands working almost unnoticed. Many of the builders already listed (Colecraft, Stowe Hill Marine, Stoke-on Trent Boat Building for instance) are known for their fitting-out as much as for their shells.

Warble Narrowboats' Kevin Wadsworth has a high profile as a prize-winning fitter-out. He has started producing off-the-peg boats alongside the more familiar bespoke boats. **Stephen Goldsbrough** fit-outs are numerous and he too has won several 'best boat' awards. Goldsbrough is one of the few fitters-out that has an active owners' club. **Blue Haven Marine** was formed by two ex-Rugby Boatbuilders fitters, Robin Bourne and Barry Smith and produces imaginative interiors for private customers and for the Challenger Syndicateships fleet. Serial award-winners, **Kingsground Narrowboats,** was set up by Richard Haynes in 1996 and produces thoughtfully detailed, well crafted boats.

Barry Hawkins, **Jeff Corbett** and **Braidbar Boats** may not have such a high profile but their boats have a great sense of style. Occupying the solid middle ground of boat fitting are **Lexden Swan, Merlin Narrowboats, Milburn**

Jeff Corbett's boats have a great sense of style.

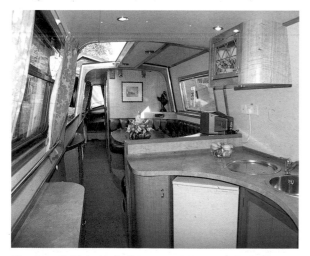

Stephen Goldsbrough fits out mainly for the private market but this unusual boat is available for hire.

Newcomer, Riverview Narrowboats, is typical of the solid, middle ground of the boat fitting market.

Reading Marine produces up-market boats for private customers as well as running a hire fleet.

Boats, Roger Myers, Navigation Narrowboats, Nimbus Narrowboats, Orchard Marina, Riverview Narrowboats and Sabre Narrowboats.

Several hire companies fit out, as opposed to build, for the private market. Warwickshire Narrowboats, now associated with Rose Narrowboats, is firmly established in the upper market as are Reading Marine and Weltonfield Narrowboats. J D Boat Services operates a fleet under the Viking franchise and is one of the most conscientious of fitters-out. Other names in this category are Ashby Narrow Boat Co, Britannia Narrow Boats, Calcutt Boats, Jannel Cruisers, Kate Boats and Wyvern Shipping Co.

The comments about budget shell builders apply equally to budget boat fitters.

Canal cruisers

The important four-berth glass-fibre market is presently served by three builders, Viking, Shetland and Wilderness. **Viking** is, by far, the most prolific of these with its 23, 28 and 32ft models. Its glossy, highly-styled range is marketed from the rivers Thames, Wey and Severn and the Broads by Walton Marine. **Shetland** canal cruisers are now competitors to Viking, with similar mini-river cruiser philosophy. They build a 4 berth 25 footer and a 32ft centre cockpit model with 6 berths.

Viking and Shetland are based on river cruiser designs but the **Wilderness** range sacrifices outward style for maximum internal space and ease of handling. The three model range can even be used, in conjunction with the purpose-built trailer, as a caravan. The smallest 17ft 6in model can be towed behind a medium-sized car and, although not built in large numbers, they out number other makes among serious trailable cruiser enthusiasts.

Viking's three narrowbeam glass fibre cruisers.

CHAPTER 10

ENGINES AND ENGINE INSTALLATION

The special priorities of an engine for a modern inland waterway boat should be:

1) The ability to run indefinitely at pottering speeds without temperament.
2) Good response at low speeds so that the boat will manoeuvre and stop without drama.
3) Reasonable fuel economy.
4) Noise levels that do not intrude on enjoyment of the waterways.
5) Low risk of fire or explosion.

Although neither meets these criteria entirely, inboard diesel engines and four-stroke petrol outboards still dominate the inland market.

Beta's 28hp BD1005

Diesels – engine size

The question often asked is 'how many horse-power are needed?' In practice, not many. The average engine installed in narrowboats today can produce around 30hp at its maximum speed. Yet if the propeller delivers much more than 3hp into a canal, the consequent wash may draw complaints.

Even ploughing against a strong river current, the propeller is probably delivering between 5hp and 10hp (depending on size of boat). Substantial power losses are incurred all the way along the transmission line from gearbox to propeller. Gearbox, alternator, water pump, shaft bearings and general misalignment absorb approximately 10% of the engine's power. Efficiency of propellers varies according to relative size and shape. One to fit a 3:1 gearbox reduction may be 60% efficient while that one on a shaft without any reduction might be less than 45% efficient.

So, to cope with large rivers, a small narrowboat needs an engine rated at around 10hp and the largest needs no more than 20hp. However, while the engines of offshore powercraft are expected to work hard for most of their cruising time, busy engines intrude on the relative peace of canal cruising. Consequently a generous power margin is usually specified so that the engine sounds comfortable at river speeds and totally relaxed on canals – hence the original 30hp.

Torque and engine capacity

The trend in diesel technology is towards lighter units producing higher power outputs. This is fine for yachts and most motor cruisers where light weight is an asset. Narrowboats, on the other hand, are inescapably heavy – the owner of a 45ft/nine tons narrowboat need take only a single glance at the average compact modern 20hp diesel to know that it lacks the necessary guts and durability for emergency stops, and for punching out across weir-streams. 20hp may be sufficient theoretically, but the engine needs torque to wind itself up to enough speed, under heavy load, to deliver that power – as soon as it is needed. So, the question that should be asked is 'How much torque is needed?'

When shown in engine manufacturers' brochures, it is often found in a graph adjacent to one for power. From

these it is immediately clear that while power increases with speed, torque output varies less – and its maximum is often at quite low rpm. This low speed gutsiness is just what heavy narrowboats appreciate. In fact, it can be taken for granted that, if an engine's torque output is high enough, its power output is also bound to be adequate.

For example, according to the engine chart in Appendix 2, Beta Marine's BD1005 has a seven horsepower advantage over the traditionally-designed Russell Newbery DM2. However, the Beta's maximum torque output is 45ft-lb, less than half that of the DM2. Not

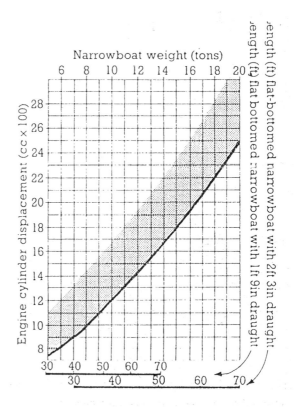

The Russell Newbery DM2 has less horsepower but can power a much larger boat.

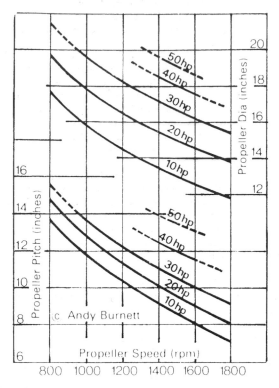

surprisingly the first engine is installed in smallish narrowboats whereas the DM2 will comfortably manage full length craft. (Beta Marine won't be too upset by the comparison; it offers several models with more torque than the DM2, including its 150ft-lb Tug engine).

Manufacturers do not always reveal torque figures. However, torque correlates quite closely to cylinder cubic capacity – in the example above, the BD1005 has a cylinder capacity of 1,001cc, the DM2, 2,628cc – so the difference in torque fairly closely follows the difference in capacity. It is this standard, familiar to any car buyer, that should be used to establish suitable engine sizes for narrowboats.

The other variable, size of boat, is not a matter of length but of weight. The momentum of a deep-draughted 45ft traditional tug at 17 tons clearly takes far more stopping than a 55ft vee-bottomed Springer narrowboat at, perhaps, 11 tons. A reasonable minimum seems to be about 125cc cylinder capacity per ton weight, although this might be increased towards 150cc per ton for smaller narrowboats – under 40ft length.

Engines can be too large. All are designed to be most efficient when working reasonably hard. Generally, the more efficient the design, the less tolerant it is of running under light loads. If a lubrication system fails to reach working temperature, sludge can be precipitated into the sump where its accumulation eventually reduces capacity for lubricating oil to inadequate levels. A water temperature gauge only indicates conditions at the top of the engine – the water may be brought up to temperature by its thermostat while the bottom end remains relatively cold. Bad practice by owners is a contributory factor – running engines off-load for long periods, just to charge the

batteries, promotes sludging and 'glazed' cylinder bores. Tolerance of low speed running varies between different types of diesel. The best automotive designs are rarely fitted to inland craft. Industrial engines, particularly those developed for agricultural use (which also involves long periods at low speeds), are generally happy when canal cruising.

An arbitrary guide to maximum engine size is that it should be no more than 25% greater than the minimum. The older, and more tolerant the engine design, the more this rule might be relaxed. The diagram shows maxima and mimima against different weights – which are then scaled against two combinations of length and draught.

Marine gearboxes are compact and operate without a clutch.

Gearboxes & reductions

The function of a marine gearbox is to provide alternatives of forward and reverse gears while reducing the engine's speed to one that can be more efficiently used by the propeller. As in a car, changing gear involves a clutch, although it is situated inside the main gearbox and operates automatically. When ordering a new engine, customers can specify from a range of gearbox reduction ratios. In addition to increasing propeller efficiency, stepping down the prop-shaft speed increases torque in proportion to the reduction ratio. However the extra gain achieved by fitting a 3:1 ratio instead of the conventional 2:1 is no real substitute for a gutsy, durable engine.

Large traditional engines like the Gardner 2LW, and Russell Newbery DM2 have so much torque to spare for pushing relatively light modern narrowboats that they can be installed without any reduction ratio. Arguably, any slight performance loss suffered would be offset by the shallower draught needed (thus less overall weight to haul). But for the typical modern narrowboat with an engine of less than 2 litres capacity, a 2:1 gearbox reduction is reasonably efficient and allows the appropriate propeller to fit behind an average stern post height of 20in-21in while still leaving at least 10% tip clearance (the minimum). Arguments for maximum possible tip clearance are that it reduces the likelihood of flotsam jamming between prop and counter and that it lessens annoying prop turbulence immediately aft of the counter. The high propeller torque of a 3:1 reduction can also magnify the stern's tendency to swing to one side when stopping or when trying to steer going astern.

Gearboxes can be mechanically or oil operated. The two makes used by most marinisers of engines for narrowboats are the German Hurth and British PRM – the former mechanical, the latter oil operated. Narrowboat engines are more at risk of exceeding their gearboxes' torque capacity than overpowering them. Torque limits for Hurth and PRM are shown in Chapter 19.

Propellers

There are so many variables to consider – length and weight of boat, efficiency of water supply to the stern post, engine power, shaft speed, stern post height, for instance – that the standard prop sizes quoted by engine builders and marinisers would seem to be fairly approximate. However, in many cases, only a couple of these variables appear to make a huge difference to the prop size needed. Against that, poor performance sometimes improves remarkably with a carefully revised choice of propeller. Many chandlers now have computer programmes that can work out your optimum propeller size in seconds.

A typical propeller size is 17in x 12in. The first figure is the diameter in inches, the second is the pitch (if the angle of the blades is imagined as a section of the thread on a screw, the pitch is the longitudinal distance moved by the thread

A conventional 3-bladed propeller.

when it has completed a full circle). The perfect propeller should just allow the engine to reach its maximum speed when pushing the boat on open water. In other applications, pitch can be traded off against diameter but, for narrowboat use, priority should be given to larger diameter for more efficient thrust. Quite a few major narrowboat engineers and chandlers can provide expert advice, and stock good ranges of new and reconditioned propellers. One manufacturer, Crowther Propellers, is uniquely dedicated to supplying special propellers for the narrowboat market. In addition to the standard version, a high-efficiency type, with several fuel saving features is offered. Both these have a blade area ratio of 50% (relative to the area contained in a circle of same diameter as the prop). For narrowboats with stern posts too short for the optimum diameter prop, the company supplies a type with increased blade area ratio (i.e. what cannot be fitted in lengthways is accommodated sideways). Crowthers also provide a prop repair service.

The diagram constructed by Andy Burnett some years ago is a general and approximate guide to narrowboat prop sizes, and may be of use for preliminary planning and costing.

Engine cooling

The majority of narrowboat engines are water cooled and linked to a hull-side skin cooling tank. The system is thus sealed and can be treated with anti-freeze to avoid winter draining-down. The arrangement is sometimes called 'keel cooling', although that really refers to cooling pipes that run in a circuit outside the hull – which is more practical for timber or glass-fibre craft than trying to cool a slab tank through the hull side.

Most skin tank-cooled engines are based on water cooled exhaust manifold jackets originally designed for fresh-water cooling. The latter system takes in canal or river

Mud box strainer for a fresh water cooling system.

The canvas duct on this Lister engine reveals that it is air-cooled.

water (through a small filter or, on inland waterways, a larger 'mud box'), then uses it to cool a separate sealed circuit via a heat exchanger mounted inside the manifold jacket.

Cooling problems sometimes arise because skin tanks are incorrectly sited or too small. If the hull-side profile at that point is heavily curved, resultant turbulence in outside water may reduce efficiency. Cooling is also much more effective if the tank is fitted with internal baffles to prevent the hot water taking a short cut from tank inlet to outlet. The only rule-of-thumb encountered for tank size recommends 1 sq ft of cooling surface for every $3^1/_2$ hp of engine power. For a typical narrowboat with 30hp diesel, this suggests a 5ft 0in x 1ft 9in panel. In practice, the average size is around 3ft 6in x 1ft 9in – which is probably adequate since most 30hp narrowboat engines never exceed 20hp for more than a few minutes. Some narrowboats have twin skin tanks, one on each side of the hull, with a two-way cock. Water runs through both tanks on rivers but is switched to by-pass one on canals.

Large traditional diesels, with generous cooling passages that are not so sensitive to built-up sludge, sometimes use raw water cooling – from a mud box direct into the block, then overboard via a water injected exhaust or separately. Raw water cooled engines can readily be adapted to a skin tank layout.

Air cooled narrowboat engines are limited mainly to Lister's secondhand S and (larger) H range. Twenty years ago the S engines (SR and ST) monopolised the narrowboat market because of their indestructibility and simplicity. Little can go wrong with air cooling provided the compartment is well ventilated and the engine ducted as necessary. On the downside, air-cooled engines are, almost without exception, noisy – and you cannot run the waste heat through a calorifier to warm the cabin water.

DIY conversions

Converting a secondhand vehicle engine for marine use looks deceptively simple. The usual candidates for narrowboat installation are BL1.5 and 1.8 diesels. The job basically involves attaching a marine gearbox via a special bell-housing and drive plate to the back end, bolting on marine engine mounting feet – and replacing the automotive exhaust manifold with a water cooled version. Some owners omit the last because some other marine engines (like air-cooled Listers, for instance) are not so fitted. Unless the compartment is well ventilated, a water-cooled manifold is necessary.

In addition to these few major items, the DIY mariniser/installer may have to obtain external water pump, sump pump kit, half-coupling, flexible coupling, intermediate shaft bearing(s), prop-shaft, stern tube & greaser, control box, cables & fitting kit, silencer, exhaust pipe, flexible exhaust bellows, fuel cock, fuel/water filter, fixed & flexible fuel lines.

Several companies supply a full range of marinising equipment but Lancing Marine deserves a mention if only because its spectacularly comprehensive brochure includes step-by-step advice on assessing secondhand base engines. It is modestly titled 'The Boat Builders Guide To Engines And Marinising And Everything'. That advice is, however, aimed at proficient DIY engineers. Another possibility (apart from buying ready marinised reconditioned engines from those companies that specialise in them) is to buy a reconditioned vehicle engine. Your local Yellow Pages should list several sources under 'Engine Reconditioning'. However, research may be worthwhile before committing yourself to a reconditioner (vehicular or marine). It is a business that attracts more than its fair share of shoddy workmanship.

Installation sundries

Fuel supply. The fuel tank filler should be on deck and unable to spill fuel inside the craft. A separate on-deck fuel vent is also needed. Narrowboat fuel tanks are usually of mild steel and integral with the shell. All supply lines and fittings should be of steel or copper, although final connections to the engine may be in approved armoured flexible hose to allow for vibration (only flexible hoses marked 'ISO 7840 – MARINE FUEL A' are now accepted). Plastic fuel tank sight gauges are not allowed, nor are soldered joints in the fuel line.

Exhaust and ventilation. Conventional narrowboat exhausts are dry rather than water-injected. Whether dry or wet, the exhaust should be fitted with a relevant silencer and dry exhaust assemblies should be lagged. Modern engines tend to be enclosed in insulated compartments but, if not provided with fresh air, they will suffer deteriorating performance as the air ingested becomes hotter and hotter. Fresh air can be drawn through the cabin bilge (usefully scavenging that space), through gaps in the engine box, through special ducts with assisting vent fans, or simply through hull side grills.

Stern bearing and seal. The stern shaft bearing, where the prop shaft passes through the hull to the propeller, is conventionally of plain metal in a steel case, with seals at either end. The forward seal, quaintly named 'stuffing box', is the main one. It consists of special rope-like packing wrapped round the shaft, compressed into place by an adjustable end cap. The space occupied by the packing is filled with grease, which, as it works its way out, is replenished from a screw greaser which should be given half a turn or so every day when cruising.

Some narrowboat builders try to make an aft-situated engine room as short as possible to leave more

Conventional stuffing box, rope and stern tube greaser.

cabin length for main accommodation. If the distance between the shaft coupling (immediately aft of the gearbox) and stern bearing is very short, sideways loads will be put on the bearing reducing its life and increasing vibration. A (very) few builders overcome this by using a cutlass stern bearing which is of neoprene (instead of plain metal) and thus allows the shaft to flex within it without loading. Cutlass bearings are potentially less noisy but more prone to wear by intruding grit. The Deep Sea Seal is an alternative to the conventional stuffing box forward seal. It is a deceptively simple two-part concoction of neoprene which makes a drip- and maintenance-free shaft seal with itself. The Deep Sea Seal can be vulnerable to grit wear but carries a spigot into which clean water can be fed, pressurising the Seal and adjacent cutlass bearing. The water is normally supplied by the engine cooling system, so will work with fresh water cooling, but not with a sealed skin tank system.

Control systems. The main choice is between single lever control boxes and traditional speedwheel systems. If your engine is a modern boxed- or decked-in unit, only the single lever type, which operates both throttle and gears, is relevant. The mechanism is almost foolproof – if set up properly. Boxes have adjustable innards to suit different engines and gearboxes.

Speedwheel systems recreate the control systems used in pre-war working narrowboats. They are fitted in traditional style narrowboats with replica boatmans cabins. The speedwheel controls the throttle with good sensitivity and the gear control is normally a push-pull lever linked via cranks. Because the two controls are not linked, care is needed to reduce revs while going from forward to reverse. Wheel-operated gear changes have traditional antecedents but may be so slow as to be almost dangerous. Linkages can range from horrific (involving cotton reels, fishing line and elastic) to ingenious.

Outdrives

Introduced to the inland waterways some forty years ago and widely fitted to off-shore craft, the outdrive is, perhaps, due for re-discovery in river and canal cruisers. Popularly called Z-drives (because that is how they direct the drive line out through a flat transom, down, then out via a submerged gearbox) outdrives simplify installation and reduce engine compartment space. They also allow easy access to the propeller – the complete external unit can be hinged up or wound up sideways. The make most commonly fitted to inland cruisers, the Enfield drive, is still available, and would marry well with modern small diesels

A selection of 'Z' drive units.

for a compact and competitive installation.

Outdrives, based on alloy castings, are more substantial than the average outboard motor but not as sturdy as a narrowboat skeg. As in an outboard motor, the gearbox is mounted underwater on the prop-shaft. So, if the shaft seal is damaged, the gear oil becomes emulsified and large bills for new gears arise – unless you make simple but regular checks.

The electric future?

It may be that most narrowboats of the immediate future will still contain conventional installations – diesel under the steerer's feet, driving a short prop shaft via a mechanical gearbox. But several unrelated factors may come together to launch the age of the electric canal boat – some twenty years after the first electric narrowboats were introduced, then faded from view for want of a nationwide charging network.

What are the benefits of electric drive anyway? It is quiet, potentially almost silent; it is clean – emitting no irritating or toxic exhaust; and it is economical in simple fuel terms – a typical overnight battery recharge costs about £1.50.

The arguments against electric drive so far? With enough dedication, a diesel engine can be made as quiet as electric. While recharging costs are low, initial outlay on batteries is high – the entire propulsion installation becomes considerably more expensive than for conventional diesel drive. And if we include pollution back at the power station......

The power output of narrowboat electric motors need only be relatively small because their inherent torque (pulling power) is massive at almost zero engine speed. A diesel engine that can manage comparable torque (although usually at around 1,200rpm) typically produces 15kW maximum power compared to about 6kW from a narrowboat electric motor. That 15kW (or 20hp) is usable on rivers, while running an electric motor at full power severely reduces the range of even a substantial battery bank.

Lack of charging points is ultimately the greatest turn-off. Electric cruising has established itself on smaller waterways like the Broads and the Monmouthshire & Brecon Canal where, with only a limited number of points, craft are never more than a few miles from a recharge. On the main canal system, narrow-boaters are put off by the idea of batteries finally flattening while out in the wilds. Authorities have succumbed to a chicken-and-egg dilemma – refusing to install a canal-wide network of charging points until sure of demand.

So far, the drawbacks of electric propulsion overwhelm its benefits. However developments started in the nineties may well tip the balance back. Some old-fashioned diesels that are well suited to running at low speed on canals may struggle to meet forthcoming exhaust pollution standards (although these will not apply to engines already installed). There is even a question mark about health risks from modern diesel designs. Research suggests that ultra-fine specks of diesel soot, called fine particulates (as against the visible smoky stuff) could be implicated in severe cardio-vascular and respiratory illnesses. The research seems to be based on studies in urban traffic but many narrowboat exhausts emerge just a few feet from the steerer's face.

Electric propulsion has also been hampered by its technological stagnation. Now the state of California has effectively demanded viable electric cars within a decade, concentrating manufacturers' minds on better batteries and drive systems. Controllers available for marine use are already more efficient than those of the early nineties. Improved and/or lower-priced batteries will increase the average cruising range.

The answer to the charging point problem could be simple: diesel engines. Extended canal cruising of the future could be based on diesel-electric drive, diesel/electric or electric backed up by diesel – depending on the exact configuration.

Diesel-electric

Many modern narrowboats demand so much cabin electric power that they carry a built-in diesel generator in addition to the diesel propulsion engine. This is because the propulsion engine is too large to run just for generating

Looking down onto the generator and double Lynch motor in a 60ft narrowboat.

electric power without risk of increased internal wear through light-load running.

On the other hand, a relatively small diesel could generate cabin power efficiently and, by driving an electric motor on the prop shaft, could replace a larger engine for propulsion. The electric transmission is a superb torque converter, endowing the little engine with torque to start and stop a large narrowboat confidently.

That small diesel can be set to run constantly at its most efficient speed, reducing exhaust pollution considerably over the tickover-plus-400rpm regime of existing narrowboat engines. The constant note and relatively light weight of the engine, mechanically isolated from the shell, is easy to insulate to near silence. The compact unit could even be moved to a position remote from front and rear decks. This is diesel-electric propulsion and it is already in existence in the form of the HFL drive/generating package. This system is based on 380 volts three-phase output to the propulsion motor, which makes it particularly efficient but does not easily allow development into . . .

Diesel/electric

Replacing the hyphen between 'diesel' and 'electric' with an oblique slash, signifies that drive can either be by diesel or electric. This might be based on a diesel-electric system (more-or-less as above) but with a bank of batteries for occasional engine-off propulsion (as when working a flight of locks in fume-free silence). For this to work simply, the propulsion motor has to be relatively low voltage DC.

The Thames Electric Launch Company offers an alternative arrangement that can be fitted to existing narrowboats (even inboard shaft-drive canal cruisers) without disturbing the conventional engine installation. A compact 36-volt electric motor sits just above the diesel's gearbox to drive the propshaft via a toothed belt and automatic clutch. It is powered by banks of batteries that fit into most engine compartments. Recharging could be from a 230-volt supply through a charger or by a special engine-driven alternator. With the former, 100% electric cruising would be possible as long as a hook-up is found every night. With an engine-driven alternator 55% diesel to 45% electric cruising might be possible (but bear in mind that, unlike the tickover of a diesel, when the electric drive is not driving, it is not consuming power). Whichever option you choose, the TELCo system offers electric cruising with complete peace-of-mind – if your propulsion batteries flatten in the back of beyond, you resort to diesel drive.

More recently, a system based on a 96-volt double Lynch motor has been installed in a 60ft narrowboat It performs as well as a 1.9 litre diesel engine for up to 10 hours before the battery bank needs a charge from a land line or the 12kW inboard generator.

Electric with diesel back-up

The distinction between the first type of diesel/electric described above, and electric with diesel back-up could be just of emphasis. The Herbert Wood hire fleet introduced an electric hire cruiser in 1995 – but with diesel generator for back-up. *Quiet Light* has battery range for two days' cruising and, with the Broads network of charging points, rarely has need of the generator. But it can recharge batteries, or it can propel the boat without recharging, or it could work with the batteries to power the boat against a flood.

Beta Marine's PropGen unit with part of the acoustic enclosure removed.

The set-up undoubtedly removes hirers' lingering doubts about being stranded but has even more relevance to the canal system.

While electric with diesel back-up adds up to a particularly expensive installation, it does, like TELCo's diesel/electric system, provide electric cruising with total independence. But electric drive with diesel back-up is more likely to be specified in new boats.

Recent developments

In the late nineties, Beta Marine developed a package called the PropGen. The aim is to provide a single power source capable, simultaneously, of propelling the boat and producing enough electricity to enable it to be completely gasless. It does this with a 30hp BV 2203 or 40hp BF 2803 engine set to a fixed speed of 1500rpm and coupled, at the forward end, to an 11.3 kVA Genko generator. A Newage hydraulic gearbox is connected to the flywheel and the propeller speed can be varied from 0 to 750 rpm by a Newage trolling valve/feathering device which bleeds the clutches of oil pressure. The smaller engine is for boats up to 55 or 60ft and the larger is for boats of 60 to 70ft.

The engine speed remains constant regardless of how fast or slow the boat is travelling. The whole unit is housed in an acoustic enclosure which reduces the noise level to about 68dbA at one metre. Although the trolling valve is new to the inland waterways, it is fairly common on fishing boats which need power for auxiliary equipment like winches while, at the same time, the boat is being manoeuvred about.

Quietening diesels

Perhaps you aren't convinced about the merits of electric drive or maybe you are but can't afford the high prices of electric installations. Those prices are, for the moment at least, inescapable. However, you can take steps to make a diesel quieter and cleaner.

The factors that affect diesel noise include combustion cylinder head design, weight and configuration of the engine, propeller size, engine mounts and coupling, engine alignment, compartment insulation and type of exhaust. Engine position is a consideration too – it is much quieter ten feet away than under your feet.

Direct fuel injection is noisier than injecting diesel fuel into a small ante-chamber (indirect injection). Most modern narrowboat diesels use indirect injection but the Lister Alpha, for instance, is built in both versions – the direct injection LPW range is noisier than the indirect injection LPWS.

Flexible couplings prevent engine vibration from being transmitted to the hull.

More cylinders, and less weight make for less noise than a slow-revving heavy twin. However, if you buy the latter, you will almost certainly be more interested in a measured vintage kerdonk kerdonk than suppression. In fact lighter engines are not necessarily quieter than heavier ones – but their noise is mainly at higher frequencies which are easier to dampen out.

The note of an engine becomes more strident when coupled to a smaller propeller – much as a car sounds busier in a low gear. Latitude in propeller sizing is very limited though – an inch off both diameter and pitch can make the difference between underpropping and overpropping. While the latter is quieter, severe overpropping may reduce canal cruising rpm enough to produce black smoke and affect the engine's long-term health.

With smaller, faster revving engines, less vibration is transmitted to the steel hull when the engine sits on flexible mounts. Marine mounts are individually designed to cope with the weight and speed of different engines. Unlike the car-type, they are also capable of taking the propeller's full thrust load. Any engine larger and heavier than a Perkins D3 will normally vibrate less if bolted to hardwood bearers.

Most engines, even if solid mounted, are fitted with a flexible coupling between engine and propeller shaft. Couplings vary from simple plastic-based discs with limited flexibility to the Aquadrive coupling. Unlike ordinary flexible types, the Aquadrive contains sideways engine shake and allows significant angular misalignment. It also

Acoustic foam with an internal sound-deadening membrane and a washable outer face.

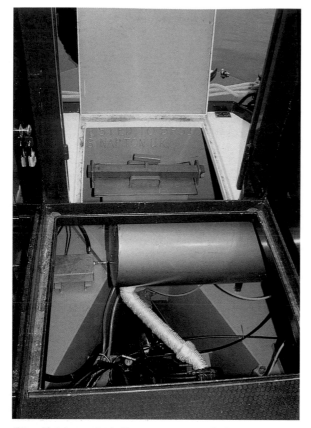

'Hospital generator' silencers are not always easy to accommodate but they are effective.

incorporates its own thrust bearing to take the propeller's thrust, and rubber mounts to absorb vibration.

Many flexible couplings have almost no tolerance of misalignment so should not be relied upon to correct an inherent fault that needs correcting by professional re-alignment.

In narrowboats, acoustic insulation foam is usually fitted under engine compartment deck boards, and inside engine boxes. This has a substantial quietening

Mounting the engine in a box against the side of the hull reduces noise and gives more space.

effect. Builders of glass-fibre offshore cruisers tend to plaster the stuff on every hard surface in the compartment so that noise has nowhere to bounce. The improvement would be even more marked in steel hulls. When engine noise has been curtailed, other sounds become intrusive – like the exhaust note, wash and propeller turbulence against the swim plate. Insulating the swim plate could reduce the last two. Acoustic foam is carefully engineered – sometimes it sandwiches a heavy lead-like membrane for extra deadening – and is faced with fire retardant, washable plastic. While the foam is available from most larger chandlers, one company, TW Marine, specialises in total acoustic treatment.

Most narrowboat diesel exhausts carry a single silencer. A few owners have fitted additional expansion boxes with considerable softening of the exhaust note. Very large 'hospital generator' silencers have also been used to good effect. Thse are so large that they often have to be installed across the engine compartment.

If you are concerned about health risk from exhaust gases, a water-injected exhaust with water-lock/sump will wash out soot, although not necessarily fine particulates. Water-injected exhausts are standard on inboard powered craft other than narrowboats. A large filter (such as a 'mud box') should ensure that the inlet for the raw water involved does not become blocked with canal weed and rubbish. Water-injected exhausts may be regarded as antisocial if they spray sooty water over boats in locks. This problem can be overcome by using a separator silencer which, as its name implies, separates the exhaust gases from the cooling water and emits the former above the water level and the latter, silently, below.

Remote installations

Traditional enthusiasts know that a vintage engine sounds mellower, when distanced by a 9ft boatmans cabin. The standard shaft arrangement for this installation – a hollow intermediate prop shaft with a universal joint at each end – can be adapted to make a compact and quiet installation for a modern engine. Cranking the shaft allows the engine to be fitted in an insulated (but ventilated) box right against the hull-side. This makes almost no intrusion on cabin accommodation and, at 10ft forward of the steerer, is barely audible to him/her or to the forward cockpit. Wilson Drive Shafts of Nottingham are the specialists for this type of assembly. The universal joints involved can work up to 23° out of line; and linked drive lines have included up to three shafts.

Unlike other radical steps towards noise reduction, this one might be immediately cost-effective – because, by eliminating the engine room, it could fit planned accommodation into a shorter boat.

Hydraulic drive

Hydraulic drive has often been used to link remote-mounted engines to the prop shaft. The system allows all mechanical contact to be broken between shell and engine – reducing opportunities for transmitted vibration. It is particularly suitable for narrowboats as the engine can be mounted in the bow – as far away from the steerer as possible – with long straight hydraulic pipes incurring very little power loss. At thirty-or-so feet distance, an insulated diesel should be virtually inaudible. Fitting the engine in the bow can offer other advantages – it sits sideways, taking up little space, and leaving the cabin entirely free for accommodation. Once installed, the hydraulic pump can also be used to power a bow thruster and generator.

Hydraulic drive systems are generally more expensive than extended drive shafts (above), but less so than diesel-electric drive. However, the latter has several other advantages. It provides cabin power as well as motive power and its high-torque-at-zero-speed characteristic could reduce the engine size needed. Hydraulic systems are widely used in industry so mechanically adventurous owners could save considerable cost by sourcing their own drive parts. Of the marine providers of hydraulic drive, ARS Anglian Diesels is the most familiar name to narrowboaters.

Steam

Steam has its own magic. Some of the UK's thousands of steam train and traction engine enthusiasts are interested in canal boating and, not surprisingly, a few of these have specified steam to drive their narrowboats. The first mechanically propelled working narrowboats were, after all, steam driven. Steam generally does not make for

10hp steam engine in a 65ft narrowboat.

convenience. Rather than just turning a key, it demands time for building up steam. Systems can be gas-, oil- or coal-fired – the last requires careful and regular tending while cruising. If this sounds attractive, the Steam Boat Association of Great Britain (Tel: 0115 922 7654) will tell you more.

Outboard motors

Forty years ago, the majority of inland waterways cruisers (as apart from narrowboats) were powered by inboard petrol engines. While diesel engines displaced them in larger boats, the four-stroke petrol outboard became universal for budget-priced canal craft in the seventies. After near-total decline in the early eighties, outboard-powered canal cruisers re-invented themselves as entry-level buys for aspiring river boaters – some of whom pay over £25,000 for a new boat/motor package. With the advent of larger four-stroke outboards, the concept has been extended to wide-beam cruisers, where discreet outboard wells save on the high cost of river-sized inboard diesels.

Why four-stroke?

A review of outboards suitable for inland cruising can only consider four-stroke types. Traditionally, outboard motors have always been based on lightweight, fast revving engines. These are fine for lots of power on the back of light offshore craft – which accounts for the vast majority of the outboard market. For that sort of use, low speed guts (which two-strokes lack) is not a priority but it is a necessity for inland waterways use and four-strokes inherently pull better at low revs.

Lubrication oil for two-strokes is mixed in with the petrol. At low engine speeds the spark plug is often not hot enough to burn off an accumulation of oil on its electrode which can kill the spark. Over the years, as lubrication technology has improved, oil:petrol ratios have become smaller. With the introduction of more powerful electronic ignition and variable-mixture oil injection, two-strokes are far less temperamental than they used to be – but still not as happy as four strokes, when ticking over for long periods in locks.

Four-strokes are more fuel-economical too and, the lower the speed, the greater the saving. The fuel bill for the average 10hp four-stroke used on canals might be less than £100 for the same number of hours cruising – not a significant figure in overall annual running costs. The figure for a comparable two-stroke would be at least twice as much.

Four-strokes are arguably cleaner. Their exhaust emissions do not include burnt oil. However, quantities of toxic carbon monoxide are present and they are injected into the water through the underwater exhausts that all outboards use – to the discomfort of aquatic life. Larger four-strokes can be converted to run on LPG, which is less polluting than straight petrol.

Four-strokes enjoy one major advantage over almost every other type of propulsion. In a light, unballasted craft, a slow-running four-stroke petrol outboard competes even with electric propulsion for quietness.

The conventional way to install outboard motors is with wheel steering. However they lend themselves well to tiller steering in inland craft, providing a more direct response. And where steering a narrowboat involves some thinking ahead, tiller steering a light canal cruiser is dodgem-car instant – and fun.

Installation and spares

The particular advantage of outboards is that they need little installation compared to inboards. This saves many hundreds of pounds and means that the engine can be easily removed to the specialised facilities of a repair shop

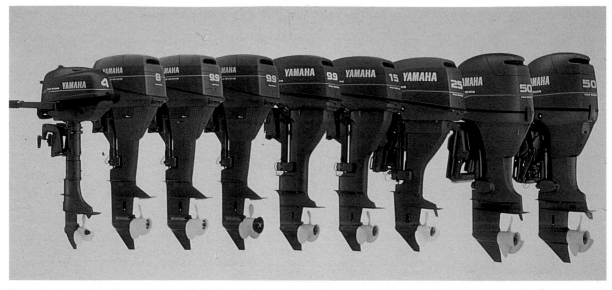

Four-stroke outboards are now available in all sizes.

– rather than suffering repair on an inhospitable towpath.

A by-product of hanging-on as against fitting-in is lower fire risk. If fuel leaks from an outboard powerblock, it usually runs overboard. The standard fuel tank is portable and, in modern glass-fibre craft, is housed in a sealed locker. However, most canal-size four-strokes are supplied with a smallish fuel tank which, on the average canal cruise, has to be refilled roughly every one-and-a-half days. This is when the risk of accident is greatest. If fuel is to be transferred, say from a jerrican, the operation should take place on shore where spillages cannot enter the hull. Ideally (but expensively) a spare outboard tank should be carried so that it can simply be plugged in. Owners should reject the temptation to fit inboard tanks – although the range is greatly increased, so is the risk of fire and explosion.

The high cost of extra outboard fuel tanks is just one example of the high cost of outboard spares. Since they were introduced to the UK in the seventies, Honda four-strokes, particularly, have enjoyed a reputation for reliability but, when spares are needed, they cost dear relative to those for British-built inboard engines. But then again, major outboard manufacturers establish widespread service dealer networks supported by formal mechanic training – not a common practice among inboard engine builders.

CHAPTER 11

WHO'S WHO IN MODERN ENGINES

Inboard diesel engines

The table in Appendix 2 lists nearly 100 diesel engines that could be fitted in inland waterways craft – from inboard canal cruisers to wide-beam barges. All are new units although several companies volunteered reconditioned engines – mainly based on BMC 1.5s and 1.8s. The forebears of that venerable but still popular design go back to a petrol engine of the thirties. Two companies supply new BMCs, both necessarily imported since the 1.5 ceased UK production in 1987. **AMC Engineering's** 1.5 is from India and **Calcutt Boats'** 1.8 is Turkish. Both are well proven in narrowboat use.

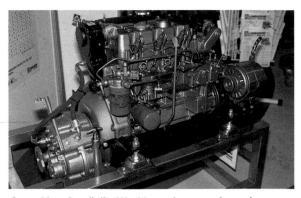

One of Lombardini's 'Workhorse' range of canal engines.

A BMC 1.8 imported from Turkey and marinised by Calcutt Boats.

Not so long ago, the CB 1.8 contended as narrowboating's most popular engine. The title probably now belongs to **Beta Marine's** range of Kubotas – smooth-running Japanese engines that appear to be quite tolerant of canal cruising regimes. Another manufacturer competing for the title is **Lister** which has long narrowboat associations. Its Canal Stars are based on the entirely British

industrial LPW Alpha range – all water-cooled, unlike the earlier SR, ST and TS Canal Star designs. Beta also faces competition from Nanni, the other company to offer Kubotas. Nanni is one of Europe's largest engine marinisers.

Japanese Mitsubishis have been fitted in narrowboats since the early seventies. The major Dutch mariniser **Vetus** continues to offer them and the **Thornycroft** name is now associated with Mitsubishi on which it has based its Kaizen range. Italy is another source of narrowboat engines with 2 new **Lombardini** 'Workhorse' engines being offered by Sowester. From the other end of Europe, the Danish **Bukh** is fairly modern, but probably too well-made (and therefore expensive) to fit into the mass narrowboat market.

All so far are lightish industrial-based engines, intended for discreet installations. Ford's XLD is also available in industrial form, although the overhead camshaft betrays its origin as an automotive engine. Nevertheless the XLD has proved quiet and reliable in narrowboats and **Club Line, Lancing Marine and Mermaid** are all long-time XLD marinisers. Vetus' larger engines are based on Peugeot automotive diesels – the 2.5 litre unit has been fitted in canal craft, while the

The all British Lister Canal Star 36.

Yanmar 'Shire' engines being run on a test rig at E P Barrus.

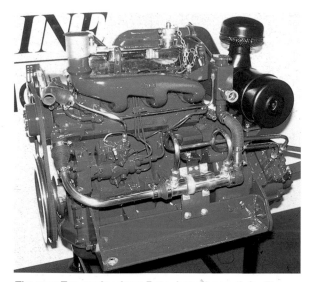

The new Tug engine from Beta, based on a John Deere engine.

A Russell Newbery DM2.

sophisticated (and less canal-proven) 1.7 and 1.9 litre designs are based on highly successful car engines. The Japanese **Yanmar** company is a world-wide mariniser producing yacht and workboat engines entirely with in-house parts – including its own gearboxes. It has recently entered the canal market with its impressive range of Shire engines.

Gardner re-introduced the 1930s designed 2LW in 1993.

Lancing Marine also listed Ford's 2.5 litre FSD engine, as fitted to Transit vans and it volunteered the 5 litre New Holland which, in a staid 2,000rpm rating, looks suitable for large wide-beam Europe-bound barges. However, if that engine interests you, it is also marinised by other companies including **Mermaid** and **Watermota.**

Conspicuous (as against concealed) engines are those intended for open engine rooms and for an exhaust stack to emphasise their ponderous note. These can be divided into wannabe and real vintage engines. The former include **Beta Marine's** Tug Engine – now a John Deere tractor diesel that has been derated and considerably worked on to make a fairly convincing and eye-catching traditional engine. **Perkins'** 3HD46 has plenty of guts, a slow tickover, ancestry in a fairly venerable Perkins design, and a respectable record in narrowboats. However, you can buy the same engine cheaper (and ticking over more slowly) from Calcutt Boats. Norwegian **SABBs** (not Saabs) are slow-revving traditional fishing boat diesels that are convincing as narrowboat engines except that the only model now available, the 10hp GG, only displaces 760cc. Its sturdy, well-balanced, single cylinder is a jewel of an engine in a small narrowboat.

For many years, narrowboaters could only buy one vintage engine – the **Russell Newbery** DM2. With changes of company ownership and competition from other rebuilt vintage engines, the DM2 lost some of its cult status for a while. However, an active owners club has done much to restore this and, with all optional brasswork, it is hard to beat for engine room glitz. The 'most desirable new vintage engine' title must now be shared with the **Gardner** 2LW, relaunched in 1993, and precision-built to a 1930 design by the original factory.

Four-stroke outboard engines

Honda was the pioneer, and still dominates in four-stroke outboards. The original 7.5hp version was introduced in 1972. A 10hp model followed in 1978 and a 15hp in 1988. The latter used a 280cc engine – still with two cylinders but featuring sophisticated gear-driven balance shafts to minimise vibration. Battery charging capability was increased to a canal-useful 10-amps and – at last – electric

Outboard diesel engines are a rarity but this Yanmar would push a 6 ton boat.

Electric outboards are almost silent and ideal for dinghies.

start became available. These last two features greatly increase the engine's potential as an alternative to inboard engines.

The advent of the 15hp, after some years of market speculation, was probably triggered by **Yamaha**'s introduction of a four-stroke outboard in 1985. This was a 323cc/10hp unit, offered in two versions. Model B had a conventional gearbox ratio but the lower revving model A was designed to push heavy displacement craft and features a larger reduction ratio through which it can drive a super-large (by outboard standards) 12.3in diameter propeller. 10-amp battery charging and electric start were included – and an elaborate automatic choke. The range has now grown to 15 engines from 4hp to 115hp, including 3 high thrust models which are particularly suited to inland boating.

Other manufacturers of two-stroke outboards were united in their scorn, until 1993, when they all announced their own ranges of four-strokes. This was forced upon them by impending anti-pollution legislation. However, the Mercury and Mariner ranges are both based on Yamaha's engines (but not legs). Evinrude's four-strokes look very competitive, particularly its 10hp model with standard 12-amp battery charging.

Honda has ventured into larger outboards in the nineties, with three- and four-cylinder units from 25hp to 90hp. The 75hp is a de-rated 90hp and is really too sporty for inland use although, ironically, it is based on a Honda engine that is particularly popular with sedately inclined UK car owners.

Diesel-powered outboard motors are mainly used by commercial operators. A diesel outboard is bound to be noisier than a petrol model, and, without careful installation (in an enclosed and insulated well), noisier than a comparable inboard diesel.

Many manufacturers now produce electric drive outboards, operating in near silence from a 12-volt battery. They are ideal for powering dinghies across a nearby lake or back to the pub you cruised past thinking there would be another one round the corner.

LEFT: Honda started the vogue for four-stroke outboards. This is their 9.9.

CHAPTER 12

WHO'S WHO IN VINTAGE ENGINES

It may seem odd to include a chapter on vintage engines in this section but the majority of refurbished engines are installed in new boats nowadays. Although they arrived relatively late in the history of working boats, and were described at the time as 'high speed diesels', vintage engines – their sound and profile particularly – are one of the essential attractions of narrowboating for many enthusiasts.

Until a few years ago, you needed to be mechanically adept and resourceful to own one but vintage diesels have become quite big business, supported by a growing number of canalside engineers. For some makes, parts and service are now only marginally less convenient than for modern engines. Demand is so great that Gardner has put its 2LW back into production after a 22 year lapse. The following thumbnail sketches cover six of the most well known vintage makes.

Bolinder

First, the exception to the generalisations above. Bolinders were among the first internal combustion engines to be fitted in narrowboats, pre-date 'high-speed' vintage engines by nearly thirty years and are not at all convenient to use.

Bolinder semi-diesels were among the first internal combustion engines used in working boats.

The Swedish company, set up in 1844, introduced its first two-stroke, hot-bulb, semi-diesel in 1902. Because it only partly followed Dr Diesel's principle (which involves applying enough compression in the cylinder to achieve combustion without external assistance), this design is called a semi-diesel and needs a blow-lamp to heat the cylinder head before start-up. A retractable stud in the face of the flywheel is used to kick the engine into life – hopefully without breaking the operative's leg if it decides to kick back.

Cadbury Bros fitted Bolinders in two narrowboats in 1911. Fellows Morton & Clayton (one of the two great pre-war fleets) followed Cadbury's example in 1912 – and fitted only Bolinders during the rest of its trading years.

The statistics of vintage engines look odd compared to modern ones – those for Bolinders particularly so. The first E-type engine produced just 15hp from a single cylinder, at a maximum speed of 450rpm (tickover was 100rpm). However, the capacity of that cylinder was 8.35 litres, and the engine weighed 3,350lb, without gearbox.

Most Bolinders were never fitted with gearboxes. The engine could be stopped and made to run backwards – all within a few seconds. A special pump injected fuel at bottom dead centre, causing the engine to stop and, with luck, kicking it back in the opposite direction. Occasionally, Bolinders would tickover so slowly as to take it into their cylinder heads to go backwards anyway.

The sound is unique and immediately recognisable. Where other vintage full diesels go kerdonk, kerdonk, a Bolinder goes kerdoinkk. Speed control was not by varying the amount of fuel injected but by deciding whether to inject at all on each revolution. Kerdoinkk. So at tickover, combustion might occur every fourth stroke. Bolinders' other idiosyncrasies include an ability to blow smoke rings from the exhaust stack. Kerdoinkk – about that often.

FMC probably persevered with Bolinders because they are incredibly sturdy. The most common models fitted to narrowboats were the BM 15hp (5,950cc) and BM9hp (3,200cc) – both with a single cylinder. Few spares are needed for existing engines today. Bolinder owners tend to be dedicated to their engines and on phone call terms with each other when problems arise. Not surprisingly the make has an owners club – the Bolinder Register. Kerdoinkk.

Russell Newbery/ National

Russell Newbery is famous as the engine fitted in the narrowboats that launched the massive fleet expansion of the thirties. RN introduced its first diesel engine in 1930

The National was built under licence from Russell Newbery.

and the DM2 was selected for six new narrowboats commissioned by the Grand Union Canal Carrying Company in 1934. By 1938, RN had supplied 38 engines to GUCCC but, early on, had licensed production to the National Gas & Oil Engine Company to build another 136 for GUCCC's boatbuilding programme. National's version was not identical to Russell Newbery's and, over the years, they grew further apart.

The RN head design was remarkable for its day, with a small pre-chamber for more efficient combustion, and valves that could be removed without taking off the head. Russell Newberys, though more lightly constructed than Lister JPs, are easy to work on. The basic design has been built in one, two, three and four-cylinder form and the specification statistics listed under new engines (in Appendix 2), are basically representative of past production, except that older engines were heavier and fitted with different gearboxes.

The DM2 remained in production for many years despite several changes of company ownership. For several decades it was the only authentically traditional engine available and, as such, gained cult status among narrowboaters in the eighties. At the time of writing, The RN Engine Co and RW Davis & Son have acquired the name and assets from the last owner, Vero, and are hoping to resume manufacture in the near future.

Lister

The Lister JP2 is probably the most popular vintage engine among narrowboaters even though it did not figure in original thirties fleet installations – perhaps because it was too well made to be competitive. The initials JP stand for 'joint production' – the project was launched in co-operation with Ruston & Hornsby, although the companies went in their own directions within a few years. Lister's JP series was built in large numbers between 1930 and 1952 and, even by narrowboat standards, has a reputation for reliability. Bearing surfaces were always generous, requiring only low pressure lubrication. Wet cylinder liners were treated with the patented Listard hard chrome process and the engines could be adjusted (by a distinctive wheel on the side of the head) to run on high or low compression, depending on the load involved.

A relatively large number survive today (including the three-cylinder JP3), and spares are reasonably available (not from the factory, although it is

still a major builder of modern narrowboat engines). The JP2 was invariably fitted with a Lister 3G gearbox, which survived in production until quite recently for use on the company's HR engine. Like many vintage engines, pre-war versions often lacked electric start but canalside vintage specialists can make neat conversions. JP2s were usually rated at 21hp at 1,200rpm, displacing 2,860cc, and weighing just under one ton.

The CE range, introduced after the JP in 1933, is not as well known and is slightly smaller and lighter. The post-war FR range was smaller still – displacing 814cc in each cylinder. It remained in production until 1964 but is generally accepted as 'vintage'. Lister's special relationship with narrowboating is mostly due to the more modern SR range, which, in air-cooled form, dominated the leisure narrowboat market in the sixties and seventies. It is too numerous, indestructible (and noisy) to be regarded as a classic engine – yet. The contemporary, larger H series can look quite convincing in a traditional engine room

Ruston & Hornsby

The first Akroyd-Hornsby hot-bulb compression-ignition oil engine was sold for marine use in 1895. That company's descendant, Ruston & Hornsby, was the other half of the JP partnership with Lister although its version (also called the JP) ended production sixteen years before Lister's. However, the company's later VR range had identical bore and stroke and was listed in production until 1958. VT and VS ranges, exactly contemporary with the VR, are both smaller. All were eventually overtaken by Ruston & Hornsby's YB, YC, YD and YW ranges which were first introduced in 1950. Although slightly smaller, the YD makes some claim to be descended from the JP engines.

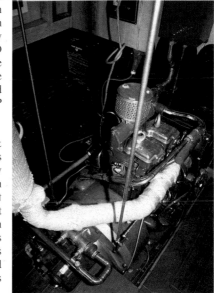

Ruston & Hornsbys played very little part in working boat history but were built in large numbers – both as marine and industrial units – so second-hand engines are readily available for narrowboat

This Greaves engine is based on a Ruston & Hornsby design and was built in India.

installation. All are suitably heavy and slow-revving to be convincing in traditional craft. The 1.17 litre 2VS, for instance, weighed 16½ cwt, ticked over at 400rpm and produced its 15hp at 1,000rpm. The company gradually transferred production of the 2YD to an Indian subsidiary. Some of these engines were imported in the early nineties under the name Greaves.

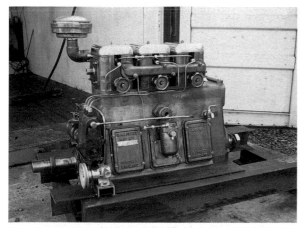

A restored Lister JP3 awaiting its characteristic green paint.

A single cylinder Gardner being restored.

The Kelvin J3 is a more sensibly sized engine for a narrowboat than the K series.

Gardner

Sometimes described as the Rolls-Royce of diesels, Gardner's reputation is based on its precision of manufacture and care in building. Typically, when the host vehicle goes to the scrapyard, an automotive Gardner is snapped up for overseas marine use. The narrowboat-sized ones usually have an industrial history – Gardners were always too well made to be viable for original installation in working narrowboats.

The company introduced an innovative 'high speed' diesel in 1929. The L2 produced an impressive $9\frac{1}{2}$ hp at 1,000rpm, made an impact on diesel engine design generally, and Gardner's fortunes in particular. By 1931, a 'lightweight' version had been developed and this, the LW, remained in production until 1972. Remarkably, a two-cylinder version was reintroduced in 1994, partly to satisfy overseas industrial demand, and partly to exploit the vintage narrowboat market. Gardner's reputation made it the 'ultimate' narrowboat engine as soon as availability was announced. Like Ruston & Hornsby and Kelvin, Gardner has, in its time, been swallowed up by a large engineering combine but the 2LW was re-launched when Gardner was later bought by a smaller group. The company still operates from its original (and famous) West Manchester premises.

The 2LW is similarly composed to its main vintage competitors – two cylinders, 2,780cc, 28hp at 1,300rpm – but it is remarkably smooth-running for a twin. Modern technology has reduced its weight to 1,040lb compared to around 1,800lb for original Gardner twins although those lightweight alloy parts account for part of the loss too.

Kelvin

Kelvin vies with Gardner for reputation. While the latter's precision is legendary, Kelvin built marine engines, rather than adapting industrial ones. The make could be found in high quality pleasure boats as much as in commercial craft.

Corrosion resistance is exceptional.

The Scottish company introduced the K series, its first diesel, in 1932. At 4,000cc per cylinder, it is rather large for narrowboat installation although several owners have installed them. The J series followed in 1933 and the J2, producing 22hp at 1,000rpm from a total capacity of 2,960cc, is directly comparable to all the other vintage 'twins'.

Kelvin built paraffin-powered engines until well after WWII and fitted a remarkable dual-fuel system to both K and J ranges. The engines could be started easily on petrol (using low-compression and spark plugs) then switched, cylinder by cylinder, to diesel. Vintage owners love this ritual and the involved brassware that graces the cylinder head. It is made redundant on engines fitted with electric start, but kept as a showpiece. The J series' tickover is decidedly slow – official speed was 225rpm but some say the engine is happy at 160rpm.

Kelvin's two- and four-cylinder P range was not introduced until 1954 and remained in production until the eighties but it has true vintage quality. Tickover is 350rpm, while at 1,500rpm, the P4's 2,176cc produces 20hp. It looks right and runs smoothly, comparing well with modern diesels.

Kelvins were always expensive engines. The final price of the P4, in 1983, was equivalent to £11,000 at 1995 levels. J, K and P engines and their spares are available, particularly in their Scottish homeland.

Other vintage engines you may come across in narrowboats include Armstrong Siddeley, Dorman, Petter, Ailsa Craig, Fowler, Hercules, Kromhout, Seffle, Widdop and Perkins – some of which have been featured in *Waterways World*.

Not all vintage engines are found in pristine condition.

CHAPTER 13

ELECTRICAL INSTALLATIONS

The typical narrowboat, used for weekends and holidays, has a 12-volt engine system, separate cabin 12-volt system, and (sometimes) a simple 230-volt circuit which can be plugged to a landline supply or generator.

Official guidelines for inland boat electrics are in the Boat Safety Standards, which are fairly sketchy, and in the British Marine Electronics Association's Code of Practice, which is not so accessible or readable. However, although it contains much that does not concern inland boats, it is comprehensive, and is useful reference material for electricity-minded owners. Further requirements will be published as supporting standards for the European Recreational Craft Directive (see Chapter 7).

Low voltage systems – 12-Volt or 24-Volt?

Although basic boat electrics are usually thought of as 12-volt systems, quite a few boats are fitted with 24-volt systems which greatly reduce the problems of voltage drop. This is because the long wiring runs which tend to occur in long narrowboats cause a fall-off in voltage and, the lower the voltage, the more pronounced this becomes.

If your boat is fitted with high consumption appliances (such as a bow thruster), 24-volt systems look increasingly attractive. However, the entire system usually has to be geared to the higher voltage – from engine alternator to cabin light bulbs. 24-volt versions of most appliances are available from major chandlers. You may need to carry more spares – replacement 12-volt water pumps, for instance, are readily available in local boatyards, but 24-volt ones are a rarity.

230-Volt systems

Most narrowboats are fitted with a basic 230-volt circuit to allow use of mains appliances when tied up near to a landline supply. At its simplest, the circuit is simply an household extension lead. However, the 13-amp plug that hangs off these is not intended for exposed use – the approved type is the blue 'Marechal' circular plug to be found in chandlers and caravan shops. It is not unusual to find connection leads with 13-amp plugs at either end, so that one can be plugged into the land supply; and the other into a socket on the boat. This is lethal – if the plug is pulled out of the boat socket, its exposed blades are live.

The simple extension lead is not, in any case, adequate. An onboard circuit should be protected by a Residual Current Breaker, which trips when it senses even a minute leakage of current to earth (as when you touch a live wire). 230-volt circuits should also be protected against overload by fuses or circuit breakers. RCBs look similar to circuit breakers but have a distinguishing test button.

BMEA's Code of Practice stipulates that wiring (12/24- and 230-voltage) should be multi-stranded – and not the domestic 230-volt 'twin-flat & earth' cable, which is single-core.

Installation checkpoints

The real quality of a boat can be found in the parts you are not supposed to look at. This applies particularly to the electric system. Some builders take pride in

12- and 230-volt systems are both run through this board but are kept totally separate.

immaculately ordered wiring, others leave tangled spaghetti of questionable thickness – and this difference is discernible, even to the untutored eye.

Both 12/24-volt and 230-volt systems should have isolation switches so that you can cut off supplies quickly. Some 12/24-volt appliances, like an automatic bilge, or burglar alarm may by-pass the isolator. All circuits must be protected by fuses or circuit breakers. You can ask your builder to order an integrated control panel, which handles the 230-volt supply and has separate fuses, switches and lights to show when individual 12/24-volt circuits are on. It often includes a battery condition meter too.

The alternative fuse box is a small, simple line of fuses. Domestic 230-volt fuse boxes can be used for 12/24-volt systems without any alteration but both voltages should not be routed through one box and, if two identical boxes are used for different voltages, they must be permanently distinguished. Wiring of any voltage may not use the boat's steel shell as part of the circuit. The exception to this is the starter motor circuit – a relic of most boat engines' automobile origins.

Wiring should be properly supported, or harnessed in unsupported runs. Pvc-coated wire, as pointed out in Chapter 7, should not be in contact with polystyrene insulation which eventually damages the pvc and reduces its electrical resistance. Cables (carrying 230-volt or 12/24-volt) must avoid gas and fuel pipes and sources of heat. As a general priority, water pipes should run as low as possible, gas as high as practicable (but usually under one side deck), electric harnesses under the other side deck, or behind service panels in the deckhead. 12/24-volt wiring plans in inland boats are relatively simple, as the diagram indicates. However, one major consideration in specifying wiring remains:

Voltage drop

A 12-volt water pump draws about 10 amps when working. A cable of 2.5mm2 cross-section has a nominal current-carrying capacity of 15 amps so you might conclude that this cable is sufficient to supply the pump. Unfortunately, it is not that simple – 15 amps is only the maximum it can carry to avoid overload and consequent overheating. Voltage drop is a different consideration and a particular

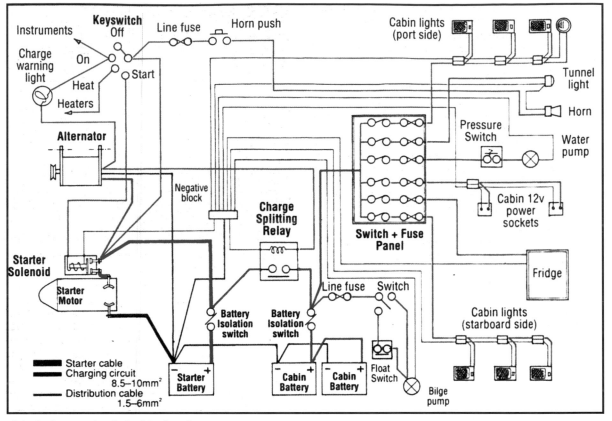

A typical narrowboat electrical system.

problem with high consumption 12/24-volt appliances (like water pumps) on the end of long supply cables (as in narrowboats). If voltage drops, the current increases to compensate, and reduces the working life of the pump.

The other implication of inadequate wiring thicknesses is that a surveyor may condemn it and require major sections to be replaced. The critical cabling in a 50ft narrowboat with conventional layout might be to water pump (typically needing $6mm^2$ wire), main lighting supply line, colour TV (both $4.5mm^2$) and fridge (6 to $10mm^2$). These are guide approximations but, while a local marine electrician will make exact calculations for your boat, the sizes here are a substantial improvement on the high consumption/long run wiring in many existing narrowboats.

Batteries

Batteries designed for engine starting are expected to produce considerable cranking power for short periods – a regime that does not deplete the battery's charge state significantly. The cabin system of a modern narrowboat requires much deeper discharges and does so frequently. This sort of work can cause damage to the plates of starter-type batteries (even the ones described as 'heavy duty'). The most suitable types for cabin use are those labelled 'traction', 'semi-traction', 'deep-cycle' or 'leisure'. Their internal construction is beefed-up to resist plate damage. Gel batteries are maintenance free and so can be installed in more out-of-the-way places.

Battery sizes

Finding a replacement for an engine battery is simple. Your local battery specialist can simply look it up,

although it helps if you can tell him/her what industrial diesel your narrowboat engine is based on. In practice, any 90amp-hour starter battery should be able to start any well maintained engine.

Apart from a few major chandlers, battery suppliers are not equipped to calculate your cabin's needs. Over the years *Waterways World* has tried several methods for this. As a starting point, the cabin system should be separate from the engine system so that, even if you flatten the cabin battery(ies), you can still start the engine and replenish the cabin system. Capacity of the typical single

Heavy duty engine battery (right), deep cycle batteries for domestic supply, a relay to keep the two systems apart and a battery management system.

cabin battery is, for some reason, around 90 or 100 amp-hours. One such is sufficient in a small (35ft to 35ft) narrowboat with unsophisticated requirements. Two in parallel will support a similar cabin in a medium-sized boat. Running an electric fridge calls for another battery, still in parallel with the other(s).

More complicated needs call for an 'energy audit' as described by Peter Hopley in *Waterways World's 'Narrowboat Builder's Book'*. This involves looking at each appliance to find out how many amps it consumes, then estimating how many hours it will be working each day. If the appliance quotes its rating in watts, divide that by 12 (or by 24, if a 24-volt appliance) to obtain amps. (But note that the figure for the fridge below is an average – a typical fridge draws 4.5 amps when its compressor is running which is about 30 minutes in every hour).

Audit example:

	Load (amps)	Time on (hrs)	Audit (Amp-hrs)
5 fluor lights @ 1.3 amps	6.5	2	13
3 fil lamps @ 2 amps	6	2	12
Water pump	10	0.25	2.5
C/heating pump	2	4	8
Electric fridge	2.25	24	54
Colour TV	5	2	10
TOTAL			**99.5**

Multiply the audit total by 3 to obtain the battery capacity needed – 298.5 amp-hours, which could be provided by three, 100 amp-hours batteries in parallel. The reason for multiplying the final number of amp-hours by 3 is that a battery's usable energy is normally reckoned to be about one third of its stated capacity. This is because batteries are rarely charged to more than 80% or 90% of their stated capacity and, by the time they drop to 50%, the voltage is so low as to be unusable. The difference between these 2 levels is about 35%, hence the rule of thumb factor of 3.

Very high consumption appliances – like bow thrusters – need their own separate battery systems, so that the engine alternator is supporting three systems (cabin, bow thruster, engine starter) via two charge splitting devices. Suppliers of these special appliances should be able to recommend battery sizes. (The battery for a bow thruster, incidentally, is usually mounted close to the thruster, where all others are invariably in the engine compartment and none in the cabin itself).

Charge control & splitting

In many narrowboats and cruisers, the only power source is the engine's 12-volt, 36-amp alternator. During much of its working time, output is considerably lower than 36 amps, even if the batteries' needs are more – the alternator is controlled by an internal regulator designed to cope with the limited demands of a starter battery and easily confused by the different regime of cabin batteries.

Inefficient recharging causes deeply discharged batteries to build up a surface resistance on internal plates, which itself prevents full recharging – so your 100 amp-hours battery's capacity reduces to about 80 amp-hours and its life expectancy is also lessened.

The engine alternator charges the engine start and domestic batteries.

Special regulators or battery management systems, like Acorn and Sterling controllers and the Adverc battery management system, provide the solution. These encourage the alternator to charge at relatively high voltage to 'burn' through the battery plate resistance. The most sophisticated do this in repeated cycles of high, medium and low charge pulses to avoid battery damage, and they also monitor the batteries' state closely. Some 230-volt inverter/chargers (as from Mastervolt, Victron and Heart) offer similarly sophisticated charging, but only from a 230-volt source.

As we have already seen, batteries supported by conventional regulators run between approximately 50% and 80% capacity which is about one third of the nominal output. More efficient charging systems increase the upper limit to 95%, giving $1\frac{1}{2}$ times the available power from the same battery bank.

While controlled by conventional regulators, the benefits of larger engine-driven 12-volt (or 24-volt) alternators are limited but sophisticated controllers take advantage of larger sizes now available. The typical standard alternator on a modern narrowboat diesel used to be rated at 50 amps output but 70 amps is now more usual and 100-amp-plus units are available.

Most narrowboats have two separate systems – one for engine starting, one for cabin appliances. Some builders specify separate ones for the inverter, the bow thruster and, sometimes, the fridge. Keeping these systems separate can be simplified by using separate engine-driven alternators but if a single alternator charges the batteries of more than one system, a charge splitting device is needed.

Most common is the relay. When the engine is running, a heavy duty switch automatically connects two battery systems allowing the alternator to charge both. Marginal disadvantage: if the cabin system suffers a massive discharge while the engine is running, it could overwhelm alternator output and flatten the engine battery. However that eventuality is rare, and relays are inexpensive.

The blocking diode is also popular. It works as a one-way switch when the engine is running but the charge suffers a small voltage drop when passing through it. This can be countered by using an alternator controller (as above) that measures the necessary alternator output at the battery's terminals – downstream of the blocking diode. Some electronic charge splitters now available work like blocking diodes but do not suffer voltage drop. Their disadvantage is cost.

The other option is a selective master switch. This requires you to remember to switch all batteries on when the engine is running, and to isolate the engine battery when tied up for the night. The disadvantage of this is your unreliability.

Inverters & chargers

Inverters do not generate power; they convert battery power (12 volts or 24 volts DC) to mains voltage

Inverters convert the battery's 12-volt power to mains voltage but cannot generate electricity.

(230 volts AC). Small inverters (down to about 100 watts output) are available for running small individual appliances. Larger ones manage up to 2kW and more – requiring a considerable battery bank. Inverters are less intrusive than generators and more efficient for continuous, light loads. Although their efficiency has improved in recent years, capacity to run heavy loads for any length of time is decidedly limited. Given the losses involved in power generation and battery storage, an engine alternator has to work long and hard to replenish the drain of a largish inverter. At this level, a sophisticated alternator controller and deep-cycle batteries are not just desirable – they are essential.

Inverters convert direct current (DC) into alternating current (AC) by electronic chopping. The simplest types produce a simple square wave AC pattern whereas the most sophisticated recreate the sine wave pattern of landline supplies which is necessary to run some sophisticated electronic appliances. Between these in cost and performance is the modified sine wave inverter, which runs most electronic items.

Battery charging is almost the reverse of inverting so many devices combine both functions, usually with enhanced charging routines. Devices are also available to run 12-volts DC appliances direct from a 230-volts AC supply, avoiding charger and batteries.

Renewable energy

With careful planning, you can harness natural energy to avoid having to start the engine just for battery charging. The overall cost might be more than for a substantial portable generator – £1,000 or £1,200. While the power immediately available might be only 5% of that from the generator, it is produced seven-days-a-week with little noise and no fuel cost.

Wind generators are not as powerful as alternators but they work whenever there is a breeze.

Wind power cannot be guaranteed and solar power is only available in daytime but that £1,000 to £1,200 budget will buy a wind generator and reasonable area of solar panels – enough to free you from charging worries on most days of the year.

To achieve this end, the cabin has to be designed around low consumption, with efficient lights (such as 2D compact colour-corrected fluorescent units), pump-free central heating system, and a low consumption fridge.

Wind generators are often mounted on hinged masts for canal cruising, and Ampair makes flexible solar panels that conform to the shape of a cabin top, and resist impact damage.

Solar panels can reduce battery drain considerably.

CHAPTER 14

APPLIANCES AND SYSTEMS

The simplest and most convenient way to cook on inland waterway craft is by gas. Gas cookers do not tend to asphyxiate (appliances with faulty flues are more often guilty – but this does not mean that cookers should be left alight for cabin heating). And, if all burners are fitted with flame failure devices (new ones have to be), they cannot leak explosive quantities of gas after blowing out.

Stoves' free-standing Vanette 5000 WL.

Separate oven/hob combinations are now more popular on narrowboats.

The smallest cruiser may be fitted with a simple two-burner or two-burner-and-grill unit. Many larger continental craft only carry these because eating out is so popular there – and there is at least one narrowboat where the cook has refused to have a larger cooker aboard as emphasis that this is as much his/her holiday too. A combination unit – burners, sink and basin together – may be more space effective in a small boat than separate units. Caravan centres and coastal chandlers stock a variety of combination units but make sure they have flame failure devices.

The most popular cooker, until recently, was Stoves' Vanette. It qualifies as full-size although it is slightly smaller (21in wide) than some domestic cookers (24in wide). The design was introduced in the seventies as a white free-standing ugly duckling which is still available but it is also produced in brown, green and cream.

Most boats nowadays have a separate, built in oven and hob – also made by Stoves. The GG7000 oven unit contains a large grill compartment and a good size oven. It comes in a variety of colour and trim options. The hob choices are between the 4000 and 5000 – both smaller than a domestic hob – or the 600 GXS which is normal size. Before the introduction of BS 5482, boaters often teamed a Stoves oven/grill with a domestic LPG hob, bought from a gas showroom. This is not possible now unless the latter has flame failure devices.

Alternatives to gas

Boats equipped with 230-volt power from a decent size inverter or a generator can use a domestic microwave although models using a simple clockwork timer are less likely to suffer incompatibility problems than those using an electronic one. The other consideration is that microwaves have a high start up requirement and consume roughly twice their stated cooking power. This means that, for a standard 600 Watt microwave, you would need a 1200Watt inverter that has a surge rating of between 30% and 50%. It is also claimed that, with most inverters, domestic microwaves can only run at about 85% of their stated maximum power because of power losses.

If you don't want to install an inverter, it is possible to buy a 12-volt microwave, although some of these are simply 230-volt models mounted on a dedicated inverter. Others, like the Vibocold, Whispaire and Mobitherm, are more sophisticated and are claimed to deliver their full stated power – taking the guesswork out of setting the timer. They

Full electric cooking is possible if you have a large generator.

also have a built-in low-voltage cut-out to avoid flattening your batteries. All 12-volt microwaves need fairly hefty cables to carry the current and avoid voltage drop. Assuming the galley is about 10 metres from the battery bank, 35mm² cable is require.

Narrowboats with very sophisticated electrics – like many of the next decade, will have sufficient onboard resources to cook only by electricity. Switch on the microwave and the inverter will swing into action. Increase demand with, for instance, an electric grill or hotplate, and a sensor will fire up the boat's built-in generator. For full electric cooking, you need a 10 or 11kVA generator. Some systems have a 7kVA unit but, with these, it is not possible to use all the burners at the same time.

Solid fuel cookers are usually additional to gas ones – but for traditional virtues rather than convenience. The smallest are boatmans cabin-sized ranges, which need plinths to stand on. The largest are farmhouse-sized Agas, so heavy as to cause a pronounced list unless you can adjust underfloor ballast. In winter, these are the heart of the boat, cooking all your meals, heating radiators and providing hot water too. They are extremely expensive to buy (although some dealers sell secondhand ones). And your galley will need an alternative gas cooker and water heater to avoid torrid heat in summer.

Dickinsons' stoves are a popular choice on gasless boats.

Diesel offers the best immediate alternative to gas. You can buy diesel-fired Aga ranges but Dickinsons' much lighter stainless steel cookers use low-voltage fans to speed heat-up time. The most popular Pacific model is claimed to boil a simmering kettle from tickover in a couple of minutes. It has a hot plate and approximately 1 cu ft oven, and can be fitted with a water heating coil. At maximum 5kW output, it can cook, heat the boat and a calorifier. The 2kW tickover setting is less than from a large range and some of it is absorbed into water heating. Even so, an adjacent side door, pigeon box or houdini hatch is handy in summer for losing excess heat.

A Dickinson diesel cooker may cost you more than an Alde gas central heating boiler and a Vanette cooker together but it has an additional advantage. A Vanette cooker accounts for 37sq in of the 45sq in ventilation needed in a typical narrowboat. Replacing the Vanette (maximum output 11kW and unflued) with the Pacific (5kW flued) reduces the total mandatory ventilation requirement to 12sq in – which is much less draughty.

More sophisticated still is the Wallas range of diesel hobs and ovens. These use pumped air and diesel oil and give a performance that is nearly as quick as gas. The exhaust is so clean that it can be taken through the cabin side if required. Their disadvantage is initial cost.

Fridges & freezers

The smallest gas fridges are economical to run. For liveaboards, with limited power available, a gas fridge was always the favoured option until BS 5482 part 3 effectively outlawed its use on new installations. The main manufacturer, Electrolux, always refused to approve the use of its products on boats but it is developing a new model which has a balanced flue to satisfy the BS and which they will approve. It is due for release in July 2000 at a price still to be announced at the time of writing.

Electric fridges

Electric fridges avoid all the safety problems of gas but they do require adequate wiring and battery bank – which usually means three rather than two cabin batteries in a typical cruising narrowboat. Technology has advanced since the first Engel electric fridges were fitted in narrowboats twenty years ago – designs are more economical and quieter.

Power consumption depends on the amount and temperature of contents, the target temperature, ambient temperature and the number of times the door is opened.

Average consumption is between 2 amps and 3 amps.

Until the nineties electric fridges meant Engel (and Electrolux marine models). Now the narrowboat market is led by Inlander and Shoreline, which convert a range of LEC domestic units to 12/24-volts, employing a Danfoss compressor. The range is from 2.2 cu ft freezer and 2.9 cu ft fridge (which can stack on each other) to 6.9 cu ft fridge/freezer. The most popular model is the 4 cu ft fridge with a small icebox. However, an even wider choice, at competitive prices, is available if you can use an unconverted 230-volt fridge, either running off the boat's main inverter or with its own local inverter.

A 4 cu ft Lec fridge with a 12-volt compressor.

The trend in up-market narrowboat fridges may be towards custom-made compartments with remote-mounted

A small chest type freezer.

refrigeration units. This promises more flexible utilisation of valuable galley space and easier access to the working bits. Coolmatic and Isotherm offer suitable compressor-driven systems. They also offer fridges which use a holding plate in place of the evaporator to store cold energy in the way that night storage heaters store heat. These are mainly designed for yachts which use their engines – and therefore, alternators – for only a small part of the time they are cruising but some narrowboat owners may find that they suit their pattern of use.

Heating a small boat

The options for staying warm in a small boat are fewer than in a large one. Gas catalytic types were the most popular choice but, as these are totally unflued, they cannot be fitted in new boats or replaced in existing ones. Current makes of gas heater which have a balanced flue are the Truma range comprising warm air heaters, water boilers and combination units, the Carver P4 warm

The Trumatic C provides hot water and space heating on smaller boats.

air heater and boilers by Atwood and Belling. Solid fuel stoves are generally too heavy although the TorGem or Faversham could be used with care.

The Canadian Dickinson company (marketing through Kuranda Marine in the UK), sells a tiny wall-mounted stove which burns charcoal, wood or solid fuel. A natural draught diesel version is available. The British company, Blakes/Lavac/Taylors, produces the 'Taylors' bulkhead mounted diesel units.

The most expensive, but still compact, type of heating is diesel forced combustion. Ardic, Webasto, Mikuni all offer small models, but most common is Eberspacher's D1L 1,800 watt warm air heater. The disadvantage of these is that they consume fairly large quantities of electricity.

Heating a narrowboat

Many narrowboating images are to do with solid

The popular Squirrel stove is very easy to control.

fuel stoves – smoke curling from the chimney, water lapping against the hull as the glowing fire toasts your toes but the popularity has practical advantages too. Solid fuel stoves suffuse a gentle drying warmth through the cabin and they are cost-effective. Until they have used one for a while, owners are reluctant to accept that a single stove can heat a longish cabin without assistance from radiators (moral: plan your new boat for a solid fuel central heating system, but try it without first). You can also eke out bought fuel with driftwood and fallen branches.

The TorGem represents the budget end of the stove market. It was the only stove fitted in narrowboats for many years but now has several well-priced competitors – principally the Villager Puffin (née Heron). The Squirrel stove dominates the upper end of the stove market, with choice of wood- or solid-fuel settings, and a high level of

Boatman's cabin stoves provide heat and are good for gentle cooking.

controllability. Small solid fuel ranges, like the Epping and Premier, are not too expensive to buy, add character to a saloon (particularly if set in an arched, tiled and scumbled shrine) – and are marvellous for gentle cooking.

Natural draught diesel heaters match all the practical advantages of solid fuel stoves – they also require less looking after and spread less ash dust around the cabin. Their exhaust is not so picturesque or aromatic

and, until 1995, their cylindrical steel cases were something of an acquired taste. The principal makes – Kabola, Somy, Refleks – are all built in Europe.

Kuranda Marine started the fashion for 'fireplace stoves' with its Old English – a disguised Kabola central heating boiler, with low radiant output. This has now been joined by the Bubble stove by Harwood Heating and Lockgate Marine Stoves. Natural draught diesel boilers – in fireplace or concealed under airing cupboard) are particularly suited to residential use.

Some natural draught diesel stoves look just like solid fuel stoves.

The cruising boat's favourite central heating system was, for a long time, the Alde gas boiler. The tall, slim unit was designed to heat caravans but has a long history of supporting radiators and calorifier in narrowboats – hire and private. It is competitive to buy, although LPG central heating is not economical or convenient (the bottles need more frequent changing) for year-round residential use. All Aldes sold today have balanced flue (ie scaled – and safe) combustion systems. They are also available with heat exchangers that avoid the need for a calorifier and provide almost instant hot water.

Their popularity has been challenged in recent years by forced combustion diesel heaters (Eberspacher, Ardic, Webasto, Mikuni) which are the 'wet' type (supplying radiators and calorifier). They are more compact than natural draught diesel heaters but consume relatively large amounts of electricity and will not run if batteries are flat. They can also be rather noisy – particularly from outside the boat – if not silenced effectively. Seven-day timers are available for many types of narrowboat central heating

Forced combustion diesel boilers like this Eberspacher are easy to accommodate and convenient to use but consume relatively large amounts of electricity.

so you can set the system to heat your boat before you arrive on a Friday evening. Forced combustion types score high marks for combined convenience and safety and are found in many upper market craft.

Most narrowboat central heating systems feature domestic-type panel radiators. If relying on these, provide roughly 1sq ft of area for every 2$^1/_2$ ft run of cabin. Large bore supply pipes can be almost as effective. While copper pipe is expensive, your shell builder may be able to rig up a convection central heating run based entirely on 2in diameter steel pipes.

In a typical pump-free convection-driven layout, the heat source is a solid fuel or diesel stove, usually at the forward end of the boat. The pipe rise towards the stern has to allow for the fact that all boats sit slightly tail down. Opting for a utility boiler like the Kabola E series and locating it in the engine room means that the boat and the pipes rise together.

You can dry your smalls on panel radiators and 2in pipe but they are not discreet (although radiators can be encased in hardwood surrounds and brass grilles). Skirting radiators are discreet. They stand 6in up from the floor and are often disguised by a colour-matched steel or even hardwood fascia. Skirting radiators can resolve space problems if they are recessed into berth fronts – or even, treated with scumble, in the side bed of a traditional boatmans cabin.

The benefits of gas

A small but growing band of boat owners go to extreme lengths to exclude gas from their boats. Chapter 18, concerning secondhand craft, deals with the safety considerations of gas because it is a frequent – and dangerous – fault area. However, there is no reason why a properly fitted gas system should not be entirely safe and those available for new boats are even safer. Gas cooking is hard to beat for convenience and gas appliances are usually less expensive to buy than those consuming competitive fuels.

The main supplier of LPG (liquefied petroleum gas) on UK inland waterways is Calor although it is not, by any means, the only one. Some other companies offer better prices but you cannot exchange their empties for full Calor bottles. Two types of gas and four bottle sizes are available.

The most popular gas for inland boating is propane (sold in red bottles). Butane, the alternative (and in blue bottles), freezes unusably in winter and does not burn so cleanly. Propane is offered in 3.9kg, 6kg, 13 kg and 19kg sizes. 13kg is by far the most common in narrowboats. 3.9kg bottles are used in small cruisers, 6kg is a new size; at 19$^1/_2$ in high it fits into lockers where builders (surprisingly often) fail to accommodate the 13kg's 24in height. The economy-sized 19kg bottle fits in to 32in – but is very heavy to carry over any distance (many owners resort to hand trolleys for 13kg bottles). Butane is available only in 4.3kg and 15kg sizes.

Two bottles are typically linked by 'pigtails' to a common regulator in the gas locker. The regulator is often fitted with an automatic changeover valve although, since you won't know when it switches from one to the other, your locker should carry a third bottle loose (but vertical) as back-up when the second bottle runs out. With a manual changeover, you can get away with 2 bottles.

At the other end of the system, in the cabin, you can fit a gas alarm to give early warning of leakage.

Sometimes these work too well – they go off when sensing other gases – like hairspray. After they have cried wolf a few times, owners turn them off and they aren't working on the rare occasion of need. The pipe system in between is not suitable for DIY installation or changes – work should be done by marine gas fitters.

Water

Most cruisers, whatever their size, can accommodate a built-in water system. The most basic consists of a soft neoprene bag or rigid small plastic tank, linked to a manual pump or simple electric pump.

The basis of the system in larger cruisers and narrowboats is a more substantial electric pump that is wired through a pressure switch. When a tap is turned on, allowing pressure in the pipes to drop, the switch activates the pump until cut-out pressure is achieved. Turning a tap half-on will sometimes cause a pump to rattle on and off

Water pump (left), pressure accumulator and optional pressure switch.

like a machine gun and a dripping tap will bring the pump alive for a few heart-stopping seconds in the small hours of the night. Fitting an accumulator tank reduces this tendency by compressing air which effectively stores pumping energy.

The most popular water pump is the Shurflo, usually installed with integral pressure switch. Although that switch's pressure range is adjustable, Shurflos are sometimes fitted in-line with a more sophisticated Square D switch. Other makes include ITT-Par, Johnson, Flojet, Fiamma, Whale.

Of necessity, glass-fibre cruisers use water tanks that are not integral with the hull – usually of polypropylene, galvanised steel or stainless steel. Many narrowboats use these too but the integral steel tank has been a popular alternative (although decreasingly so). For many years, the fashion was to incorporate this under the front deck. Problems occur when foot pressure causes the joint of the inspection hatch, which is flush with the deck, to flex and allow contaminated matter to seep in.

A potentially better integral design uses the bow locker (otherwise given over to gas bottle storage) as a water tank. The flange of the hinged lid should keep contaminants out provided there is an efficient gasket, and the lid itself allows a clear view of the tank's condition at every fill. A variation of this, which restores the gas bottles

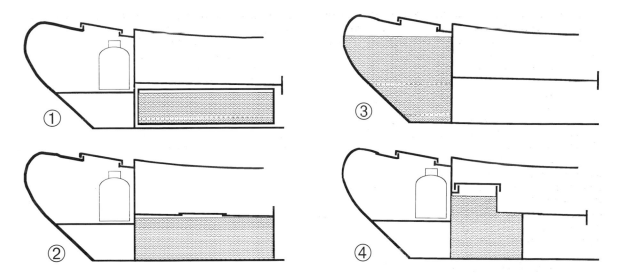

Sections showing (1) a separate water tank, (2) an integral under-deck water tank, (3) a bow locker water tank and (4) an integral but easily accessible water tank.

to their original position, is to construct an integral tank under a full width seat across the forward cockpit – still with large, deep-flanged lid.

The simple way to get hot water in boats with closed-circuit engine cooling systems is to exploit the hot coolant to heat a calorifer (ie lagged storage tank of strong enough construction to withstand the relatively high pressures of marine pumps). Calorifiers are surprisingly effective; most engines will heat a typical 11-gallon calorifier in half-an-hour and the tank's lagging will keep the stored water hot overnight. The engine coolant passes through a coil inside the calorifier and does not mix with the stored water. Running the engine without load, on a regular basis, just to heat water is bad practice – it can lead to severe long-term engine wear. Many calorifiers have two separate coils so that a gas, diesel or solid fuel boiler can also heat water.

The diagram shows the layout for a twin-coil calorifier system. Among its details are a non-return valve at the inlet to the calorifier so that warm water cannot find its way back to encourage bacteria in the cold (drinking) water line. To cope with expansion downstream of the NR valve as the water heats, a pressure relief valve is fitted in a position where its drips do no harm. Every calorifier carries a

Hep[2]0 plastic plumbing (right) compared with the brass/copper alternative.

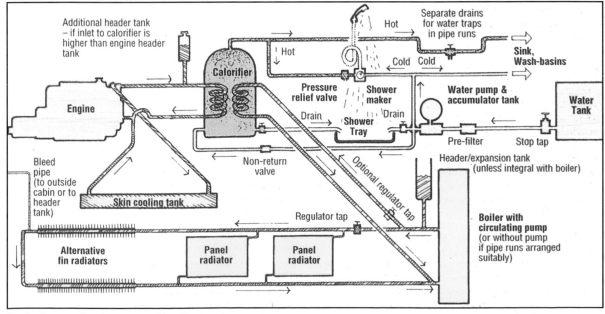

Typical narrowboat water and heating system.

bung for winter draining-down. This too should be arranged so that it does not dump the contents haphazardly to end up in the boat's bilge.

The diagram shows how a boiler also supports a central heating system. A regulating tap cuts off supply to the radiators in warm weather.

Apart from copper (which does look more attractive), the generally accepted material for boat piping is Hep^{2}O (previously known as 'Acorn') plumbing. This proprietary system consists of rigid plastic piping with push-fit plastic jointing – all very easy to cut and assemble.

Hep^{2}O cannot be used with a solid fuel or 'drip-feed' diesel stove as these are not thermostatically controlled. For the most part, the boiler capability of these is used for central heating where copper or steel pipe radiates heat better anyway.

Showers & baths

A shower is one of the amenities that make the difference between a cruiser and a cruising home. As long as you have enough space to fit a small shower tray (about 24in x 24in) and curtain, you don't need much technology to take a shower – camping types are based on a plastic water container with hand-pumped pressure reservoir.

Narrowboat size baths are available with or without an integral seat.

Small narrowboats and cruisers use that size of tray in electric-pressurised systems, although 24in x 24in confines movement and fails to contain all the water. Domestic size – 30in x 30in – is most effective, and less restricting if installed with bulkheads on three sides and a door on the fourth.

The 'squat bath' is half way between shower and bath. The plastic moulding has seats on either side of a deep shower tray so it is large enough to turn round in, deep enough for dunking small children and more comfortable than a standing-room-only shower. Proper narrowboat-size baths are designed to fit into 4ft length. Even then they are not often used for adult-depth baths which would quickly empty the average water tank. They almost always carry shower fittings, take up only a little more room than a 30in x 30in tray, and are not too extravagant of water for dunking kids and dogs. They also add status to your toilet compartment – a bath, after all, is widely regarded as less makeshift than a shower.

Chandlers sell electric pumps specifically designed to empty showers and baths. Note that the pipe from shower/bath drain to pump should be about twice as long as that from pump to hull side fitting – so that any water not cleared overboard when the pump is switched off stays in the pipes and does not run back into the shower/bath. The alternative is to drain the shower/bath to a sump containing a suitable automatic pump (one not readily damaged by hair and fluff). This switches itself on and off depending on level in the sump – and avoids risk of the bather leaving the pump on to burn itself out.

Lavatories

In the beginning was the bucket-and-chuck-it – a portable container with a lavatory seat on top. Elsan still make versions and they have a number of advantages. The plastic construction does not corrode, has no moving parts, is totally space efficient, and is very easy to clean. The original alternative was a marine WC – a small porcelain device that flushes overboard. Quite rightly, they are no longer permitted on canals.

The Thetford Porta Potti.

Portable flush WCs (often generically called 'Porta Potti' – although that is the product of one particular company) arrived in the seventies. Most current types have detachable holding tanks so you can keep spares. They have toilet bowls and a shutter to screen the effluent from view.

Cartridge WCs look more permanent and this one has a swivelling pan for better use of space in a tight bathroom.

The Mansfield Traveler is the most popular narrowboat toilet.

Electric and manual pump-out kits can soon pay for themselves.

Cartridge WCs, originally intended for caravans, are an installed development of the same idea. The holding tank is designed to be removed through a hatch in the outside wall – unless it is installed inside a boat, where it has to be removed via the corridor. While that particular benefit of the cartridge WC is lost, it does look more substantial than portable units. 1995 saw a variation on the cartridge WC – the swivelling lavatory. Setting the top at a variable angle on the base allows ergonomic use to be made of the compartment, which is often not as spacious as when drawn on paper.

Non-portable holding tanks have to be emptied with a pump – usually at a pump-out station although a few owners carry their own self-pump-out kits. The most popular narrowboat WC, for many years, has been the Mansfield Traveler (as spelt in America). It uses a small amount of fresh water for flushing and is relatively simple to install on top of a separate stainless steel (best), polypropylene (not quite so rigid, but more common), or

mild steel (liable to corrode) holding tank. Effluent dumps straight through. Keeping smells at bay depends on a seal good enough to retain a pool of fresh water at the bottom of the bowl.

The traditional liquids for treating effluent are based on formaldehyde, although it inhibits the natural processes of sewage treatment works and is decidedly toxic. Non-formaldehyde liquids have been available since the early nineties but the trend is towards more natural degradation – sometimes assisted by brewer's yeast – while in the holding tank. That necessarily means a remote tank with little risk of smells travelling back through the WC.

Many simple flush WCs – like the Mansfield and Lavac – can be linked to remote tanks. But this type of system has attracted a variety of new and sophisticated models, all with push-button flush. Most involve electric macerator or vacuum pumps but the Microphor is compressor driven. This can be a mixed blessing. The flush itself is reasonably quiet but the compressor cuts in after four or so flushes and the noise, usually from a installation under your berth, can be heart-stopping if you forget to turn it off before retiring.

Pump-outs are done by appropriately equipped boatyards into shore tanks approved and emptied by the local authority. Service to boats is not available outside business hours and, sometimes, out-of-season. Some boat owners keep a self-pump-out kit on board. If they cannot find an approved station, a minority of these manage to swamp emptying points for portable wcs. A few owners eventually leave their posh pump-out WCs unused in favour of simpler portable types.

One company which specialises in lavatory technology for inland waterways craft is Lee Sanitation.

Staying in touch

Although inland boating is partly about escapism, most owners still need to stay in touch either with land-based relatives and friends, with lock keepers, or just with each other. You might find three different systems on inland waterways craft that meet at least some of these needs.

The poshest is marine VHF. Although mainly used by sea-going craft, it is particularly popular with boaters on North-East waterways for communicating with lock- and bridge-keepers on the region's rivers and canals. These waterways can be considerably more intimidating than the Midlands' 'narrow' canals. Probably for that same

A selection of vacuum, compressor and macerator toilets.

A small, hand-held, marine VHF.

reason, British Waterways also operates marine VHF services on the river Weaver (in Cheshire), Caledonian and Crinan canals (in Scotland), and (for urgent calls only) on the river Severn and Gloucester & Sharpness Canal. It is useful (and mandatory for larger craft) on the tidal Thames for communicating with the Port of London Authority.

Boaters do use marine VHF for talking to each other but the strict protocols include a ban on idle chat. Sets may only be used under the direct supervision of certified operators, who, typically, pass a one-time examination at evening courses run under approval of the Royal Yachting Association. Marine VHF sets must be licensed annually (£25 for pleasure craft use in 2000) and the sets themselves have to meet type approval standards. The system is designed for sea use and range on inland waterways is considerably reduced by obstacles and clutter. Installed sets (slightly larger than a car radio) are allowed to transmit with up to 25 watts output, portables (similar to mobile phones), only 5 watts. However, an installed set with 6ft aerial mounted at maximum feasible height can communicate over 15 miles in flat countryside. Typical price for an installable unit, complete with aerial and fittings: around £300. Portables are only slightly cheaper.

The easiest system to buy and use is CB (Citizen's Band) radio although this also needs a licence. Once you have one, you simply buy an installable or portable from a radio shop (like Tandy) – and switch it on.

CB sets are useful for communicating between boats in convoy or between boat and a crew on the towpath – as when sending someone on to prepare locks – although this can be annoying to other canal users. Installed sets might be used for the former, portable 'walkie-talkies' for the latter. If you are easily embarrassed, turn your CB radio off near roads and housing estates otherwise the various channels will burst out with expletive-enhanced chatter from lorry drivers and teenage gangs. Fortunately the three mile range of a typical 4 watts radio loses most intrusions once you are on rural canals. A decent installable set is priced between £60 and £90. Portables are generally less powerful and costly – starting at about £25.

Mobile phones are now owned by half the population so there can be few narrowboats that do not enjoy their benefits – and disbenefits. The major networks were launched in the UK in 1985 and the market is now well past the poseur phase. Suppliers are inventive in applying charges to exploit demand. The phones themselves are usually subsidised in price and you may be offered free connection to a network. Nevertheless, monthly service fees and call charges mean that your phone could cost between £150 and £500 a year to run depending on how much you use it. Increased competition between the four networks is adding features and bringing down costs almost monthly. As well as conventional tariffs, you can now opt for pay-as-you-go deals or buy a year's rental and some 'free' air time in advance. Insurance is worth considering in the first year but, after that, it is cheaper to start a new contract if the phone is lost.

The networks claim to cover around 98% of the country with their analogue networks but the future lies in digital mobile phones which provide much clearer speech and cannot be 'cloned'. When first introduced, digital coverage was limited to the country's heartland and urban areas. It is now claimed to be around 95% but both percentages are of the population, not land mass, so rural canals are often on or beyond the fringe of even analogue networks. Performance, in any case, is greatly affected by local obstacles.

Residential boats used to be fitted with 'Class 2' car phones but improvements in hand-held, Class 4 phones have made them a rarity. If you find yourself at Braunston – or any similar 'signal desert' on the network – a magnetically mounted external aerial that plugs into a socket on most phone bodies will add 2 bars to your signal strength for about £30.

Details on marine VHF courses from: The Royal Yachting Association, RYA House, Romsey Road, Eastleigh, Hants S05. Tel: 023 8062 7400.

Aerial boosters make a big difference in poor signal areas.

CHAPTER 15

DECK & SAFETY EQUIPMENT

Anchors

One of the attractions of inland boating is its relative safety. However, if your boat ever goes near a river, an efficient anchor is essential. The most popular type for inland waterways use is the Danforth and its variations. These have broad blades to hold well in soft river beds but stow reasonably flat.

This type of anchor is designed to lie naturally on the bed with flukes inclined down so that a horizontal pulling force on the anchor also makes it dig in. A vertical force, or in fact any more than 10° above horizontal, will tend to lift it out. For this reason, heavy chain is used to make sure that the anchoring line descends in a curve, transforming the boat's side and downwards pull into a

The Danforth anchor holds well in soft river beds.

horizontal one. So it is particularly important that heavy craft like narrowboats should put out sufficiently long and heavy anchor line to prevent dragging. To save on cost, the boat end of the line is sometimes of rope – nylon not polypropylene, whose floating properties are counter-productive.

The anchor line acts as a shock absorber. In deep water, where a lot of line is paid out, it less likely to be pulled taught. On rivers, rarely deeper than 20ft, a relatively high line-length to depth-of-water ratio is needed to contain the load of a narrowboat easing and then suddenly pulling. If an all-chain line is used, a 5:1 length:depth ratio should be paid out. If nylon rope (called a warp) is introduced the ratio should be as high as 9:1, depending how much chain is used – 20ft of chain is a minimum.

The line should be permanently attached to the boat – don't wait until the anchor has to be used because, in haste, you might throw anchor and all the line overboard. However, if all-chain is used it should not be shackled or welded to the hull – the final connection should be rope so that it can be cut quickly in an emergency. The chain can be stored in a locker, coming out through a proprietary chain-pipe. A large deck cleat, additional to the mooring cleat, should be on hand to tie off the chain or warp once sufficient is paid out.

Don't take it for granted that the anchor has to be dropped from the bow. In narrowboats, particularly longer ones, anchoring from the stern can save valuable distance in the typical emergency of approaching a weir. This is because the boat does not have to turn through 180° before the anchor can bite and because the anchor is already to hand for the boat's most vigilant crew member – the steerer.

Raising the anchor requires the boat to be motored slowly towards the anchor, the line being brought in until it descends almost vertically. The anchor should then pull out.

The following weights suggested for narrowboats are in a range because the heaviest (and most effective) may be too heavy for some crew to handle. A lighter anchor will be of more use to them if it can be deployed quickly, with plenty of anchor chain to make sure that the lesser blade area bites. Dimensions shown under chain/warp are thicknesses of link and rope.

Narrowboat – length (ft)	Anchor weight (kg)	Chain/ warp(mm)
30	7-10	8/12
45	8-12	8/14
60	12-16	10/18
70	14-18	10/20

Other safety equipment

Does your boat carry a lifebuoy? It should – and perhaps a throwing line. Various types are made, based on a ball that pays out a line as it is hurled towards its target. Life jackets are recommended for children but these should not be too large or the child may be trapped in a semi-submerged position. Adult crew may be reassured by life jackets on rivers but they are not often worn by adults on canals. Some might feel slightly ridiculous wearing one – until the occasion it saves their life. Life jackets are even available for dogs and cats which might prevent a human from risking his/her life to save a pet.

The cabin-top companion set is boat hook, pole and plank. Boat hooks are of aluminium or steel-capped timber. A long wooden pole (referred to as a shaft on narrowboats) allows you to push through the mud of most canal beds to move a heavy narrowboat out of shallow water, or even punt it along. It should be made of ash and not softwood which may snap, impaling you in the process. Don't be tempted to fend off another boat with it unless it has a padded end. The boarding plank should have a small timber lip on either end of the bottom side, to hook over cockpit coamings, and anti-slip paint or transverse slats on the top side to provide grip. You can make brackets out of timber to store pole, plank and rack or you can buy brass ones to screw to the cabin top or your builder may have included them in the steelwork.

Fenders

Narrowboats are equipped with heavy rope-bound fenders on bow and stern. The forward one is a single unit but as many as three cantilever out from the counter to protect the rudder. Bow fenders should be suspended and not fixed with chains from below so that they can ride up if trapped on a lock gate while the boat is descending. The chain fixings should also have a weak link so that they will break if the fender catches while rising in a lock. Plastic balloon fenders protect lighter hulls but are usually too frail to withstand squashing by narrowboats. These sometimes use rather unsightly but practical car tyres. Lengths of softwood or plastic pipe, hanging down on lines, are an alternative but rope side fenders, matching those on bow and stern, are smartest for narrowboats.

Mooring lines

An advantage of low-cost (but durable) polypropylene is that the most unskilled boater can usually splice loops into it so that it can be quickly switched from one mooring dolly to another. 10mm dia should suffice for an 18ft canal cruiser, 14mm to 20mm for large narrowboats. As a guide, a narrowboat bow line should measure between 23ft and 33ft long, stern lines between 15ft and 20ft. Experts advise against coiling the aft line and hanging it on the tiller pin because it can catch feet and/or fall into the water and tangle round the prop. It looks naff anyway.

The front fender should be suspended from the cants.

Fixing the fender from below increases the chance of being hung up on a lock gate and causes wear.

Most young narrowboats carry a midships cabin-top mooring cleat/ring for single rope lock handling. If your narrowboat lacks one, and does not have raised steel handrails through which you can loop a midships line, consider welding a ring to the inside face of the traditional handrail. This will minimise the risk of heat damage to insulation and linings (or even a fire) from welding through the cabin top.

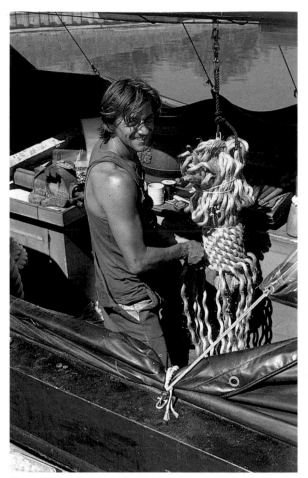

Fender making is a skilled occupation.

To reduce scrubbing, particularly over winter, long diagonal lines called 'springs' can also be set to prevent the boat running forward and back. The well set-up owner will have mooring lines for cruising, lighter but longer ropes for springs – and a couple of short straps looped at each end and measured to neatly fit the home mooring.

The standard of deck design in narrowboats is often wanting. Builders compete fiercely for orders, but few have asked themselves how the product could be improved in use. This might include somewhere neat, safe and convenient to stow mooring lines and smart fender bins so that side fenders can lie out of sight but be deployed instantly when needed. Occasionally builders fit open-fronted lockers as a single store for lock keys, spikes, hammer – so that you can check at a glance whether any have been left behind. Minimise that risk by painting them a bright colour. And carry covers to place over mooring spikes (washing-up liquid bottles will do) to warn passers-by of the obstruction.

Rear fenders should also be hung and extend beyond the rudder.

Mooring ropes should have an eye splice at one end and a back splice at the other.

CHAPTER 16

BUYING A NEW BOAT

This is one of the shortest chapters in this book but, if you are considering buying a new boat, it may well contain the advice which will save you the most heartache. In the last edition, this part was entitled 'Hell knoweth no fury like a punter scorned'.

Having a narrowboat built sometimes provokes extreme emotions in the new owner. He/she eats, drinks and dreams narrowboats during the building period. He/she is inordinately proud of, and well disposed towards, the builder and cannot imagine the he is not equally enthusiastic about the project, just because this is the 43rd boat he has built. In this sort of condition, the besotted buyer may not be concerned if the builder does not offer a written contract, asks for large sums of money in advance or is slow in receipting stage payments.

He/she may well be lucky and find that the builder repays his/her optimism with honesty and reliability but marine surveyors nearly all have horror stories about deals which have gone wrong and customers whose lives have been ruined by the experience. There are no sure-fire ways of avoiding all the pitfalls but here are a few suggested ways to help minimise the risk.

Unless you are a seasoned boater and know exactly what you want, look at as many boats and builders as you can before placing your order. Newcomers face a fairly steep learning curve but there is plenty of help around if you take the time to seek it out.

Once you have narrowed down the field, speak to as many of the builder's previous customers as possible. Some builders hold open days which are an ideal opportunity to find out how the boats, and the builder, perform. If not, a good builder with nothing to hide should be willing to put you in touch with some of his customers.

Ask for a written specification of all the materials and equipment that will be used in the boat. This will enable you to compare one offer with another more accurately and is a useful record if the builder changes the specification during construction.

Try to discover the builder's financial standing. No sector of the market or size of company is immune from bankruptcy but those working with minimal profit margins and no cash reserves are particularly prone. Finding hard evidence is not easy. You may be able to get information on larger builders from a search at Companies House but, with the smaller ones, you just have to rely on observation and instinct.

Be suspicious of requests for large sums of money in advance. Most reputable builders ask for a nominal sum as a gesture of goodwill on placing the order and more substantial payments only when materials have been bought or work carried out. Some builders, particularly at the budget end of the market, finance work in hand with deposits on future orders. If they cease trading, these deposits are usually lost.

Use a proper contract to record the agreement. The British Marine Industries Federation/Canalboat Builders Association has a contract which suggests stages when interim payments should be made. It also establishes the buyers' ownership of all work paid for if the builder goes into liquidation, provided the items are properly marked. If things don't go as smoothly as you hoped, it contains procedures for dealing with disputes. This contract can only be used by members of the CBA.

If you chose a builder who is not a member of the CBA, make sure they offer you a contract at least as good as the BMIF/CBA's. There are many good builders who have their own reasons for not being members of the CBA although several of these are realising the advantages of membership with the introduction of the Recreational Craft Directive.

Confirm that the builder with whom you have signed a contract will be responsible for doing all of the work including fitting out. Some builders sub-contract this work to other companies without notice and the customer can be left not knowing who to pursue in the case of a dispute.

Once the contract has been signed, try not to vary it or you may be opening the door to a host of costly extras. If changes are essential, obtain a written quotation before the new work is carried out.

Make sure that the builder is aware of his responsibilities under the Recreational Craft Directive and intends to give you full CE marking and documentation with the completed boat. If, as some do, he offers to give a Boat Safety Certificate as well, so much the better. Dealing with RCD documentation imposes additional costs on boat builders. Some are able to absorb this or pass it on without affecting their price too much while others mistakenly assume that it does not apply to them and ignore it.

If the delivery date has to fit in with other important events – like moving out of a house, for example – make sure that this is noted in the contract. If late delivery is likely to result in you being involved in extra expense, you could try adding a clause to the contract making the builder pick up the tab. Here, it is even more important not to make changes to the design while the boat is being built as these will almost certainly make such a clause unenforceable.

If you have worries while the boat is being built, seek the advice of a local marine surveyor. For a modest fee, he or she should be able to carry out a pre-purchase survey. A small investment at this stage could save a lot of heartache later on.

If things do go wrong and you end up in dispute, take heart from the fact that it is no defence for the builder to say that, because his boats are £20,000 cheaper than someone else's, they can't be expected to perform properly. The Sale of Goods Act states that all items offered for sale should be fit for their purpose and of 'merchantable quality'. That requirement applies to narrowboats just as much as it does to toothbrushes.

Finally, don't have nightmares. The majority of builders are simply trying to earn a modest living doing the thing they enjoy best. The advice given here is intended to help you avoid the one or two who aren't.

CHAPTER 17

THE MARKET

What your budget buys

Here is a rough guide to the sort of boat your budget will buy in 2000:

£2,500: Twenty year old, 19ft four-berth Dawncraft Dandy glass-fibre canal cruiser with Honda four-stroke outboard. Or: Twenty year old, 22ft Norman cruiser with Honda four-stroke outboard.

£5,000: Eighteen year old, Norman 27 four-berth canal cruiser with Yamaha four-stroke outboard. 40ft narrowboat of uncertain age and parentage, requiring a complete re-fit and engine overhaul.

£7,500: Nine year old, 20ft Springer Water Bug four-berth steel mini-narrowboat with Honda four-stroke outboard. Or: Twelve year old, 25ft Romero (Dawncraft) with Johnson 9.9hp outboard.

£10,000: Twelve year old, 35 to 40ft steel ex-hireboat. Or: Fourteen year old, 28ft Dawncraft with 15hp four-stroke outboard.

£15,000: Twenty year old, 40ft Hancock & Lane steel narrowboat, with sound DIY fit-out. Or: Eight year old, Viking 28 glass-fibre cruiser with 15hp four-stroke outboard.

£20,000: Ten year old, 45ft Harborough Marine trad narrowboat with Perkins diesel engine.

£25,000: Five year old, 35ft cruiser style narrowboat by Bridgewater Boatbuilders. Or: Fourteen year old, 60ft Colecraft with Lister ST3 diesel engine. Or: Almost new 23ft Wilderness Beaver, glass-fibre canal cruiser with Yamaha four-stroke outboard and trailer. Or: Sixty year old, unconverted, riveted-steel working motor narrowboat in reasonable condition.

£30,000: Eight year old, 50ft trad narrowboat built by Mike Heywood. Or: New Viking 28 glass-fibre canal cruiser with 15hp Honda outboard.

£40,000: Seven year old, 60ft Colecraft trad, fitted out by established professional with boatman's cabin and traditional diesel. Or: New 55ft trad or semi-trad from a budget range builder. Or: New 50ft x 12ft 'wide-beam' narrowboat from budget builder – excluding your own free-standing furniture.

£50,000: Most newish secondhand narrowboats you care to consider. Or: Typical new 50ft narrowboat from a mid-range builder.

£70,000: Three year old, up-market narrowboat, well equipped and with boatman's cabin and vintage engine. Or: Seventy year old, 60ft x 13ft converted luxemotor (Dutch barge) in sound condition.

£95,000: Almost any new top-of-the-range narrowboat with almost any specification (like built-in generator and inverter/chargers) you care to consider.

Names on the secondhand narrowboat market

Many of the names you will come across when looking for a secondhand narrowboat are listed in Chapter 9. The following are the names of companies that have stopped trading but whose boats still appear on the market. The thumbnail sketches provided may help to give some idea of what to expect.

Alphafax: Shell builder in Cheshire/ Liverpool area during early/mid-eighties.

Barney Boats: A class of craft rather than a builder. Braunston Boats, set up by Chris Barney in late sixties, built a popular and durable steel-hulled, glass-fibre topped traditional-style boat, that attracted considerable owner loyalty. All-steel version was built latterly by Union Canal Carriers.

The original Barney boat (right) and the 1993 all-steel version.

Bingley Marine: Popular builder of conventional cruiser-style boats in seventies. From West Yorkshire.

Braine, Malcolm: Most sought-after builder of seventies. Typically built in BCN style with strong traditional leaning – including oak-clad side decks and Masonite-skinned superstructures. Retired in mid-eighties, to concentrate on surveying. Yard taken over by Norton Canes Boat Builders (see Chapter 9).

Brummagem Boats: All-steel boats, built in reasonable numbers. mostly for hire although some later ones show relatively ambitious fitting-out. Brummagem merged into Alvechurch Boat Centres (see Chapter 9) and disappeared as a name in the early nineties.

Canal & Rivercraft: Busy builder, mainly of glass-fibre-topped hire narrowboats in seventies.

Chappel & Wright: Shell builders near Manchester, not well known outside the area, but well spoken of.

Cleaver Marine: Hire operator on river Avon in late seventies.

Coles Morton: Ambitious multi-based hire company of late seventies/early eighties. Built large numbers of all-steel narrowboats, including some for private market. Conventional, almost pert styling. Many boats fitted with Danish Bukh diesels (small but sturdy).

Colliery Narrowboat Company: Previous name of Wincham Wharf Yacht & Boat Builders (see Chapter 9).

Conmac Boats: Popular shell builder in Cheshire/Liverpool area from early-eighties. Briefly changed name to Alphafax (qv) in mid eighties.

Cox, Charles: BCN builder in late eighties/early nineties, mainly of tug-style shells with generous sheer.

Crestelle Marine: Builder in ambitious (and quite convincing) traditional style in Burton-upon-Trent. Now trades as Tony Francis & Son (see Chapter 9)

Crook, J&J : Originally working boat operators on the Leeds & Liverpool Canal. But also the employers of Doug Moore (qv), who later set up under his own name.

Dalescraft: Unusual builder based on edge of Yorkshire Dales in seventies and early eighties. Built canal cruisers and narrowboats. Styling details included glazed aft bulkhead on one model that sloped forward like a garden cold frame, and narrow side decks. Experimented with gas-powered engines.

Davison Brothers: Changed name to Sawley Marina in 1991. Narrowboat building dates back to fifties and has been in wide variety of styles: all-timber, ferro-concrete (with exceptionally fine swimming hulls), modernistic cruiser-style, and traditional-style all-steel. Derrick Davison (see list of surveyors in Appendix 4) recalls most boats built.

Delph Lock Narrowboats: Related to Screwcraft (qv).

Dunston, Richard: Thorne-based shipbuilder, produced some narrowboat shells. Ex-employees now run French & Peel, narrowboat builders.

Duval, Brian: Built in exaggerated trad style (great sweeping curves) in seventies.

Eggbridge Cruisers: Over-ambitious budget/mid-range Cheshire-based builder of early eighties. Conmac Boats (qv) was former Eggbridge supplier.

Faulkner: Early Cosgove-based builder of budget narrowboats, possibly based on Springer hulls (qv). Last known output in early seventies.

Fenmatch: Evesham-based production narrowboat builder from later seventies to early nineties – many for hire use.

Fernie Fabrications: Produced a similar style to Harborough Marine (qv) in seventies – primarily for hire fleets. The name went on to be adopted as a style by successive builders.

Forth, David: Very relaxed boatbuilder in East Yorkshire – has built one narrowboat a year for several years. Used to cruise canals for several months in new boat before selling it. Has also built inspection launches. Favours timber-framed windows.

Goldalming Narrowboats: Fitter-out, particularly of hire boats for own and other fleets in late seventies/early eighties. Generally based on Colecraft shells, and with deep (24in) windows.

Greentour: Was Steelcraft and is now M G Fabrication. Run by Mike Gration who was at Hancock & Lane (qv), finishing as works manager. Has built all types from Dutch barges to hire boat shells.

Gregory: Small fleet of Wolverhampton hire boats, built in-house with erratic plating.

GM Engineering: Black Country engineering company that diversified into sturdy, good-looking tug-style narrowboats in late seventies/early eighties.

Hancock & Lane: Prolific production narrowboat builder of seventies and early eighties. Slightly chubby, unremarkable styling but quality so consistent that design was copied by some – and may be passed off as H&L. Builders' stamp often found on rudder bearing and in front deck. Standard styles were 'Norsman' and 'Marlin' (a compact design) but the company also built for many trade customers. Several owners claim to possess the 'last H&L ever built' (in 1984), although Hancock & Lane is still in the engineering business.

Harborough Marine: Built in large numbers during seventies. Typically ex-hire. Characterised by long, sweeping high bows and long sterns. Most with glass-fibre tops, louvre windows and air-cooled Lister engines. Well maintained as hire boats, but most are on second or third private owners and a few date back before 1970. All-steel range, some built as budget-priced fully-fitted narrowboats for private market, date from around 1981.

Characteristically high-bowed Market Harborough boat.

Harris, L R: Budget builder with fairly abrupt styling, based on river Soar.

Hesford Marine: Prefers character to conventional styling, popular on Bridgewater Canal.

Heywood, Mike: Prolific, low-priced builder of good-looking shells in eighties and early nineties. Has influenced the industry through pricing, and through the number of ex-employees who later set up as narrowboat builders. Now works for Evans & Son (see Chapter 9).

Hopwood: Company owned by current builder John Pinder (see Chapter 9) from mid-sixties. He set up under his own name in 1974.

Hurst, M: Builder of chunky, budget narrowboats, based at Mirfield.

Jenkins, Barry: Nottinghamshire-based shell builder, particularly of very low, rakish tug-style narrowboats, in eighties. Also worked as Eddishaw & Jenkins.

Ladyline: Aggressive multi-based company of seventies sold mainly glass-fibre canal cruisers, but also commissioned a range of narrowboats. Specs were surprisingly good. Shells by Hancock & Lane, fitting out by Len Beauchamp (now the fitting-out director of Colecraft).

Lofthouse & Wilson: Quality fitters-out from Whaley Bridge.

Lloyd, Chris: Traditional but imaginative boat fitter. Stopped fitting-out in the early nineties. His use of colour and the technique of spreading boatmans cabin character throughout the whole interior have been influential.

Mastercraft: Unique cruiser-style narrowboats of late seventies. Lynton Engineering (a Manchester caravan manufacturer) built fully-fitted aluminium-clad cabin modules to drop into steel narrowboat hulls. Although they did not look substantial, quite a few are still about. Two were even in a hire fleet in 1993.

Mindon Marine: Quality builder/fitter-out of seventies and early eighties. Easily identified by builder's dated plaque. Square transom stern, unusual upswept bow. Some ex-hire, but also attracted loyal private owners. Version built by Sandall Marine in early eighties although Mindon Engineering is still in business.

Moore, Doug: Highly respected builder of traditional boats. Continuous sheer from stem to stern prohibits lengthening. Worked latterly at Lower Park Marina but has now retired.

The elegant lines of a Doug Moore shell.

Newman, Pete: Built small number of pleasant traditional-style narrowboats in late eighties/early nineties, from Langley Mill on Erewash Canal. Now active again at Langley Mill Boatyard.

Original Boat Company: Hire company on Avon with individual style in craft – all trad with very low side-decks and deep windows. The pioneer of electric drive – several craft so powered, but later converted to diesel. Shells built by Colecraft.

Parker, Graham: Builder in BCN style – early examples have aluminium-on-ply superstructures. Most boats date from early seventies. Graham Parker retired, then returned in early eighties to join a partnership as current builder Canal Craft (see Chapter 9) then retired again.

Pearson, Malcolm: Builder of fine BCN style narrowboats and, especially, tugs. Boats were very well finished and detailed – even below the waterline. Alternated spells of boatbuilding with computing. Not active at present.

Peakland Narrowboats: Short-lived builder of early nineties, based close to Chesterfield.

Peter Keay & Sons: Walsall-based builder mainly working in timber, leaning towards working boats. Most prominent in seventies.

Phoenix Narrowboats: Very imaginative fitting out company, employing an interior designer. Flourished in early nineties but went into liquidation in 1998.

Rickaby, John: Built small number of traditional-style craft near Kegworth in mid eighties – notably a striking Bridgewater Canal tug.

Rugby Boatbuilders: Fitter-out, rather than builder but produced large number of craft (glass-fibre-topped and all-steel) with characteristic deep top panel round bow, and double-decker foredeck cants. Gravel ballast under cabin floors in older versions – not accepted practice today. Rugby Boatbuilders ceased business in the early nineties but two ex-employees now run Blue Haven Marine.

Screwcraft: Budget-class narrowboat built by Dennis Grainger near Birmingham in seventies and eighties.

Seasteel: Worcestershire-based builder with some original ideas – including a 23ft all-steel canal cruiser with wheelhouse steering.

Severn City Boats: Hire boat operator in Worcester, built in quantity (but not quality) to satisfy hire boat boom of late seventies. Not to be confused with Severn Valley Boat Centre. (see Chapter 9).

Shropshire Union Cruises: One of the earliest leisure narrowboat builders – its Cutlass style dates back to early sixties. 'Frobisher' class has sliding roof over centre section. Later taken over by Dartline which was, in turn, taken over by Anglo Welsh (Falcon). (see Chapter 9).

Simolda: Cruiser-style narrowboats, mostly ex-hire, decidedly chunky in shape.

Smith Bros (of Goole): Built some very boxy narrowboat shells in eighties.

Sovereign Marine: An associate company of Severn City Boats (qv), in later seventies/early eighties.

Springer Engineering: The canals' most prolific narrowboat builder started production in early sixties. Most are instantly recognisable, from 'moustache' over the stem post, to no-frills welding finish. Plating tended to be thinner than competitors (although Springer's vee-bottomed hull arguably needed plating no thicker than hull sides) but many elderly Springers remain afloat. Pre-1981 boats have vee-shaped transoms and ridged cabin tops – those of later boats are rounded. A large proportion were sold fully-fitted. Springers were entirely honest boats, but the company went out of business in 1994, probably defeated by recent competition from boats that looked better but were just as cheap. The company invented the mini-narrowboat by designing a 20ft boat to be outboard-powered. It also built some large wide-beam craft, including peniche/barges with wheelhouses.

Steelcraft: Now trades as Greentour (qv).

Stone Boat Building: Current company, best known for its narrowboat chandlery but built a line of carefully-detailed cruiser-style narrowboats – most with glass-fibre tops. Still builds the occasional, all-steel traditional narrowboat with high quality fit out.

Swan Line: Cruiser-style boats of recognisable style – transom stern, no tumblehome at top of hull, but plenty of hull curvature (sheer) looking from side. Seventies boats stood out through quality fitting-out, with imaginative use of colour. Most of this earlier production had glass-fibre tops.

Teddesley Boats: Popular builder of glass-fibre topped narrowboats in seventies. Later output of stylish all-steel trads (from current company) has been less numerous.

Thomas, Ernie: Owner of Hatherton Marina until late eighties. Had a fleet of hire narrowboats built, with beautifully engineered hulls, quiet engines, handsome (but timber) tops.

Tinker, R: Manchester-based shell builder in eighties.

Tolladine Boat Services: Produced elegant narrowboats from Worcestershire in seventies – most with timber detailing that made cabin particularly vulnerable to rot. Characterised by aft cabin line that rose in trad-style – but with long cruiser-style aft deck. Quite a few are ex-hire.

TT Marine: Mid-market production narrowboat builder, based at Doncaster then Thorne from early eighties until company went out of business in 1994. Staff took over to run it as Thorne Boat Builders.

Walsh, Seamus: Pioneering shell builder, was asked to build a narrowboat shell at Stone in sixties. Then built for Shropshire Union Cruises (qv), alongside David Piper. Now near Market Drayton, specialising in marine ironmongery.

Water Travel: Respected builder in BCN traditional style in seventies and early eighties. Some shells built by David Harris. Still current as a hire company.

Watercraft: Evesham-based shell builder.

Watson, Albert: Builder on Macclesfield Canal in seventies. Small output but discerning clientele (including Chris Coburn), and good lines. Timber-, Masonite- or steel-topped.

Whalley Boats: Set up by ex-employee of Hopwood (qv) at Burton-upon-Trent in mid-seventies.

Wharfside Boatfitters: The one-man company of the late John Woollard, whose atmospheric style, based on stained timbers, placed him towards the top of the eighties' fitting-out market.

Whittle Boats: Marketed narrowboats in approximate butty-style in late seventies. Based near Chorley.

Willoughby Fabrications: Production shell builder, based near Braunston, in early seventies. Several current shell builders worked there, including Colecraft, R&D Marine, Dave Clarke (see Chapter 9).

Willow Wren: Typically timber-topped boats from seventies, with simple, beefy but striking cabins. Many used for hire. Early hulls supplied by Hopwood/John Pinder (qv), later ones by Hancock & Lane, although Willow Wren all-steel shells of eighties/nineties from Braunston Canal Services in its own style.

Wilson, Jonathan: Talented nephew of Mike Heywood (qv), with nice line in Josher-ish shells. Traded for a while with Gary Gorton as Wilson & Gorton in Market Drayton. Moved to Rotherham to set up as Steelmart but now builds there under his own name. (see Chapter 9).

Wroe, A&B: Shell builder in Doncaster area.

WW Fabrications: Budget/mid-range shell builder, based at Market Harborough. Dates back to seventies.

Names on the second-hand glass fibre market

Current manufacturers of glass-fibre boats suitable for the inland waterways can be counted on the fingers of one hand but it wasn't always like that. If you are looking for an older boat, the chances are it is no longer in production so here

A Romero 25, externally identical to a Dawncraft 25.

The Atlanta24 mould started life as a Norman but is now producing Shetlands.

are some pen portraits of the names you might come across. One defunct range of canal cruisers stands out from all others as a particularly popular secondhand buy. The **Dawncraft** range was introduced in the sixties, initially with plywood hulls, although most are glass-fibre. The seven-model range was generally built to keen prices but all seem to survive canal cruising. They are boxily spacious and many spare parts are still available via the original builder's present company Wilson Marine (Tel: 01384 872983). The 19ft Dandy, with four berths and separate toilet compartment inside its cabin, is a particularly useful starter cruiser – basically sound examples change hands for as little as £2,500. During the company's death throes, similar models were built under the name Romero.

Norman canal cruisers were also built in large numbers but are less common because they went out of production some years earlier (one model re-emerged as the Atlanta 24 and, more recently, the Shetland 25). Normans were slightly better built, but less spacious than Dawncraft. One Dawncraft model, the Crusader, was developed by another manufacturer, **Highbridge,** into several lengths. It was a sturdy glass-fibre hybrid cruiser/narrowboat of great practicality.

The Dawncraft Crusader was later developed by Highbridge.

Buckingham's 20ft and 25ft canal cruisers were introduced in the sixties, but renamed and restyled as Leisurecraft in the seventies. Well made, they eventually became the 21ft Shetland Saxon and the basis for Viking's 26ft canal cruiser. **Dolphins** go even further back but most were built of ply, so are dodgy buys. Just a few later twenty footers were glass-fibre-based.

Nauticus 27s (and the less common 22) were ambitiously advertised as the 'Rolls-Royce' of canal cruisers, and were certainly well-made. **Freeman's** narrow-beam 22 was much better built – a neo-vintage concoction of glass-fibre, walnut and tapestry upholstery. However many Freeman 22s were tantalisingly just wider than canal-beam and most Nauticus and Freemans were fitted with inboard petrol engines (although several engine marinisers offer drop-in diesel conversions).

The **Burland** 26, built by Stone Boatbuilding, had a 9 inch keel giving excellent handling. The **Dobson** 24 by Dobsons of Shardlow, the forward-steering **Trentcraft** range by Sawley Marina and the **Mayland** 16ft and 20ft canal cruisers were all good, middle-market cruisers. The centre-cockpit **Creighton** Inlander was built in numbers, later as the **Ribble** and **Stirling.** Other reputable names from the past in the 20ft to 30ft class include **Callumcraft, Charnwood, Classic, Ormelite, Teal** (some of which were wider than canal beam), **Ensign, Headline, Enterprise, Dalescraft.**

One or two builders have offered a boat that looks like a modern canal cruiser – but is built of steel. You may come across examples of Brummagem Boats' Clipper or Arcrite Fabrications' Sun Cruiser – both wheel-steered, centre-cockpit craft in the 26ft to 33ft length range. These are more suited to the rough and tumble of canal use and should be judged on narrowboat criteria.

Car-towable cruisers
Several builders already mentioned included car- (as against four-wheel-drive-) towable glass-fibre canal cruisers in their ranges. Norman was one of the most prolific with four separate models – one of which was a four-berth centre-cockpit 20 footer. The 19ft Dawncraft Dandy, though bulky, is light enough buts needs careful choice of trailer to fit its semi-catamaran hull. Flat-bottomed Wilderness boats are designed to be easy to recover on to a custom built trailer.

Unusual car-towable craft include the caravan-cum-boat Caracruiser and the Wavey Rider Wanderer, a light 18-footer that is entirely cabin, from estate car-type aft bulkhead to its stem. Headroom is good but it is not an easy boat to handle, particularly in windy conditions.

The 18ft Birchwood Continental is simple, stable and spacious, with wide folding door and single floor level that allows canopied cockpit and cabin to run together as a single space. The Continental, which was built in the early seventies, is a reminder of Birchwood's humble beginnings. This large company now builds only large and luxurious coastal cruisers but you might find a modest and basically sound Continental for well under £2,000 – a good towable starter/ camper boat for a tight budget. An owner's club was formed in 1999 and can be contacted on 01462 670793.

Names on the vintage market

Ex-working boats are almost all over fifty years old, and need dedicated maintenance. A few years ago, they were generally regarded as very cheap houseboats or toys for penniless enthusiasts. However, several builders now specialise in rescuing neglected working boats, not least because pristine restorations provide ultimate canal-credibility to deep-pocketed narrowboaters. Among the major names in working narrowboats were:

British Waterways: Owner of the post-1948 nationalised working narrowboat fleet, BW commissioned two modern designs in the fifties – the River class with glass-fibre hold covers and steering by swivelling propeller, and the more conventional but also unlovely Admiral class.

Clayton, Thomas: Carrier of bulk liquids, like tar, in narrowboats with decked-over and compartmented holds. Formed in 1889, remained in existence until 1966. Many Clayton boats were built by Nursers (qv).

Fellows, Morton & Clayton: Merger of several carriers created FMC in 1889. It become one of the largest and best known of canal carrying companies. The term 'Josher', applied to an FMC-style boat with fine double-curved bows, is derived from co-founder Joshua Fellows. The company built iron composite (iron hull sides, elm bottom) at Saltley, and in wood (mainly butties) at Uxbridge. Some of the older and more majestic FMC boats were built as steamers. Early livery was black and white but later changed to red and green. Absorbed into British Waterways on 1st January 1949.

Grand Union Canal Carrying Company: Five canal companies amalgamated in 1929. Their carrying subsidiary then took on this name in 1934 and set about an amazing expansion. GUCCCo only existed for another thirteen years, but a large proportion of ex-working boats remaining afloat today were built for it between 1934 and 1938. Boats were supplied by Yarwoods of Northwich (qv), Harland & Wolff of Woolwich, and Walkers of Rickmansworth. They were popularly identified by their sources: 'Northwichs', 'Woolwichs', and 'Rickies'. GUCCCo ordered later batches to be larger (ie deeper), so these names are further qualified by 'Small', 'Large' (and even 'Middle' in the case of Northwich). Early Northwichs and Woolwichs were of composite hull construction (iron sides, elm bottom), later ones of steel. Walkers built in timber. All the 'Small' boats were named after stars and are thus Star class; the 'Large' boats are similarly Town class. Real traditionalists are attracted to GUCCCo boats as much as to Joshers – not least for the way they swim. The most sophisticated part of vintage working boats is hidden below water.

Joeys: Day boats on the Birmingham Canal Navigations, usually without cabins, and with provision for hanging the rudder at either end. Not built to last.

Nursers: Family of boat builders, based at Braunston from 1870 to 1958 (although latterly owned by Samuel Barlow). Builders of wooden narrowboats.

Station boats: Built for the LMS railway as day boats on the Birmingham Canal Navigations but with finer lines and better construction than joeys (qv). Relatively shallow draughted, so popular for conversion to leisure boats.

Yarwoods: Northwich-based ship and barge builder. Supplied narrowboats to major carriers – Fellows, Morton & Clayton (qv), Grand Union Canal Carrying Company (qv), LMS Railway (see Station boats), and Cowburn & Cowpar.

A Large Northwich Town class motor boat.

CHAPTER 18

WHAT TO LOOK FOR IN A SECOND-HAND NARROWBOAT

The vast majority of craft sold on the inland waterways every year are secondhand. The market for used narrowboats is particularly busy – and potentially confusing. Variables that determine a narrowboat's place in the secondhand market are, in approximate descending order of buyers' priority:

- Type of shell construction (i.e. all-steel, steel/timber, steel/glass-fibre)

- Shell builder's name

- Standard of maintenance

- Fitting-out appearance

- Sophistication of shell style

- Professional fitter-out's name

- Quality of plating

- Cabin layout & equipment specification

- Engine type

- Integrity of fitting-out.

When looking at a second-hand narrowboat with a view to buying, it is easy to become baffled. Just what should you be checking out? Here are a few points to help you through the maze:

Shell construction

The leisure narrowboat market is now really only interested in all-steel craft. Any narrowboat you are offered with a glass-fibre or timber superstructure was almost certainly built before 1982. Large glass-topped boats in good condition are not likely to exceed £14,000 in value; small ones will fall below £10,000. Timber superstructures are valued even lower. Quite a few good quality traditional-style narrowboats of the seventies were built with Masonite cabin skins. In its old age, this oil-tempered board is considerably more troublesome than glass-fibre but the builder's reputation may have lasted long enough to hold the value to glass-topped levels or higher. One or two builders specialise in putting steel superstructures over timber cabins but this has to be done with great care to make sure that the heat from welding does not ignite the timber.

Wooden, composite (iron sides and elm bottom), and riveted iron and steel hulls belong to the specialised vintage narrowboat market – if they are rejected there as being too tired and hacked about, they will have very little appeal to the conventional narrowboat market.

10/6/4? 6/5/3?

The conventional quick description of narrowboat plating lists the thickness of the flat bottom plate, then that of the hull sides, then the superstructure – all in millimetres. The modern norm is 10/6/4 but a few narrowboats have cabin

tops and cabin sides of different thickness so four figures are shown – 10/6/5/4, for instance. Until around 1980, the average all-steel narrowboat was based on 6/5/3 plating. Posher ones ran to 6/6/3. Competition between builders in the early/mid eighties caused escalation to 8/6/4 then 10/6/4. A few boats are built to 12/6/4, and 25/6/4 is not unknown. The merits of different thicknesses are discussed in Chapter 8, concerning new boats.

You may be able to deduce bottom plate and hull sides original thicknesses from two measurements. The bottom plate usually stands sufficiently proud of the hull sides to be measured with callipers. You will probably have to wade in to measure around the bow. Feel about to establish that the protrusion retains its original square edge and is not worn thin. You could risk a measurement off the horizontal Uxter or cavitation plate over the propeller which is usually cut from the same plate as the bottom. This only requires you to immerse hands a couple of inches, with no wading in.

The only easy access to the thickness of hull side plates is at the forward cockpit's drain holes or engine vent grilles. If these are large enough, you can pass a simple vernier gauge or hand micrometer through. However, the drain holes are nearly always in the curved bow plating rather than in the straight main section. Occasionally builders fabricate the bow and stern from plates of different thickness from the middle (either thinner, to bend the plates more easily, or thicker, for better resistance to impact damage).

Hulls are threatened principally by wear on the bottom plate (particularly towards the stern and at the edges), and by corrosion around the waterline. Hire boat hulls wear much more quickly than private ones – but often corrode less. A well-maintained 6/5/3 shell can be a better secondhand bet than a neglected 10/6/4.

Both wear and corrosion need expert assessment. Surveyors sound the steelwork with hammers to check for thin patches as well as making a grid of ultrasonic thickness measurements but other evidence of poor maintenance and likely corrosion is often easily spotted. Lift the engine floor boards, and look inside steel lockers. Is the hull flaking internally with rust? Check under cabin floor boards – if they are readily liftable – for rusting floor bearers. Small areas of rust are acceptable (narrowboat plating, after all, is much thicker than car body panels), extensive corrosion isn't.

Considerable hull denting points to a history in a hire fleet which may not be admitted (or even known) by the present owner. Hire boats were built in large numbers and, sometimes, to mediocre standards in the late seventies but improved so much in the eighties that later ones are often a more sensible proposition than DIY-fitted contemporaries.

There are no simple check points for plating. Are the cabin sides and top wavy? Almost every narrowboat has some irregularity along the superstructure and this is accepted in moderate amounts. For instant comparison, look at a decent sample of nearby narrowboats from other builders. Are details like cockpit drain holes cut raggedly? Compare welded seams with those on other narrowboats.

Are the lines of weld irregular and blobby? Is the steelwork spattered by molten debris? Or scarred by careless grinding of welds?

If your secondhand purchase is priced over £30,000, steelwork finish should be a real priority. In the low teens, it is barely a consideration – your concern then should be does corrosion threaten to sink it and do superstructure and decking details (like doors, hatches, vents) keep the weather out?

Beam, length and draught

The width of a modern narrowboat from an experienced builder is not likely to be wider than 6ft 10in – the accepted figure for passing through narrow locks. But if the boat has been lengthened, check that is has not 'sprung' wider. If it is from an inexperienced builder, do not take the width for granted – measure it. Reject any 'narrow-beam' hull that is more than 7ft wide.

Narrowboats are sometimes not the length that sellers claim – usually because they never been measured by their owners. Often they are longer (because the builder couldn't be bothered to trim standard sheet sizes), rarely shorter (except by a few inches – it is regarded as picky to complain that a 50ft narrowboat only measures 49ft 7in). Length is measured from stem post to counter (so does not include fenders or rudder blade).

Sellers often have little idea how much water their boat draws and frequently volunteer a misleading figure. For a rough idea, measure the height of the stern post from inside and add a couple of inches. Check that the prop shaft exits half way up the stern post. If lower, the boat has a 'dropped skeg' (a guard that projects several inches below the bottom plate). In this case, measure from the top of the stern post to the centre line of the prop shaft. Double that figure and add about four inches. Narrowboat draughts vary between approximately 1ft 6in and 2ft 9in – see Chapter 8 for the reasons why. Height above water is rarely a problem. The maximum fixed 'air draught' should not exceed 6ft.

Age

First time buyers often ask how long modern narrowboats last. The usual answer is that no one knows because most narrowboats built for leisure (i.e. from about 1960, with welded steel hulls) are still afloat. Underwater plating may need patching or more extensive overplating after fifteen or so years of wear and corrosion. This is fairly easily done and may give the hull as long again before further work is needed.

The standard of narrowboat construction and maintenance has improved steadily over the last thirty years so that the average young boat may go much longer than fifteen years before needing steelwork repairs. Plating is thicker, sacrificial anodes are more widely used to protect against corrosion and internal plating is kept drier and better coated.

The history of modern narrowboat building might be divided into phases: the concept of sturdy canal leisure boats became established in the sixties and builders experimented with widely different styles and materials. Was the future in long, narrow versions of centre-cockpit river cruisers? In modern-style narrowboats with huge windows? Was it in glass-fibre hulls or ferro-concrete? Most 'conventional' new narrowboats were based on steel hulls and uninsulated timber superstuctures. Sixties-built

boats were often more adventurous than narrowboats of the eighties and nineties but many fitting-out details fell a long way short of today's safety standards. Very few sixties-built narrowboats would sell today for more than £8,000, with typical price in basically good condition – if you can find one – around £5,000.

The all-steel narrowboat, with sealed cabin bilge, started to appear in the seventies. The inland waterways market finally decided that it was less interested in modernistic styles than in ersatz traditional narrowboats so a few (generally up-market) boats achieved the general lines and approximate specification of modern narrowboats. However, as the number of hire narrowboats reached its peak towards the end of the seventies, quite a high proportion of craft from this decade are ex-fleet and in cruiser style. Only an exceptional narrowboat from this period would better £15,000 in price; average is around £10,000.

British Waterways introduced its Safety Standards in 1979 although, at first, it only applied to hire boats. Nevertheless, they had a gradual regularising effect on narrowboat design, particularly on fuel, gas, electric and ventilation systems. The modern 'floating cottage' with double bed, central heating, solid fuel stove, pump-out WC, free-standing furniture was well established by the early eighties.

The second half of that decade is a watershed in terms of narrowboat age. So many boats were built between 1987 and 1991 that any from before that bulge appear middle-aged at least.

Since 1987, lines, plating standards, equipment and fitting-out tastes have changed only little. Different models of built-in cooker and electric fridge have become popular for instance and on-board 230-volt power has become more common with the aid of inverters and generators. As the guide in Chapter 17 suggests, the spread of prices for younger boats is wide.

Underwater

This checklist is not intended to substitute for a surveyor. You particularly need his advice when looking at underwater steelwork but if, before engaging him, you see a potential buy out of water, extensive pitting (like the surface of the moon) and scaling (as if steel has lifted off in areas) should be a cause for concern. However, very young boats sometimes show initial high rates of corrosion where the plating loses mill scale and adjacent to weld seams.

The bottom plate usually stands proud of the hull side plates to make a wearing edge. If it is particularly worn towards the aft end of the hull, suspect that the full width of bottom plate there is also thin. While in the area, is the bottom rudder bearing worn or corroded? Is the skeg undamaged? Propeller blades ditto? Can you rattle the prop shaft in its bearing? Does the bottom of the weedhatch sit approximately flush with the cavitation plate?

Is the hull fitted with sacrificial anodes? Are they magnesium (for fresh water protection) rather than zinc? (for salt water). Are the anodes' mounts damaged? (if contact with the hull is not good, they will not work). Ask the owner when they were fitted. The best answer is "less than four years ago", the worst, "ten years ago but they have worn barely at all" (because this means they have not been working). How often has the hull been out of water? Every two or three years is desirable.

Older modern leisure narrowboats, and those from inexperienced builders, tend to have shorter swims. You can check the aft swim length from inside while the boat is still afloat. A taper over 10ft length or more is good. At 6ft (about the shortest possible length) the flow of water is severely compromised, inducing turbulent wash and (possibly) poor grip by the propeller. The prop's efficiency is also reduced by a flat broad stern post (more than two inches wide), rather than the sharp edge of most current shells.

Hull corrosion

If it didn't corrode, steel would be the perfect material for the hurly-burly of inland waterways cruising. It is undeniably the most practicable for narrow canal cruising

Corrosion needs expert assessment.

so narrowboat owners have to identify what it is that eats their hulls and try to inhibit the process.

The culprit is electrolytic (or galvanic) action. When two dissimilar metals are immersed in water, an electric current is set up between them. They are acting just like the plates in a battery. As this takes place, one metal is eroded as particles are drawn from it, through the liquid, onto the other metal. The metal that loses is called the anode – that which wins, the cathode. A set pecking order determines which of a particular combination of metals is to be the anode and which the cathode.

The variation in impurity content even between different areas of a single steel plate is sufficient to set up electrolytic action. The ferocity of the process increases in proportion to the difference between the metals and to external factors – salt water causes faster corrosion than fresh and so can industrial or agricultural pollution of canals and rivers. Persistent use of the hull as a current conductor in the boat's electric system also promotes electrolytic action. Hulls have even been affected by current leakage on adjacent boats. Apart from the earth strap that forms part of the engine starter motor circuit, all boat circuitry should be insulated from the steel shell.

The simple overall solution is to establish a new electrolytic pecking order so that all the hull's steel plating works as a cathode. This is done by introducing sacrificial anodes. Lumps of a metal that is further down the order are attached to the hull, solely to be eaten away. In sea water, zinc is used but in fresh water, which is less electrolytically

active, a larger pecking order difference is needed to ensure the cathode-anode relationship, so magnesium is employed.

The benefits of sacrificial anodes are seldom questioned but the claim is still occasionally heard that they don't work. If anodes are not effective, they have probably not been fitted properly. The lumps of magnesium are cast round a steel mounting strap, which should be welded to the hull to guarantee electrolytic contact. Likewise, anodes should not be painted or allowed to become heavily over-coated with trapped weed.

Anodes usually take between three and five years to erode away. As the surface area is reduced, so is effectiveness. Anode manufacturers MG Duff suggest that the active life of anode is two years. Their size recommendations are:

Wetted Surface Area	Type of Anode
Up to 300 sq ft (Up to 30ft x 2ft draught narrowboat)	4 @ 32lb
300 to 450 sq ft (up to 50ft x 2ft draught narrowboat)	4 @ 7lb
450 to 550 sq ft (up to 62ft x 2ft draught narrowboat)	4 @ 10lb or 6 @ 7lb

For surface areas over 550 sq ft, add 2 @7lb for every 200 sq ft.

Anodes are normally mounted on the hull side plates, two on the bow taper, two on the stern. They should be well immersed, taking into account the considerable variation in waterline level at the bow between water tank full and water tank empty. If six anodes are to be fitted, two should be midships, ideally in a recess to avoid increasing the overall beam and reduce the risk of being pulled off.

MG Duff point out that fitting anodes may make enamel paint on the waterline brittle and will cause some oil based paints (like red lead) to break down. More dramatically, it will cause scale – formed when the steel was being rolled into plate at the rolling mill – to lift off. However this is not detrimental – in fact the shell, once repainted, will be better off without this scale.

Mill scale and other rust layers can, in any case, be removed by grit blasting. This has to done by a professional and an antisocial residue of dust and grit is left behind on the ground and/or neighbouring stored boats. Grit blasting not only takes the surface back to bare, unrusted steel but also leaves a good texture for paint to key into. The surface should be coated within an hour or two of blasting and, to gain most advantage, the hull should be painted with an epoxy pitch or tar, so establishing a really hard and tenacious finish. Typical cost of grit blasting a hull: £700.

External fittings

The more your potential narrowboat uses steel for external fittings like door skins, hatches, plank & pole racks and cockpit lockers, the less it will cost to maintain. Rotten ply deck panels over the engine compartment can be surprisingly expensive to replace and so can fitted vinyl cratch and cockpit covers.

A steel slide would have lasted much longer.

Some DIY builders choose to fit timber-framed windows, which have a much shorter life than the standard aluminium-framed type. These, and the frameless hopper windows, found on some older boats, are more liable to leak and to use plain rather than toughened glass. Check aluminium frames to ensure that sliding panels move in their channels and that condensation drains have not been blocked for so long that they cause leakage into the cabin.

Paintwork

The black-painted part of the hull, normally below the top rubbing strake is not intended to remain in perfect condition so scraped paint here is not untoward. Many owners paint the panel above the top strake in a gloss colour. Marks here cannot be prevented either. Rust spots and chipped paint on decks and superstructure might indicate neglect but, even here, the average narrowboat picks up scrapes from bridgeholes and overhanging branches.

A fresh paint scheme on a boat put up for sale should not be as convincing as a mature scheme that the owner has touched up regularly, and repainted gradually in panels. If the owner quotes paint brands and shades off the top of his head, the names 'Masons', 'Tekaloid' and 'International Paint' score brownie points.

Surface rusting indicates neglect but is not too difficult to remedy.

Brush painting, the norm for narrowboats ten years ago, is not as immediately cosmetic as sprayed enamel but it provides a thicker protective build-up. Sprayed paint, in the early nineties, was mainly applied by budget builders. Three thin coats (the norm then) quickly let rust through. It is also more difficult to touch up than a brush applied finish. However, spray painting is likely to become more widespread – and better applied.

Glass fibre & timber superstructures

Timber-topped boats should be checked at handrails, window surrounds and bulkhead joints and where the cabin fastens to the hull. Unless that joint is properly sealed or given a sizeable air gap, water can climb up by capillary action. Parana pine t&g, favoured as a cabin lining by some timber-top builders for its golden, knot-free hue, is more vulnerable to rot than most – so beware damp stains, which may be the first signs of rot working through from the outside.

Glass-fibre tops take the form of structural mouldings or of glass-fibre skinned ply panels. Both are liable to delaminate on cabin tops – indicated by flexing when walked on. Timber fore and aft bulkheads should be checked at their bottoms for rot – difficult if, as was often the case, the inside surface is faced with laminate. The forward bulkhead's joints with the shell are sometimes opened by impact.

Lengthening

Steel is not just a rugged material – it is remarkably versatile. What type of boat, other than an all-steel narrowboat or barge, could you easily lengthen by letting an extra section into the midships? Arguably, lengthening needs less boatbuilding skill than constructing the bow and stern sections but it does call for conscientious welding and framing to match the existing structure. The boat's original builder is probably best qualified for the job but some companies specialise in lengthening. They can advise on whether the hull is sound enough to for the purpose, whether the extra (disproportionate) amount of ballast needed can be accommodated and whether the existing engine has sufficient

The rear half of a narrowboat awaits lengthening.

power. You should also consider what the original, possibly short, bow and stern would look like on a much longer boat. Fitting-out considerations include wiring and gas – will cables and pipes need beefing up to avoid unacceptable voltage and pressure drop?

In terms of resale value, lengthening is more cost-effective for some lengths than others. Inserting 15ft into a 33ft narrowboat takes it into a more popular size range – adding the same to a 55 footer has the reverse effect.

Inside the shell

Modern narrowboats have sealed steel bulkheads between cabin and engine compartment and between cabin and forward cockpit so water should not be able to enter the cabin bilge. In fact it can, and air, often, cannot. Water drains down as condensation, leaks from windows or leaks from the cabin water system. The bilge lacks air movement to evaporate standing water – so it builds up over years, corroding the bottom plate, internal steel framing, and timber floors.

Look for an inspection hatch at the aft (lowest) end of the cabin. If the bilge there is dry and clean (particularly if it retains an original coating of bitumen paint or Waxoyl), you probably need search no further for internal problems. If it is dry and clean but the floor and floor bearers are damp, the owner has beaten you to it and you may be suspicious. A deep cabin bilge (about 5in) is obviously better than a shallow one (minimum about 2in).

Engineering brick ballast is easy to move to inspect the inside of the base plate.

A bilge with no ballast at all is best of all (as in boats with very thick/heavy bottom plates or very shallow draught), engineering bricks are well thought-of (expensive, durable, and thus generally fitted to high quality craft), concrete slab ballast is widely used. Poured concrete ballast was employed by a few builders in the sixties and seventies. It did away with the need for a timber floor – but hides what may be happening to the bottom plate and cannot be altered easily. Gravel ballast is undesirable – it retains damp and you cannot be sure that it has been washed clean of corrosive impurities like salt.

Internal bulkheads are particularly vulnerable to movement under impact if, as is often the case, they are lightly attached to the shell's internal linings. Ill-fitting cabin doors are a symptom. In older boats, particularly if not all-steel, look for softness in cabin end bulkheads, aft floor panels, floor panels adjacent to the shower tray, and under windows. Surveyors can (literally) smell rot in a cabin. And if your nose is good enough, so might you, in the moments after a cabin is opened up.

Secondhand narrowboats – fitting-out

Over twenty years narrowboat cabins have emerged from a gloomy brownness based on varnished ply and pine t&g boarding. Although not exciting, these were forgiving finishes because they masked poor joinery details and were easy to renovate. A typical young narrowboat is now based on light hardwood veneers (usually oak or ash) with routed trim. Oak does seem durable internally, although ash grain has a tendency to blacken with age.

DIY fitting-out in older narrowboats is sometimes based on chipboard, which will not withstand immersion. Coarse resin-bonded chipboard is accepted for floors. MDF (medium density fibreboard) is sometimes seen in younger narrowboats but is not looked upon too kindly. Older narrowboats sometimes have deckheads (ceilings) lined in light laminate. This should be ply-backed; the hardboard-backed version will almost certainly have warped. The best material to find for cabin linings and bulkheads is ply but blockboard is widely used, if not always admitted.

Above £30,000, you should expect thoroughly professional standards of joinery – tight joints, orderly discreet fixings. In the most popular secondhand price range (£20,000 to £30,000) joinery must be presentable even if less precise in detail. You should not, for instance, expect to see raw edges of ply.

Soft furnishings transform many narrowboats. Make sure that swathes of lace, Laura Ashley prints and chunky dralon upholstery do not cloud your judgement. On the other hand, curtaining, carpeting and upholstering most narrowboats takes up £1,000 or more, so make due allowance if your proposed purchase needs these.

Cabin appliances

Models of cabin appliances often give clues to the real age of a boat. Conversely, if your needs are for particular creature comforts in a secondhand boat (diesel-fired radiator heating, for instance), your choice may be limited to boats of a certain age

The Tor Gem solid fuel stove dates back to the early days of leisure narrowboating. A larger version, the Tor Glo, is rarely seen on younger boats. The Parkray stove, also found on older boats, is larger again and almost always runs back-boiler central heating. *WW's* first recorded mention of the deservedly popular Squirrel stove was in 1985.

Seventies narrowboats tended to be fitted with Flavel/Calor Courier free-standing cookers or Flavel's prettier Colette. The first Valor Vanette cookers arrived in the late seventies and were bleakly white. Smaller boats of that time preferred the Calor/Flavel B600 and B700 – ancestors of Flavel's compact Vanessa cooker.

Electrolux gas fridges have been fitted in inland boats for several decades (even though the manufacturer has always refused to approve them for boat use). They cannot be fitted in new boats or used to replace defunct units but, as long as they remain serviceable in a secondhand boat, they are legal. Engel electric fridges date from the early eighties. Batts electric fridges (a Lec fridge with a transplanted 12-volt compressor) made a big impact considering they were only produced for a relatively short time. Since the company went into liquidation in the mid nineties, this type of fridge has been made by Shoreline and Ranger Refrigeration.

Mansfield pump-out WCs have been fitted in boats since the seventies. They may lack the sophistication of compressor or vacuum models but many boaters see this as an advantage. Recirculating pump-out WCs, usually found in ex-hire craft, were made by Elsan and Hampton. These use strained effluent for flushing and tend to smell. Their only virtue is that they don't need a large separate holding tank.

Flavel pioneered gas central heating in narrowboats and led that market until Alde central heating boilers were introduced (originally under the Optimus name) in the seventies. The Flavel boiler, more conventional in shape than the slim Alde, was eventually taken over by Ellis & Son, which still provides service support.

In the seventies, the German Vaillant gas water heater ruled supreme – but was ousted in the eighties by the now-almost-universal Japanese Paloma. The same restrictions now apply to these as apply to gas fridges.

Diesel-fired central heating of the forced combustion type has also been around for a surprisingly long time. Webasto systems have been promoted (by Water Travel of Wolverhampton) on the canals since the early seventies. A few Eberspacher units can be found in boats of that period but most use ducted warm air systems. The Eberspacher-type central heating that is now popular is radiator-based and, in canal terms, really dates from the mid/late eighties. A similar unit is made by Mikuni.

CHAPTER 19

WHAT TO LOOK FOR IN A SECOND-HAND INBOARD ENGINE

The mainstays of narrowboat propulsion for nearly thirty years were Lister's air-cooled diesels and British Leyland's 1.5 and 1.8 diesels (still referred to in the canal world as BMC1.5 and 1.8). The Lister range is essentially four engines: the twin-cylinder SR2, three-cylinder SR3, and the ST2 and ST3 which succeeded them. The twins are suitable for standard-draught narrowboats up to approximately 45ft long, the three-cylinder engines for full-length boats. The age of these Listers barely matters; they are extremely rugged and always repairable. Oil dilution is the only significant fault to which they are prone – the diesel fuel system runs inside the engine so any leakage tends to enter the sump, diluting the oil.

In the sixties, air-cooled Listers were universal in narrowboats and quite a few die-hards cannot understand why they aren't now. Try telling one that they are unacceptably noisy compared to today's 'quiet' diesels and he'll simply reply "half-past three". SRs and STs are not related in any way to Lister's current water-cooled LPW Alpha range, although both have at various times been labelled Canal Star by the manufacturer. The original age of an SR or ST can be worked out from the serial number, by adding 50 to the two digits after the model. 152 SR3 24, for example, is a 1974 engine.

The British Leyland 1.5 diesel was based on a four-cylinder petrol engine designed in the late thirties. By modern automotive standards, it is heavy and inefficient but it is also more tolerant than most of low-speed running. Relative to Lister's air-cooled engines, the water-cooled BMC1.5 is quiet running. A more powerful version, the BMC1.8, has also been popular in narrowboats. Owners are sometimes uncertain which engine they have; but the two can be identified from the cast number 1500D or 1800D on the left side of the block when looking forward. The engines were marinised by a wide number of companies. J G Meakes' version was particularly popular until the early eighties, then it was Thornycroft's, until the 1.5 ceased production in the late eighties. Owners often claim that their Thornycroft/BMC1.8s were fitted as new engines but, if the bell housing plate identifies it as 108R, it was based on a factory reconditioned unit.

Unlike its current MC42 engine, Perkins never had much success with its 4.99, 4.107 and 4.108 four-cylinder diesels, which did not seem as happy in narrowboat running conditions as BMCs. The 4.108 continued into the early nineties as the Waterways Four, partially re-designed to make it more canal-tolerant.

Ford's 1.6 litre and later 1.8 litre XLD four-cylinder diesels have been widely marinised and reasonably successful on canals. Unusually for narrowboat engines, their valves are operated by belt-driven camshafts. Unless the owner can assure you when the belt was last changed, renew it as an early priority after purchase – a broken belt can cause considerable damage in the cylinders. Check to see that the plastic tubing between the injectors that takes unused fuel back to the tank has been replaced with metal as required by the BSS.

Japanese engines are commonly regarded as recent intruders to the canal market but Mitsubishi's K series three- and four-cylinder engines have been fitted in

Plastic tubing between the injectors should have been replaced by metal piping.

narrowboats since the early seventies. First to use them was CT Marine, then (and still currently) the Dutch company Vetus (as the M3.10 and M4.14), then Thornycroft (as models 60 and 80) and Boatserve. Thornycroft now uses the SL and SQ series.

Since introduction as a narrowboat range in 1989, Kubota's range of quiet running diesels has probably become market leader. Kubotas are marinised by Nannidiesel and Beta Marine. Make sure that the Beta Kubota you are offered is not an Isuzu – which that company marinised for a while before switching to Kubota.

Appendix 2 lists manufacturers and models of current narrowboat diesels and Chapter 12 profiles popular vintage engines. While vintage narrowboats appear to be restricted to a dedicated market, vintage diesels are frequently found in modern narrowboats. The most prominent vintage names, for which spares are available through specialists, are: Lister, Petter, National, Kelvin, Ruston & Hornsby, Gardner and Russell Newbery. Semi-diesel Bolinders are held in universal awe but are best appreciated on someone else's boat.

Engine faults account for a large proportion of friction between sellers and buyers of secondhand boats. Detailed assessment of an engine should be a surveyor's job although only a few offer particular expertise in engines.

The following are pre-survey pointers:

An untidy compartment does not bode well. Look for neatly clipped fuel lines, harnessed electrics, and provision on pipes, prop shaft and exhaust for vibration. It is best to hear an engine start from cold – particularly if, as with the BMC1.5, heater plugs are involved. Reluctance may be due to a variety of causes – worn battery, faulty injection equipment or low cylinder compression. Excessive black smoke when running points to injection problems, blue smoke to worn cylinders. Check for fumes blowing out of the oil filler; listen for knocks, especially on the over-run as you blip the throttle and at idle. Good oil pressure for BMC or Lister, when hot, is 40lb/sq in. Below 20lb/sq in is dubious (more so for BMCs than Listers though). If individual cylinder compressors are fitted, uneven compression can be identified. Excessive engine vibration may be caused by bad engine alignment, bent prop shaft or damaged prop.

Most modern narrowboat engines are cooled by a skin tank on the hull bottom or (preferably) side. If the tank is too small or poorly designed, the engine may be liable to overheat when working harder on rivers. Some older narrowboats employ fresh water cooling – where water from the canal is drawn in to cool the block via a heat exchanger. This is not as fool proof as a sealed skin tank circuit and the water inlet should be protected by a large mud box then finer filter.

Narrowboat engines, particularly BMCs, are quite often DIY marinised. Lack of water cooled manifold is questionable. Lack of marine bell housing between engine and gearbox should cause real concern.

Sometimes the gearbox fitted is not man enough to cope with the engine's torque. Hurth's HBW 50 with 2:1 reduction for instance, is rated to 36lb.ft (equivalent to approximately 1 litre engine capacity), HBW 100 up to 75lb.ft (about 1.9 litres), HBW150 up to 107lb.ft (about 2.5 litres). Ratings for PRM gearboxes (also with 2:1 reduction): 150: 110lb.ft (about 2.5 litres), 260: 180lb.ft (about 4 litres).

An engine installation with neatly clipped fuel lines inspires confidence.

CHAPTER 20

WHAT TO LOOK FOR IN A SECOND-HAND GLASS-FIBRE BOAT AND OUTBOARD ENGINE

Relative to narrowboating, a larger proportion of inland glass-fibre boat owners are first-time buyers and the average boat is slightly older. Consequently, a significant number of sellers is not sure of the identity, age – or even real length – of their craft. Some models look narrow beam but are just over canal width. If in doubt, take photos and measurements to show to a friendly and relevantly experienced boatyard or surveyor.

One of the major structural risks is osmosis damage to the underwater hull section. Constant water pressure can cause moisture penetration of the hull on a scale that is microscopic but sufficient to raise blisters of gas by chemical reaction with improperly cured constituents of the glass-fibre. Many canal craft are moulded in unsophisticated conditions which increases their vulnerability.

Taking DIY steps to pre-empt osmosis could be cost-effective, just by increasing a craft's value by more than the cost of materials involved (around £150 for a 25ft canal cruiser). International's Gel-Shield, an epoxy resin coating that is impermeable to water, is a well-known treatment. If osmosis is caught at a very early stage – where pimples are barely discernible – coating can take place after the hull has been thoroughly dried out by lying up ashore over winter (moisture content should not exceed 5%). If osmosis is more advanced, the glass-fibre surface must be taken off until all bubbles are destroyed. This can be done by abrasive blasting or in specialist treatment centres by gel-coat peeling machines. After the exposed surface has dried out (during prolonged lay-up ashore or under special heat lamps), a thicker coating of Gel-shield (three coats instead of two) is applied – or five coats of epoxy paint. Overall eradication of advanced osmosis is quoted by a professional treatment centre at around £100 per foot length of boat.

Apart from osmosis, the hull should be checked for signs of holing – if found, the repair has to be checked inside and out for integrity and the boat's interior examined for possible effects of sinking. Hull cracking may have been incurred if the boat has been inadequately supported when pulled out of water – particularly on a road trailer. Impact damage is most likely on the transom – one of the quickly-learned skills of glass-fibre boating is to avoid being hit from behind by narrowboats. Another is to avoid being hit from the side by narrowboats – bulkheads are often bonded to the hull: check that they have not been displaced and that the external joint between hull and superstructure has not been ruptured. Some transom damage is self-inflicted, particularly where outboard-powered boats have been converted to inboard without adequate transom reinforcement. Other owner failings might include poorly attached pulpit rails, fender eyes and deck cleats.

Folding canopies are quite expensive to replace so make sufficient allowance when calculating what price to offer the seller. If the basic fabric is sound, major repairs to windows and zips are cost-effective. Canopy frames too should be checked for strain. Glass windows should be toughened although a number of cruiser builders were guilty of fitting non-toughened glass which makes lethally sharp shards if broken. Reinstalled windows may leak if not properly sealed – look inside for signs. The textile material on which opening panels slide is prone to green slime, accumulated muck and to wear. Make sure that windows slide freely.

Many canal cruisers are outboard powered and, of these, the majority are fortunately now fitted with four-stroke engines – usually Honda or Yamaha, although other makes are now becoming more common. Only four-strokes will cope equally with pottering day-in, day-out at little above tickover. Despite advances in their technology, two-strokes are simply not designed for this regime and tend to oil their plugs. Four-strokes are also economical of fuel by any standards. Most two-strokes on canal craft are quite old and represent only a small proportion of the craft's value. Five or six hundred pounds, in addition to their trade-in value (assuming there is any), may be needed to buy a secondhand but serviceable four-stroke.

The only special fault of a four-stroke to check for is worn valves which may be indicated by poor starting from cold and which are not costly to repair. All outboards are attached to their clamping brackets by rubber mounts. If the engine flops about, these may be worn or, worse, castings might be broken. Check too for cracks in outboard leg castings and damage to the propeller. Home-made bolt-on rudders may overload both leg and steering system. While in this vicinity, record the serial number. From it, dealers can verify the engine's age. A missing number plate suggests that the engine may have been stolen at some time.

Examine control cables for overtight bends. Make sure that the steering arm allows full lock in both directions and permits the engine to be tilted without strain. Check the fuel line to the outboard tank for deterioration and, using the hand-primer, ensure that the end-fitting doesn't leak when plugged into the engine.

Pulling an engine over using the handstart might just reveal uneven cylinder compression. After starting, the motor should fire on all cylinders reasonably quickly. Is the water cooling tell-tale working? Repairing overheat damage to these alloy blocks can in some cases be unviably expensive. Heat discolouration round the cylinder heads should arouse suspicion.

If an engine jumps out of gear, cable adjustment is rarely a sufficient remedy – replacement of a gear may be needed. If the oil in the gearbox at the bottom of the leg is heavily emulsified, a seal and, consequently, the gears may be worn.

Chapter 2 was unenthusiastic about inboard petrol engines on safety grounds. Many DIY installations (which were popular until the mid-seventies), are frighteningly crude. Even some professional installations fall short of modern standards. Inboard petrol engines should at least be fitted with water-cooled exhaust manifold, inherently safe carburettor that cannot drip excess fuel and proper marine fuel lines – all well ventilated but enclosed by fireproof bulkheads. The fuel tank, particularly, should be in a separate sealed but drained compartment with marine standard external filler and vent. An automatic fire extinguisher in the engine compartment is a must; a reputable gas detector in the engine bilge and a spark-proof extractor fan are highly desirable.

Special installation concerns in glass-fibre craft include flexible mounts on substantial engine beds with correct alignment – the relatively light shells are intolerant of vibration. Engine cooling systems invariably involve a raw water inlet – check that it does contain a filter core of adequate size. Many glass-fibre inboards are connected to outdrive units which work just like the leg of an outboard motor. They should be checked for the same faults, except that their top ends – steering yolks and transom mounting plates – seem particularly vulnerable to impact damage. The popular makes – Enfield, Volvo Penta and Transadrive/Sonic – can be lifted for bottom end inspection. The leg should wind up freely and lock down securely.

The handling qualities of glass-fibre craft vary widely – much more than those of narrowboats. Generally, wheel steering does not allow the same directness of feel as a tiller. If you are used to narrowboats, you will probably find yourself tacking this way and that down the canal but persevere – you will soon get the hang of it. Weight, height above water and shape of keel all affect handling. Before accepting the doubtful qualities of one boat, try as many others as practical.

DIY fitting-out is markedly less popular in glass-fibre craft than in narrowboats although few boats are young enough to have escaped owner alterations entirely. Because space is more confined, special attention should be paid to gas systems and ventilation. Cabin linings tend to rely on carpet and foam-backed vinyl bonded direct to the shell to mask condensation rather than prevent it. Although the opportunities for water to creep in are slightly fewer in canal cruisers than in narrowboats, the materials used, particularly during the seventies, were often inferior.

CHAPTER 21

BUYING A SECOND-HAND BOAT

If you are seriously looking for a secondhand boat to buy, there comes a point when you must pluck up courage to commit yourself to the purchase. The possible pitfalls are probably not quite as great as when buying new but you could still lose a considerable sum of money or find you have bought the proverbial 'pup' if you are not careful. You can make the process less traumatic by working through a number of important steps.

The first is to establish whether the boat is the vendor's to sell. Do not be embarrassed to ask him/her this directly – and to ask for evidence of ownership. Make the point that you want copies to keep of documents that indicate his/her ownership so that, when you sell on, the boat has a 'line of provenance'. This is important because the only cast-iron way of registering a boat's ownership is as a ship under the Merchant Shipping Act 1894 – which no inland waterways owner would undertake on cost grounds. Registration with the Small Ships Register is not proof of ownership. The sort of documents that suggest ownership are builder's invoices and certificate, Declaration of Conformity under the Recreational Craft Directive (see chapter 7), previous owner's invoice to the present one, and chronological supporting documentation, like a series of receipts for moorings and maintenance.

You also need to know whether anyone else has an interest in the sale – a relative, for instance, who could be angry that his/her share in the boat is to be sold without consultation. And you have to be sure that the boat is not the subject of credit finance. You might check with major marine finance houses (five reportedly handle 95% of marine business) or you might seek a credit assessment on the vendor. This involves a credit agency which may only agree to do a search on instruction from your bank or solicitor. The search will not relate any outstanding loan directly to the boat but could add circumstantial evidence to any suspicions you already have.

You should check whether any debts relating to the boat are unpaid – under some boatyard mooring contracts, owners have to pay a percentage of the price of a privately-negotiated sale to the yard. Finally, you can ask the vendor to swear an affidavit before a solicitor to the effect that he/she is the rightful owner of the boat and is selling it free of any lien or encumbrance. Does all this sound like paranoia? Possibly, but bear in mind that, if you buy a boat that the vendor has no right to sell, you can lose both your money and the boat.

Privately owned secondhand boats are not liable to VAT. VAT-registered owners sometimes pass off their boats as business ventures when buying them new (it saves them $17^1/_2$ %, at least), then find that they have to charge VAT on resale. Make sure in discussions and in writing that the price agreed is either free of VAT (most are) or includes VAT.

It is important to agree when the boat and money are to be exchanged – it is not uncommon for completion of a boat purchase to hang on the sale of a house. You also need to know how much of the boat you are buying – what will be removed before the sale?

You may decide to buy the boat 'subject to survey', paying the vendor a substantial deposit (say 10% of the agreed sale price). You should establish what happens if the survey is unsatisfactory – and what constitutes 'unsatisfactory'. A surveyor's job is to present a true picture of the boat's condition but he also has to work to his client's best advantage. Sometimes his report, meant to secure a decent price reduction, is so gloomy that it frightens the novice buyer out of the sale. In this situation, the buyer has shown good faith by spending hundreds on the survey report so asks for his/her deposit back in full. The vendor has lost the sale, the boat has lost its freshness on the market, and may become stuck unless the vendor re-advertises at a lower price. So the vendor may be reluctant to repay the full deposit. Establish, before survey, what would happen in this case.

If the vendor is a private owner, he/she cannot be held liable for any faults discovered after completion of the sale. This is still true if the boat is sold through a broker. However, the buyer can justifiably claim against the vendor if the latter has misrepresented the boat.

You can enter into a written contract before or after survey. It can cover briefly all the points that you already asked about: ownership, outstanding debts, VAT, terms of payment, conditions of survey (if the contract is made before survey), what items will be removed. Make sure that the vendor, you, both addresses and the boat are all clearly identified in the contract.

It may be easier to use the Royal Yachting Association's standard agreement. This is published in 'Buying a secondhand yacht the legal aspects', available from RYA, Romsey Road, Eastleigh, Hants SO5 4YA (Tel: 023 8062 7400) at £5 including carriage. This book also includes a standard bill of sale (or invoice form). And (as a bonus) it includes a standard agreement for shared ownership.

Surveyors

All but the most technically experienced boaters need to employ a surveyor to advise whether their chosen narrowboat or large cruiser is a sound buy. No professional or academic qualification is needed to set up as an inland boat surveyor. Quite a few have marine engineering backgrounds (often as ship's engineers) and have subsequently specialised in inland waterways craft. Others are also involved with industrial survey work, so can bring special testing techniques to difficult boat problems. Many are experienced narrowboat builders who argue that they look at boats from a solidly practical (as against theoretical) viewpoint.

Most surveyors do have professional qualifications. Many are members, at varying levels, of the Institute of Marine Engineers, or Royal Institute of Naval Architects. A few, interestingly, list membership of the Chartered Institute of Arbitrators – pointing to an increasing role for surveyors in resolving post-purchase disputes without expensive and acrimonious court action.

Some of the most august surveyors list CORGI registration (approval by the Council of Registered Gas Installers for marine LPG installations), indicating just how important gas considerations are when buying a boat. They emphasise that boat owners should not allow just any CORGI-registered fitter to work on their boat's gas system. The registration may be just for natural gas work in buildings, which involve practices not permitted in boats.

Although most inland boat surveyors are approved by British Waterways to issue Boat Safety Certificates, the related inspection falls far short of a full survey – it is more of a marine MoT test than a full qualitative investigation. Where inspections for Boat Safety Certificates are undertaken by specially trained personnel (often your local boatyard engineer), these inspectors are not able to call themselves surveyors with any justification.

The most demanding qualification for marine surveyors is membership of the Yacht Designers & Surveyors Association, a long-established body which sets strict ethical and practical (as against academic) standards. Membership is at three levels: probationer, associate member and full member – and the last is usually only achieved after many years practice. All surveyors should carry relevant professional indemnity insurance protection (and it is a condition of YDSA membership).

There is no recommended fee scale for surveys. Buyers are advised by the YDSA to seek three quotations from similar, insured surveyors, making sure that the information given to each is the same. All survey costs (and costs of pulling out of water) fall to the potential buyer, so the report becomes his/her confidential property, which he/she (not the surveyor) may sell on. Hauling out of water costs between £50 and £100.

The surveyor will spend about five hours on board, inspecting behind linings, under floorboards, inside water tanks, etc and, perhaps, conducting handling trials afloat. Many surveyors specifically exclude a detailed inspection of the engine. The ensuing report can't describe the smallest narrowboat in much less than three pages. It may include a (usually pessimistic) valuation.

Clients should not be reticent to ask for explanation of points in the report that they do not understand – and for informal comments beyond those written down. See Appendix 4 for a list of inland boat surveyors.

Credit finance

Where do narrowboaters find the money to buy craft at three or four times the price of a car? From legacies, early retirement lump sums – and not infrequently by graduating from one boat to another over the years. The last course may only be possible with credit finance to make the next step up.

If you only need to borrow a small amount (relative to your financial standing) briefly, your bank may simply agree an extended overdraft. Beyond that, say to £5,000, the bank or building society may be good for a personal loan at a fixed rate of interest.

You may be able to negotiate a personal loan at a variable rate. Because the lending body no longer has to allow for the risk of interest rates going up, it should be able to offer a lower rate than for fixed rate loans. If borrowing a substantial amount from bank or building society, say above £15,000, it will want to take a second charge on your house – not a solution if you are buying a narrowboat to live on. Depending on prevailing interest rates, secured loans should be available at $3^1/_2$ % to $4^1/_2$ % above finance house base rate.

The main source for finance to buy boats is specialist marine finance houses, although these are mostly subsidiaries of high street banks. Their loans require a charge to be taken on the boat so it is a 'marine mortgage'. Narrowboats are more difficult to spirit away than yachts, attract less exotic owners, and generally require smaller loans and, therefore, some marine finance houses are prepared to offer 'unregistered marine mortgages' on narrowboats, saving expensive and time-consuming registration as a ship. A few companies specialise in inland waterways craft so may be more sympathetic to your plans (like living afloat) than conventional marine finance houses.

The interest rates offered by any of these institutions – banks, building societies, and finance houses – are worth questioning. By shopping around, and letting competitors know you are doing so, you may save half a per cent or so in interest – which could eventually work out at several hundred pounds. For this reason too, you should look into alternatives before accepting credit finance by a boat yard whose rates might be inflated by commission payments to them.

The best deal? Typically, a specialist in inland finance could arrange an unregistered marine mortgage for a five-year-old narrowboat priced at £30,000 on the following terms: 20% deposit (£6,000) with repayment of the balance over ten years at £319.68 per month – equivalent to 10.7% per annum APR. If the same loan is for residential purposes, the repayments and interest rate are higher (£384.96 and 15.9%). You will have permission from the lender to live on the boat but tax relief has now ended. Collidge & Partners (Tel: 01843 295925) specifically offers mortgages that do not involve a cost penalty for early settlement (which, as most narrowboats are sold within ten years, is a frequent catch).

All things considered, the rate for an unregistered marine mortgage is normally more competitive. It does not, for instance, involve incidental charges in the same way that a mortgage secured on a house does and it is considerably less expensive than an unsecured personal loan. All these figures are, as the finance companies solemnly chant, subject to applicant. See Appendix 4 for a list of inland credit finance specialists.

Brokers

While boats can be advertised privately, more and more sellers are using boatyards or brokers to act as agents, charging them a fee when sales are completed. At the most basic level, a broker acts as an intermediary to whom potential buyers can put searching questions that they might

Some brokers offer a wide selection of second-hand boats in one location.

Sales brochures soon start to accumulate.

be inhibited to direct to the owner. In addition to this, many arrange finance, locations for surveys, transport, repairs – and a few take buyers' existing craft in 'part-exchange'. When buying through a broker it is important to remember that the sale is still a private sale between the buyer and the owner of the boat so the principle of *caveat emptor* or 'let the buyer beware' applies.

Narrowboat brokerage emerged as big business in the nineties. The average buyer increasingly prefers to see potential purchases set out on display so narrowboat brokers encourage boat sellers to bring their craft into the sales marina. However, as the most interesting craft often have to be hunted down on their moorings, so larger brokers also prepare detailed reports of outlying craft for sale, providing a customer at one end of the country with a representative view of a boat at the other.

The first task for the broker is to inspect the boat and agree a valuation with the seller. Sellers should beware of optimistically high estimates which may be intended to secure the commission. The broker may be gambling that they will not want the bother of moving the boat to another broker when he later advises him to drop to a more realistic price. Sellers should not be tempted to inflate the price themselves either – even in a strong market, buyers quickly develop a sixth sense when it comes to over-priced boats.

Some brokers prepare highly detailed sales brochures while others rely on a side of A4. There are conflicting arguments about which approach is best and sellers have to decide which is best for their boat. Buyers can play the field and decide which type satisfies them best.

Once the buyer has found the boat of his dreams, the broker can help with finding a surveyor, although the buyer should make the final choice. The broker should also be able to prove that the boat belongs to the seller and that he has the right to sell it. Many are also licensed credit brokers so can help arrange a personal loan or marine mortgage.

On agreeing a sale the broker offers a contract that should ensure equitable exchange of boat and money. The level of commission charged on the sale – ranging from 23% for the cheapest glass-fibre day cruiser to 6% for an expensive narrowboat – is high compared to estate agents' going rates. It is justified by the high overheads involved (the estate agent does not have to provide a display lot for you to park your house in) and extra leg work involved – all against a relatively low turnover. See Appendix 4 for a list of specialist narrowboat brokers.

CHAPTER 22

MAINTENANCE, WINTERISING AND DE-WINTERISING

Repainting narrowboat hulls

Narrowboating is a contact sport; canal boating (as practised by lighter canal cruisers) isn't. A narrowboat hull is built and painted to scrape along lock walls and to suffer abrasions at a mooring. The black bitumen section below the top rubbing strake will almost always carry honourable scars – although these can be touched up quickly, with little preparation. Some hire companies redo the bitumen to waterline every week – enthusiastic owners, perhaps every three months.

The term 'bituminous paint' refers to all types of tar- and pitch-based coatings. True bitumen paints such as Sealex are fairly thick and need a bitumen primer. Then come the coal tar types, typically Bitumastic Standard Black Solution or SBS. Being more aggressive, this can be applied directly to the steel but, like the bitumen types, it suffers the drawback of being dissolved by diesel oil.

The next stage up is vinyl-modified pitch such as Comastic. This can also be applied without a primer although the manufacturer recommends – usually in vain – that the surface is first grit blasted. Two part epoxy-based pitch is more durable still, and here the finish *must* be keyed to the steel by grit blasting. If you decide to change to a

A hired pressure washer is ideal for removing slime and much of the rust from the hull.

better type of paint, all traces of the old should be removed (again by grit blasting), or your good intentions will come to nought.

Full hull reblacking is usually a DIY job, done every year or two, when the boat is pulled out of water. The slime which builds up below the waterline should be entirely cleaned off – a pressure washer is ideal for this. As the muck and loose paint is removed, quite frightening sheets of rust may come off as well. Because rusting increases the volume of steel, the damage will probably be more alarming than real. Only when all has been scraped back to bare steel can an accurate assessment be made. If in any doubt, call in an expert. Some corrosion (pitting of the bottom plate, for example) is not easily spotted. Most owners and boatyards do not paint the bottom plate – unless (as on a Springer narrowboat) it has a pronounced vee shape.

Repainting narrowboat superstructures

The enamel-painted parts above the top rubbing strake are more problematic. While most hull paints are intended to be sacrificed, elaborate cabin side paint schemes do not appear to be designed to cope with bridgeholes and projecting branches. The hull panel immediately above the rubbing strake is often in black or even coloured enamel. However, considerable time and anxiety can be saved by taking the hull paint right up to the gunwale. It also gives the boat a more purposeful look.

When you take delivery of your new boat, the builder should put together a pack of touch-up paints. The type of paint should be noted in the owner's manual which is part of the RCD documentation. This is particularly important in the case of hull paint. Likewise, when buying secondhand, ask the previous owner to list all the paint makes and shades he/she has used.

Preparing the hull for re-painting in the dry dock.

Several different types of paint are needed for the whole boat.

Keeping a touch-up kit encourages you to tackle any paint damage immediately. The kit could include rust treatment/primer, sugar soap, white spirit, lint-free rag, various grades of wet & dry paper. Inexpensive brushes are fine for painting bitumen, but not for touching up enamel.

If applying new enamel colours, stick to the proven narrowboat paint companies like Masons, Croda Tekaloid, International and Blakes. The priority for narrowboats is coverage as much as finish – to provide good abrasion resistance. Industrial finishes, like Hammerite, are frequently used in engine compartments and gas bottle lockers but do not fit harmoniously with cabin-side paint schemes. Many narrowboaters prefer to see a brush finish although rollers are sometimes used for large areas and laid off with a brush afterwards. Spray painting, done in thin coats, needs many layers and its glossy finish readily betrays steelwork imperfections, accidental damage and later touching-up marks.

Anti-slip finish, applied to cabin tops and sidedecks, provides a safer foothold when jumping down from locksides. It also hides the weld blemishes that show up, particularly, on cambered cabin tops. Anti-slip paint can be bought ready made-up or can be hand-mixed to taste. It can also be achieved by sprinkling fine, dry sand onto a wet topcoat, brushing off the excess when dry and then finishing with a final coat or two of gloss. It looks smartest if laid in large panels (which may be marked out with masking tape). Surfaces close to handrails are best left free of anti-slip to avoid abrading fingertips. Anti-slip paint on the cabin top also eliminates reflected glare.

Not a few traditional-style narrowboats appear to have cabin tops left in another matt finish – red primer. This is red oxide and is favoured for its traditional associations and because it too is a sacrificial finish – owners slap another matt coat on every few months. However, care is needed as red oxide has limited wet slip resistance. Some owners mimic the traditional 'primer' finish with more durable enamel like tile paint or Danboline bilge paint.

It may be that, having acquired a plain coloured narrowboat, you wish to brighten it up with a traditional livery. Broadly, framelines should be set-in approximately 4in from the cabin edge. The design should place windows half-way up panels and with lines not too close to window edges. Typical width of frameline ranges between $3/4$in to $1 1/2$ in.

Replacing windows

At least one maker (Channelglaze) offers a window that can be re-glazed from inside without removing the frame. In a modern all-steel shell, windows are one of the few areas where the elements can find their way in to rot timber. Leaks are usually through corroded fixings, damaged or dried sealant between frame and cabin side, or blocked condensation channels. If the old window fixings were screwed into timber inside which will not hold the new ones, consider fixing on to the steelwork by drilling and tapping the cabin side and using stainless steel bolts, with self-tappers or rivets (available from window makers in colours to match coated frames). Do not use bolts fixed into loose nuts as these cannot be re-used if the nut is dislodged.

If you need to replace complete windows, the maker's name is almost always somewhere on the glass (but should not be confused with the glass maker's stamp which is also there). If you cannot trace the maker, any reputable marine window manufacturer should be able to produce a matching replacement, given the original as sample. This is equally true of cruiser windows – whether glass or perspex.

Narrowboat windows have increased in size over the years – 48in x 24in is not so unusual. You might consider replacing existing units with larger and better shaped ones although this involves removing linings, damaging your painted livery, and probably altering internal steel framing. It will almost certainly be easier to add glazing in the cabin top – with a hinged Houdini hatch, bulls eye, pigeon box or (as seen on a few innovative narrowboats and barges) pitch-roofed skylight. Make sure that the last two do not increase the height above water beyond 6ft (and preferably less). Bulls-eyes add a surprising amount of light in dark areas like toilets but tend to focus sunlight which could start a fire if placed near a vertical surface. Some are rectangular (rather than round) with prismatic glass.

Portholes

Portholes can be added to existing cabin side elevations with less complication than conventional windows. The smallest are 7in diameter rising to approximately 12in (with brass frames) and 18in (aluminium-framed). Opening portholes in brass are expensive (although prices are reducing). Openings in aluminium-framed units are usually drop-back top vents. Their shape makes portholes more difficult than windows to trim to inside so you may have to buy internal trims of brass, aluminium, or turned hardwood.

Decking, covers & cratches

The engine access panels of cruiser-style and semi-trad narrowboats are usually of ply – which delaminates unless covered or treated with preservative. Tired panels can be improved by anti-slip facings, like Treadmaster, and neatened by aluminium edge trim. Hexastep phenol faced plywood is a popular, non-slip alternative. Replacing the panels with tread-faced aluminium is expensive (about four times the price of marine ply) but the result never needs any

A cratch cover with zips creates a valuable utility area.

maintenance, is light to lift for engine access and looks unfailingly smart.

Although modern all-steel narrowboats don't appear to need pampering, the cost of an all-over winter cover can be recovered by the extra life given to expensive superstructure paint schemes, particularly if these include labour-intensive techniques like scumbling (simulated oak-graining). Well deck covers can protect timber decks and (if cut generously) hatches.

When combined with a traditional triangular cratchboard, a fitted cover over the forward cockpit turns outside space into a valuable utility area. The cratch cover is sometimes fitted with zipped 'doors'. Modern variations on the cratchboard include hinged or removable outer panels (so that the cockpit can be opened up in fine weather, while retaining the cratch spine to carry the rolled-up cover), transparent panels, and a built-in fold-down table.

Winterising

The repair costs that you will kick yourself most for are those for frost damage. They are so avoidable that insurance companies are often reluctant to accept claims unless real evidence of adequate precautions against frost can be provided.

Winterising tasks don't require great skill and are not time consuming. The most onerous are to do with putting the engine into hibernation. The most complicated engine cooling arrangement is a sealed water system that is cooled in a heat exchanger by a separate raw water supply. The sealed circuit can be drained off (at the cylinder block plug/tap) or partly drained off and topped up with sufficient antifreeze to protect against -20° C frosts. The raw water side has to be completely drained, first by turning off the hull side inlet cock, then by disconnecting every low point where water might be trapped – like gearbox and sump coolers. External water pumps should be opened up to clear residue. A raw water system can be protected by flushing through with anti-freeze mixture – but the engine cooling water outlet should be diverted to avoid pumping toxic antifreeze overboard. If you suffer a frozen raw water

system before draining down, don't forget to turn off the hull-side inlet cock when undoing connections – otherwise the boat may sink when thaw sets in.

Skin-tank cooled engines can be treated as a sealed circuit – although there is a greater volume of water so more antifreeze is needed. Other skin-tank cooled arrangements still have two separate circuits because the intercooler cores in their heat exchangers haven't been removed. After adding antifreeze, wherever needed, run the engine to disperse it through the system.

Owners of air cooled engines don't have to bother with any of this but, whether engines are air or water cooled, this is the time to do an oil and filter change so that old oil, polluted by acid combustion products, isn't left clinging to cylinder walls through the winter.

After running the engine up to spread the clean oil around, you could spray WD40 into the inlet manifold for a few seconds immediately before shutting down. This should coat the valves with a film of oil, preventing them from sticking over the months although pouring in too much oil could be disastrous – filling the cylinder so that, when it is compressed, something has to give.

Either completely empty or, preferably, fill the fuel tank to prevent water from precipitating from the diesel into the tank bottom – possibly with calamitous results when the engine goes on to its first cruise in spring.

Traditionally, a rag is stuffed down the inlet manifold entrance. The modern alternative is to mask with wide tape. The exhaust outlet, particularly if it is a vertical stack, also needs a cover to stop rain from getting into the silencer. If you, or the boatyard staff, are able to run the engine periodically through the winter, don't forget to remove the rags/covers first.

As battery banks grow ever larger, extending their lifespan becomes more important – ruined batteries are the most common cause of post-winter expense. You may need to visit every month or six weeks through the winter to trickle charge batteries (or fit solar panels to do it for you). Otherwise your boatyard may offer a storage and charging service. If you do have to leave batteries on board and uncharged, at least disconnect them to avoid risk of flattening by the odd light left on or even self discharge. Spray vulnerable 12-volt electric connections with WD40 (both in the engine compartment and cabin).

In the cabin, turn off the water tank stop cock, disconnect the pipes to the water pump and run it for a few seconds (no longer) to clear residue. Remove the drain screw from the instantaneous water heater (checking that it is the correct screw). Open shower valve and taps throughout the boat to drain hot and cold supply pipes. Also check those pipes for low laying traps and, if necessary, blow through (preferably other than by mouth). Alternatively, your chandler may stock a 'food quality' anti-freeze that you can flush through the water system.

Disconnect piping from calorifier – except those to/from the engine and/or solid fuel stove that have been antifreezed, and bearing in mind that the tank's contents have to be emptied without flooding the floor. Central heating circuits can be treated with the domestic antifreeze that inhibits corrosion of steel radiators. Otherwise, take the same drain-off precautions.

Stack all upholstery cushions on edge or take them home to prevent condensation and mould forming. Curtains lying against wet windows are also liable to mould. If you are concerned about security, fit a makeshift winter set while the proper ones are stored. Remove berth locker lids and lift floor boards, where possible, to keep the bilges sweet (rotten floors are very expensive to replace). If your cabin bilges are inaccessible but sealed from outside decks, don't assume that they are in good, dry condition. Cut an inspection hole right at the aft end of the cabin floor – almost certainly some water will be found in this theoretically dry space.

Prop the fridge door open. Turn off the gas at the bottles. Remove all food and valuables to discourage furry and human intruders. Consider a burglar alarm – some are very simple to fit and not dependent on boat batteries.

Leave vents and some narrow window hopper tops open to maintain through ventilation. While a winter cover is a good investment to protect timber decks and fancy paint schemes, ensure that it does not restrict ventilation inside the cabin.

Check that the stern tube is reliable. If necessary, repack gland packings (don't just rely on a volume of grease) pending attention to the bearing/shaft in spring. Can the boat's mooring lines cope with increased rise and fall of water levels during the winter? In addition to the lines that hold directly onto the bank, 'springs' (ropes that run diagonally fore and aft) will restrict scrubbing of the hull.

Many boatyards and mobile marine engineers offer a comprehensive winterisation service that covers most of these tasks. If you have any doubts – particularly regarding the engine, cabin water system and stern tube – call one in. It may be cheaper than a repair bill in the spring.

... And dewinterising

Dewinterising partly involves putting back together the parts you took apart. Born engineers reassemble things in better condition than they were in the first place. Most others tend to forget to tighten up the odd hose clip – which, if it happens to be at the drinking water tank outlet or raw cooling water inlet, can result in a flooded or sunken boat.

A week or two before recommissioning the boat, check battery electrolyte levels, clean and petroleum jelly terminals, then recharge slowly – whether or not the batteries have been trickle charged over the winter. After charging, a battery will normally lose charge for 48 hours. If it continues to lose charge after that time, it may be faulty. Doubtful batteries should be taken to a reputable dealer for testing. Engine, water, lights and sometimes heating all depend on battery power so a reliable 12-volt supply is essential before attending to each system.

Clean connections to alternator and related electrics – regulators, relays, diodes etc and spray with WD40 (again) to inhibit corrosion.

If, on first attempted start-up, the engine turns only slowly, a hot starter lead points to a bad connection. Otherwise the starter motor may have suffered over winter and will need professional help. Standing unused is also a common cause of alternator failure.

If the engine turns vigorously but doesn't fire, the fuel system may need bleeding (many modern diesels are self-bleeding – BL1.5s aren't). Disconnect the return pipe on top of the fuel filter and operate the fuel pump manually until pure, airless fuel flows out. Then open the throttle lever wide, loosen the bleed screw on the injector pump and repeat the hand pumping. Finally slacken the union to each injector in turn and wind the engine over until the fuel

flowing out is free of bubbles. Take care to keep clear of the injector spray – its high pressure is capable of penetrating the skin.

If, once running, the engine fails to reach normal temperature, the thermostat may have become another victim of winter. Overheating could mean an air lock or damaged water pump impeller. Persistent black smoke from the exhaust when the engine is in gear and under load suggests that injectors and/or pump need servicing (blue smoke, however, indicates stuck piston rings or worn cylinder bores).

If you suspect that water has accumulated in the diesel fuel over winter, the contents should be drained from the bottom, where the water gravitates. Some tanks have a drain plug, otherwise fuel can be siphoned out into transparent containers, then left to settle before inspection. Keep draining until no more water is decanted.

If you didn't change the engine oil before winterising, and particularly if an oil change is well overdue, consider running the engine on flushing oil before changing oil & air filters and refilling the sump with appropriate lubricant. If you have been in the habit of running your engine just to charge batteries, regular flushing out may, in any case, be worthwhile to combat sludge build-up.

Inspect the weed hatch gasket and grease retaining screw threads. If the stern tube was leaking persistently last season, check it (or have it checked) for wear. If it needs replacing, this is the time.

Check all flues and evict anything that has nested there over winter – blockages can be lethal. Inspect all outside flue cowls for crushing. Clear rubbish from gas locker drain holes. Every other gas system job is for professionals.

Then on to the water system. After reconnecting the winterised parts, open the water tank cock, then switch on the water pump – with bucket and bowl at the ready to catch leaks from unnoticed frost damage and imperfectly tightened fittings. Pipes that habitually split are probably difficult to drain so insert a local drain tap when replacing. Gas instantaneous water heaters are frequent frost victims. In a Paloma, the entire heating matrix may need replacing – another professional job.

If the water tank is integral with the shell, remove the inspection hatch, clean and, if necessary, repaint with non-toxic water tank paint. Pay particular attention to making a good seal when replacing the hatch – leakage through it is likely to contaminate the supply. Sterilise the water system (and other types of tank) by flushing through with a proprietary additive like Puriclean or Milton. Each tankful of water can subsequently be treated with sterilising tablets, the taste of which can be removed by fitting a Freshness filter into the water line. The last, however, should not be confused with bacteriological filters. These are a separate way of making water safe and taste-free – although they restrict supply, so are usually fitted to a special drinking water tap.

Maintaining glass-fibre craft

If a glass-fibre hull is used in the open river conditions, its owner will expect to keep it in pristine condition without extreme defensive measures. A decent set of plastic side fenders, perhaps with screw-on types on the transom corners, is sufficient to keep the hull largely unmarked.

At the end of the season, tar marks can be taken out (petrol and/or Swarfega are good solvents). Running repairs to gashes or chips (that do not penetrate the gel coat) can be made by filling the damage with a gel coat kit. Minor scuffs may be rubbed out with T-Cut, wet & dry paper – or even with a Brillo pad.

For glass-fibre craft that are in regular contact with narrow locks and narrowboats, extra fixed fendering is desirable. This could mean additional substantial hardwood strakes running from transom almost to the bow and, perhaps, capped with D-section galvanised steel. To protect the transom corner against inevitable chipping, a vertical piece of hardwood can be mounted on the aft hull sides – not extending below the waterline.

Eventually the hull may become so scarred that it has to be painted, losing the original glass-fibre finish. There are two options. You can either use a conventional marine paint, accepting that regular canal cruising will cause continuing damage that, ever after, can be hidden by a quick touch-up. Alternatively, you could use a tough epoxy-based paint system – more expensive and demanding to apply, but potentially almost as smooth as the original finish. In either case, special glass-fibre primer should be used before building up with undercoat and top finishes. Epoxy-based paint below the waterline provides some protection against osmosis, an affliction that particularly affects glass-fibre hulls in fresh water (see Chapter 20 for more on osmosis).

While most glass-fibre canal craft are left unpainted below the waterline, a few are finished with bitumen paint, like a narrowboat. The posher ones, particularly those that live on rivers, use antifouling paint. This material had a (justifiably) bad press a few years ago because of the damage its tin compound ingredients were doing to shallow water life. That type has now been banned and mild variants of copper-based antifouling, designed for inland waterways conditions, are available. Conventionally, the visible band of antifouling is set off by another above it, called the `boot topping', in a contrasting antifouling colour.

Above the deckline, maintenance of glass-fibre boats is normally easier than for steel narrowboats. Finishes that dull under the sun's rays can often be recovered with cutting paste. But if the superstructure does need painting, the result has to stand comparison with the mirror flatness of moulding – only advanced paint systems, which need skilful handling, are likely to achieve this.

A folding canopy is likely to be the fastest wearing item of the boat's equipment and, at around £450 for a complete assembly, one of the most expensive. Yet most of the damage is done during winter when few boats are being used. Replacing the canopy with an inexpensive winter cockpit cover (you could even make your own) will extend its life by many years. Given the high cost of complete canopy replacement, it is worthwhile having major damage repaired, as long as the basic material is sound. Most boatyards can point the way to canopy makers who will economically replace windows and zips.

All types of alloy fendering strips are readily available from specialists.

By far the most common reader's enquiry to *Waterways World* is "Where can I find a replacement widget for my Dawncraft cruiser". Wilsons of Kinver (which now specialises in canopies and upholstery) used to build Dawncraft and can source most spares. (Tel: 01384 872983).

The alloy fendering with black plastic insert, that covers the joint between hull and superstructure on canal cruisers, eventually succumbs to repeated bashing in locks. Wilks (Rubber Plastics) (Tel: 01621 869609) has supplied various types for Norman, Dawncraft and many other glass-fibre craft and can usually match other replacement fendering if sent a sample.

Canopies are expensive to replace but can often be repaired.

APPENDIX 1

BOAT BUILDERS

This is, in fact, three lists in one. Many builders produce the whole boat from welding the first sheets of steel to laying the last piece of carpet. There are others who prefer to concentrate on building shells and, perhaps, installing the engines for completion by other professionals or by amateur fitters out. Finally, there are companies who buy in shells and fit them out for customers.

Advantages and disadvantages are fairly evenly divided. By employing one company to build the whole boat you have only one backside to kick but you may find that, while it is good at either shell building or fitting out, it is not necessarily good at both. Going to a boat fitter means that you can choose from many different shells and get the best of both worlds but each may blame the other if things go wrong or completion is delayed. However, as noted in Chapter 7, make sure that the boat fitter orders the shell. If you order and pay for the shell separately, you might inadvertently become the project manager for the boat and find yourself responsible for Recreational Craft Directive administration.

Builders are generally happy to supply a boat to any stage of completion from a bare shell to a fully fitted boat. Two options popular with DIY boat fitters are the 'sailaway', a shell fitted with engine, drive gear and ballast, and the lined sailaway which, as its name suggests, includes linings and the start of the wiring system.

For a brief pen portrait of some of the builders listed here, see chapter 9.

The telephone numbers in the following appendices are correct at the time of writing but may change in the future.

Name	Address	Phone	Shell builder	Fit out	Narrowboat	Wide beam	Cruisers	Steel	Glass fibre	Aluminium
Adelaide Marine	Adelaide Dock, Endsleigh Road Ind. Est., Norwood Green, Middlesex UB2 5QR	020 8571 5678	-	Yes	-	Yes	-	Yes	-	-
Advanced Marine Development	Woodstock House, Lockeridge, Nr Marlborough, Wiltshire SN8 4ED	01672 861307	Yes	-	Yes	Yes	Yes	-	Yes	Yes
Alexander Boatbuilders	Unit 1A, Chadwick Bank Ind Est, Stourport-on-Severn, Worcs DY13 9QW	01299 251471	Yes	-	Yes	Yes	Yes	Yes	-	-
Alvechurch Boat Centres	Scarfield Wharf, Alvechurch, Birmingham B48 7SQ	0121 445 2909	Yes	Yes	Yes	-	-	Yes	-	-
Arcrite Fabrications	Flemming Road, Earlstree Industrial Estate, Corby, Northants NN17 4SW	01536 204969	Yes	-	Yes	Yes	Yes	Yes	-	-
Ashby Canal Centre	Willow Park, Stoke Golding, Nuneaton, Warks CV13 6EU	01455 212636	-	Yes	Yes	-	Yes	Yes		
Associated Cruisers	Victoria Basins, Off Littles Lane, Wolverhampton WV1 1JJ	01902 423673	Yes	Yes	Yes	-	-	Yes	-	-
Bentlies Narrowboats	The Boatshed, Crick Wharf, West Haddon Road, Crick, Northants NN6 7XT	01788 824253	Yes	Yes	Yes	-	-	Yes	-	-
Bettisfield Boats	Canal Side, Bettisfield, Whitchurch, Shropshire SY13 2LJ	01948 710465	Yes	Yes	Yes	-	-	Yes	-	-
Black Country Narrowboats	Waterside Cottage, Prestwood Drive, Stourton, Stourbridge, West Midlands DY7 5QT	01384 872135	Yes	Yes	Yes	-	-	Yes	-	-
Blue Haven Marine	Hillmorton Wharf, Crick Road, Rugby CV21 4PD	01788 540149	-	Yes	Yes	Yes	-	-	-	-
Boat Building Services	Stanney Mill Lane, Little Stanney, Nr Chester CH2 4HY	0151 357 1949	-	Yes	Yes	Yes	-	Yes	-	-
Braidbar Boats	Lord Vernon's Wharf, Lyme Road, Higher Poynton, Cheshire SK12 1TH	01625 873471	-	Yes	Yes	-	-	Yes	-	-

Name	Address	Phone	Shell builder	Fit out	Narrowboat	Wide beam	Cruisers	Steel	Glass fibre	Aluminium
Branson Boats	Unit 4, Crowland Industrial Centre, Crowland, Peterborough PE7 0BN	01733 211966	Yes	-	-				-	-
Brent Wharf Services	198 High Street, Brentford, Middlesex TW8 8AH	020 8568 7041	Yes	Yes	Yes	Yes	Yes	Yes	-	-
Bridgewater Boatbuilders	Unit 2&3, Worsley Business Park, Mosley Common, Worsley, Manchester M28 1NL	0161 703 8297	Yes	Yes	Yes	Yes	Yes	Yes	-	-
Brinklow Boat Services	The Wharf, Stretton under Fosse, Rugby CV23 0PR	01788 833331	Yes	Yes	Yes	-	-	Yes	-	-
P.M. Buckle Narrowboats	Boat Yard, Stibbington, Peterborough, Cambs	01780 783144		Yes	Yes	Yes	Yes	Yes	-	-
Calcutt Boats	Calcutt Top Lock, Stockton, Southam, Warks CV47 8HX	01926 813757		Yes	Yes	-	-	Yes	-	-
Cambrian Cruisers	Pencelli, Brecon, Powys LD3 7LJ	01874 665315	-	Yes	Yes	-	-	Yes	-	-
Canal Cruising Co	The Wharf, Crown Street, Stone, Staffs ST15 8QN	01785 813982	-	Yes	Yes	-	-	Yes	-	-
Canal Transport Services Ltd	Norton Canes Dock, Lime Lane, Pelsall, Walsall WS3 5AP	01543 374370	Yes	Yes	Yes	Yes	Yes	Yes	-	-
Canalcraft (Boatbuilders) Ltd	The Wharf, Watling Street, Gailey, Staffs ST19 5PR	01902 791811	Yes	-	Yes	Yes	-	Yes	-	-
Castle Boatbuilders	22 Kilton Terrace, Worksop, Notts S80 2DQ	01909 478250	Yes	Yes	Yes	Yes	-	Yes	-	-
Castle Narrowboats	Church Road Wharf, Gilwern, Monmouthshire NP7 0ED	01873 830001	-	Yes	Yes	Yes	-	Yes	-	-
Classic Narrowboats	The Old Boatyard, Worsley Dry Dock, Worsley Road, Worsley, Manchester	0161 796 0626	-	Yes	Yes	-	Yes	Yes	Yes	-
Clifton Cruisers	Clifton Wharf, Vicarage Hill, Clifton-on-Dunsmore, Rugby, Warks CV23 0DG	01788 543570	-	Yes	Yes	Yes	-	Yes	-	-

Name	Address	Phone	Shell builder	Fit out	Narrowboat	Wide beam	Cruisers	Steel	Glass fibre	Aluminium
Clubline	Swan Lane Wharf, Stoke Heath, Coventry CV2 4QN	024 7625 8864	Yes	Yes	Yes	-	-	Yes	-	-
Colecraft Engineering	Southam Road, Long Itchington, Southam, Warks CV47 9QL	01926 814081	Yes	Yes	Yes	Yes	-	Yes	-	-
Colliery Narrowboats	Wincham Wharf, 220 Manchester Road, Lostock Grakam, Northwich, Cheshire CW9 7NT	01606 44672		Yes	Yes		Yes	Yes	-	-
Corbett Narrowboats	Whilton Marina, Whilton Locks, Nr Daventry NN11 5NH	01327 844044	-		Yes	–	Yes			
Cotswold Narrowboat Co	8 Severn Road, The Docks, Gloucester GL1 2LE	01452 332772	Yes	Yes	Yes	-	-	Yes	-	-
Countrywide Cruisers	The Wharf, Brewood, Staffs ST19 9BG	01902 850166	-	Yes	Yes	-	-	Yes	-	-
D.B. Boatfitting	The Wharf, Braunston Marina, Braunston, Nr Daventry, Northants NN11 7JH	01788 891727	-	Yes	Yes	Yes	-	-	-	-
Dale Leisure Marine	Unit 8, British Field Ind Est, Ollerton Road, Tuxford, Notts NG22 0PQ	01246 235599	-	Yes	Yes	Yes	-	Yes	-	-
Dale Narrowboats	Unit 8, British Field Ind Est, Ollerton Road, Tuxford, Notts NG22 0PQ	01246 235599	Yes	-	Yes	Yes	-	Yes	-	-
Davis Boatbuilders	Norwood Farm, Langwith, Mansfield, Notts NG20 9JA	01623 748592	Yes	-	Yes	Yes	Yes	Yes	-	-
R.W. Davis & Son Ltd	Junction Dry Dock, Saul, Gloucester GL2 7LA	01452 740233	Yes	Yes	Yes	Yes	Yes	Yes	-	-
Eastwood Engineering	Old Mill, Station Road, Owston Ferry, Doncaster DN9 1AW	01427 728308	Yes	Yes	Yes	Yes	Yes	Yes	-	-
Equinox Boatbuilders Ltd	Mount Pleasant Yard, White Street, Market Lavington, Nr Devizes, Wilts SN10 4DP	01380 818999	Yes	-	Yes	Yes		Yes	-	-
Evans & Son	New Road Industrial Estate, Hixon. Staffs ST18 0PJ	01889 270426	Yes	-	Yes	Yes		Yes	-	-
Falcon	Unit 5A, Waymills Ind Est, Whitchurch, Shropshire SY13 1TT	01948 66885	Yes	Yes	Yes	Yes		Yes	-	-

Name	Address	Phone	Shell builder	Fit out	Narrowboat	Wide beam	Cruisers	Steel	Glass fibre	Aluminium
Fenny Boat Services	Fenny Marina, Fenny Compton, Warks CV47 2XD	01295 770934		Yes	Yes	-	Yes	Yes		
Fibreline Boats Ltd	Unit 2, Barleyfield Industrial Estate, Barleyfield Way, Brynmawr, Gwent NP3 4LU	01495 315111	Yes	Yes	Yes	-	Yes	-	Yes	-
Five Towns Boatbuilding	Navigation House, 1 Whitebridge Lane, Stone, Staffs ST15 8LQ	01785 817506	Yes	Yes	Yes	Yes	-	Yes	-	-
C.T.&P. Fox	10 Marina Drive, March, Cambs PE15 0AU	01354 652770	Yes	Yes	Yes	Yes	-	Yes	-	-
Tony Francis & Son	41 Ironwalls Lane, Tutbury, Burton-on-Trent DE13 9NH	01283 812453	Yes	Yes	Yes	Yes	Yes	Yes	Yes	-
French & Peel Boatbuilders	Station Works, Thorne Railway Station, Selby Road, Thorne, South Yorks DN8 4HZ	01405 817954	Yes	-	Yes	Yes	Yes	Yes	-	-
G&J Reeves	Coventry Bridge Yard, Station Road, Napton, Warwickshire	01926 815581	Yes	-	Yes	Yes	Yes	Yes	-	-
G.T. Boatbuilders	Unit 10, Ladford Covert, Seighford, Stafford ST18 9QG	01785 282026	Yes	Yes	Yes	-	-	Yes	-	-
Stephen Goldsbrough Boats	Kenilworth Road, Knowle, Solihull B93 0JJ	01564 778210	-	Yes	Yes	Yes	-	Yes	-	-
Gorton Boatbuilders Ltd	The Old Sidings, Pipe Gate, Market Drayton, Shropshire TF9 4HY	01630 647090	Yes	Yes	Yes	Yes	-	Yes	-	-
Harris Boatbuilders	27 Blakeway Close, Broseley, Shropshire TF12 5SS	01952 882468	Yes	Yes	Yes	-	-	Yes	-	-
Hartford Marina	Bank Fen, Huntingdon, Cambridge PE17 2AA	01480 454677	-	Yes	Yes	Yes	Yes	-	-	-
Barry Hawkins Narrowboats Ltd	Baddesley Wharf, Holly Lane, Atherstone Warwickshire CV9 2EH	01827 711762	-	Yes	Yes	-	Yes	Yes	-	-
Heritage Boatbuilders	Evesham Marina, Kings Road, Evesham WR11 5BU	01386 48882	Yes	Yes	Yes	Yes	Yes	Yes	-	-
Heron Boatbuilders	Junction 25 Business Park, Huddersfield Road, Mirfield, West Yorkshire WF14 9DA	0500 585829	Yes	Yes	Yes	Yes	Yes	Yes	-	-

Virginia Currie →

Name	Address	Phone	Shell builder	Fit out	Narrowboat	Wide beam	Cruisers	Steel	Glass fibre	Aluminium
High Line Yachting Ltd	Mansion Lane, Iver, Bucks SL0 9RG	01753 651496	-	Yes	Yes	Yes	-	Yes	-	-
Hirst Boatbuilders	The Slipway, Farley Green Ind Estate, Knottingley WF11 3DN	01977 670834	Yes	Yes	Yes	Yes	-	Yes	-	Yes
S.M. Hudson Boatbuilders	Glascote Basin Boatyard, Basin Lane, Glascote, Tamworth, Staffs B77 2AH	01827 311317	Yes	Yes	Yes	-	-	Yes	-	-
Ivybridge Marina Ltd	Station House, Station Road, Watford, Northants NN6 7UL	01327 704847	Yes	-	Yes	Yes	-	Yes		-
J.D. Boat Services	The Wharf, Watling Street, Gailey, Staffs ST19 5PR	01902 791811		Yes	Yes	Yes	-	Yes	-	-
Jannel Cruisers	Shobnall Marina, Shobnall Road, Burton-on-Trent, Staffs DE14 2AU	01283 542718	-	Yes	Yes	-	-	Yes		-
Phil Jones	Hatherton Marina, Kings Road, Calf Heath, Wolverhampton WV10 7DV	01902 710799	Yes	-	Yes	-	-	Yes	-	-
Kate Boats	The Boatyard, Nelson Lane, Warwick CV34 5JB	01926 492968	-	Yes	Yes	-	-	Yes	-	-
Ian Kemp Restoration Services	Dadfords Wharf, Mill Street, Wordsley, Stourbridge DY8 5SX	01384 485565	Yes	-	Yes	-	-	Yes		-
Kingsground Narrowboats	Building 103, Heyford Business Park, Upper Heyford, Bicester, Oxon OX6 3AH	01869 233444	-	Yes	Yes	-	-	Yes	-	-
Ledgard Bridge Boat Co	Ledgard Wharf, Butt End Mills, Mirfield, West Yorkshire WF14 8PN	01924 491441	Yes	Yes	Yes	Yes	Yes	Yes	-	-
Lexden Swan	Pyrford Marina, Lock Lane, Woking, Surrey GU22 8XL	01252 624612	-	Yes	Yes	-	Yes	Yes		-
Limekiln Narrowboats	4 Bridgnorth Road, Compton, Wolverhampton, West Midlands WV6 8AA	01902 751147	Yes	Yes	Yes	-	-	Yes	-	-
Littleborough Boats	71 Gainsborough Avenue, Burnley, Lancashire BB11 2PD	01282 455372	Yes	-	Yes	Yes	Yes	Yes	-	-
Louis & Joshua Boatbuilders	Thorne Marine, Hatfield Road, Thorne, Nr Doncaster DN8 5RA	01405 814443	-	Yes	Yes	Yes	-	Yes	-	-

Company	Address	Phone								
Lower Park Marina	Kelbrook Road, Barnoldswick, Lancs BB18 5TB	01282 815883	Yes	Yes	Yes	Yes	Yes	Yes	-	-
M G Fabrications	Unit 2, Old Station Goods Yard, Long Buckby, Northants NN6 7QA	01604 708177	Yes	Yes	Yes	Yes	Yes	Yes	-	-
Maestermyn Marine	Ellesmere Road, Whittington, Oswestry, Salop SY11 4NU	01691 662424	-	Yes	Yes	-	Yes	-	-	-
Marine Services	Chirk Marina, Chirk, Wrexham LL14 5AD	01691 774558	Yes	Yes	Yes	-	Yes	-	-	-
Marine Services	Festival Park Marina, Etruria, Stoke-on-Trent ST1 5PS	01782 201981	Yes	Yes	Yes	-	Yes	-	-	-
Marine Technologies	The School, Forgeside, Blaenavon, Gwent NP4 9DN	01495 790400	Yes	Yes	Yes	-	-	-	-	Yes
Measham Boats	Lower Rectory Farm, Snarestone Road, Appleby Magna, Swadlincote, Derbyshire DE12 7AJ	01530 274301	Yes	-		Yes			-	-
Merlin Narrowboats	Braunston Marina, Nr Daventry, Northants NN11 7JH	01788 891750	-	Yes	Yes	Yes	Yes	Yes	-	Yes
Midland Canal Centre	Stenson Marina, Stenson, Derby DE73 3HL	01283 701933	Yes	Yes	Yes	Yes	Yes	Yes	-	-
Milburn Boats	Bridge Grounds, Staverton, Nr Daventry, Northants NN11 6BG	01327 702164	-	Yes	Yes	-	-	Yes	-	-
Roger Myers Narrowboats	Bollington Wharf, Grimshaw Lane, Bollington, Cheshire SK10 5JB	01625 575811	-	Yes	Yes	Yes	Yes	-	-	-
Navigation Narrowboats	Nantwich Canal Centre, Basin End, Chester Road, Nantwich, Cheshire CW5 8LB	01270 625122	-	Yes	Yes	-	-	-	-	-
Peter Nicholls Steel Boats	Braunston Marina Trade Centre, Daventry Road, Braunston, Northants NN11 7JH	01788 891823	Yes	Yes	Yes	Yes	Yes	Yes	-	-
Nimbus Narrowboats	The Boatyard, Mill Lane, Thurmaston, Leicester LE4 8AF	0116 269 3069	-	Yes	Yes	Yes	Yes	Yes	-	-
Northern Narrowboats	Blue Water Marina, Southend, Thorne, South Yorkshire DN8 5QR	01405 813165	Yes	Yes	Yes	-	-	-	-	-
Norton Canes Boatbuilders	Norton Canes Docks, Lime Lane, Pelsall, Walsall, West Midlands WS3 5AP	01543 374888	Yes	Yes	Yes	-	-	-	-	-

Name	Address	Phone	Shell builder	Fit out	Narrowboat	Wide beam	Cruisers	Steel	Glass fibre	Aluminium
Orchard Marina	School Road, Rode Heath, Northwich, Cheshire CW9 7RG	01606 42082	-	Yes	Yes	-	Yes	Yes	-	-
Orion Narrowboats	Ashwood Marina, Kingswinford, West Mids DY6 0AQ	01384 401464	Yes	Yes	Yes	-	-	Yes	-	-
Oxford Cruisers	Eynsham, Oxon OX8 1DA	01865 882542	-	Yes	Yes	Yes	-	Yes	-	-
Pickwell & Arnold	Unit 10, Nanholme Mill, Shaw Wood Road, Todmorden, W Yorks	01706 812411	Yes	Yes	Yes	Yes	Yes	Yes	-	-
J.L. Pinder & Sons	The Old Basin, 138 Hanbury Road, Stoke Prior, Bromsgrove, Worcs B60 4IZ	01527 876438	Yes	Yes	Yes	Yes	-	Yes	-	-
Piper Boatbuilding	Unit 3, Pins Industrial Estate, Tunstall, Biddulph, Stoke-on-Trent ST8 7BE	01782 510610	Yes	Yes	Yes	Yes	Yes	Yes	-	-
R&D Fabrications	Unit 65-67, Boughton Ind Estate, New Ollerton, Newark, Notts NG22 9LD	01623 862473	Yes	Yes	Yes	Yes	Yes	Yes	-	-
Reading Marine	Aldermaston Wharf, Padworth, Reading RG7 4JS	0118 971 3666	-	Yes	Yes	Yes	-	Yes	-	-
Riverview Narrowboats	17 Riverview, Barrow-upon-Soar, Leicestershire LE12 8LL	01509 816272	-	Yes	Yes	-	Yes	Yes	-	-
Rose Narrowboats	Fosse Way, Stretton-under-Fosse, Rugby, Warks CV23 0PU	01788 832449	-	Yes	Yes	-	-	Yes	-	-
Sabre Narrowboats Ltd	Unit 1A, Barton Business Park, Cawdor Street, Manchester M30 0QF	0161 789 3032	-	Yes	Yes	Yes	Yes	Yes	-	-
Sagar Marine	Victoria Works, Wharf Street, Brighouse, West Yorkshire HD6 1PP	01484 714541	Yes	Yes	-	Yes	-	Yes	-	-
Sandhills Narrowboats Ltd	Sandhills Farm, Edgioak Lane, Astwood Bank, Nr Redditch, Worcs B96 6BG	01527 894793	-	Yes	Yes	Yes	-	Yes	-	-
Sea Otter Boats	Unit 24, M1 Commerce Park, Duckmanton, Chesterfield, Derbyshire S44 5HS	01246 825750	Yes	Yes	Yes	Yes	Yes	-	-	Yes
Selby Boat Centre	Bawtry Road, Selby YO8 8NB	01757 212211	-	Yes	Yes	-	-	Yes	-	-
Severn Valley Boat Centre	Boat Shop, Mart Lane, Stourport-on-Severn,		Yes	Yes	Yes	-	-	Yes	-	

Builder	Address	Phone	Shell builder	Fit out	Narrowboat	Wide beam	Cruisers	Steel	Glass fibre	Aluminium
Shire Cruisers	The Wharf, Sowerby Bridge, W Yorks HX6 2AG	01422 832712	-	Yes	Yes	-	-	Yes	-	-
Sirius Boatbuilders	Redstone Wharf, Sandy Lane, Stourport-on-Severn DY13 9PN	01299 871048	Yes	Yes	Yes	Yes	Yes	Yes	-	-
South Boats	89 Condover Ind Estate, Dorrington, Shropshire SY5 7NH	01743 718415	Yes	-	Yes	Yes	Yes	Yes	-	-
South West Durham Steelcraft	Old Colliery Buildings, Trimdon Grange Industrial Estate, Trimdon Grange, County Durham TS29 6PA	01429 881300	Yes	Yes	Yes	Yes	-	Yes	-	-
Starline Narrowboats	17 Horneyold Road, Malvern, Worcs WR14 1QQ	01684 574774	-	Yes	Yes	Yes	-	Yes	-	-
Stoke-on-Trent Boatbuilding	Longport Wharf, Longport, Stoke-on-Trent ST6 4NA	01782 813831	Yes	Yes	Yes	-	-	Yes	-	-
Stone Boatbuilding Co Ltd	Newcastle Road, Stone, Staffordshire ST15 8JZ	01785 812688	Yes	Yes	Yes	Yes	Yes	Yes	-	-
Stowe Hill Marine	Stowe Hill Wharf, Weedon, Northants NN7 4RZ	01327 341365	Yes	Yes	Yes	-	-	Yes	-	-
Streethay Wharf	Streethay, Lichfield, Staffs WS13 8RJ	01543 414808	Yes	Yes	Yes	-	-	Yes	-	-
Swan Line	Fradley Junction, Alrewas, Burton-on-Trent DE13 7DN	01283 790332	-	Yes	Yes	-	-	Yes	-	-
T&T Fabrications	Ingham Works, Dragon Lane, Moston, Sandbach, Cheshire CW11 9HU	0976 377425	Yes	Yes	Yes	Yes	Yes	Yes	-	-
Tayberg Steel Boats	Brookfoot Mills, Elland Road, Brighouse, West Yorkshire HD6 2QS	01484 400221	Yes	Yes	Yes	Yes	Yes	Yes	-	-
Teddesley Boat Co	Park Gate Lock, Teddesley Road, Penkridge, Staffs ST19 5TH	01785 714692	Yes	Yes	Yes	Yes	-	Yes	-	-
Dave Thomas	The Trade Centre, Unit 2, Braunston Marina, London Road, Braunston, Northants NN11 7JH	01788 891181	Yes	Yes	Yes	Yes	-	Yes	-	-
R. Tinker	Baytree Lane, Middleton, Nr Manchester M24 2EL	0161 643 3652	Yes	Yes	Yes	-	Yes	Yes	-	-
Valley Cruisers	Springwood Haven, Mancetter Road, Nuneaton CV10 0RZ	024 7639 3333	-	Yes	Yes	-	-	Yes	-	-

Name	Address	Phone	Shell builder	Fit out	Narrowboat	Wide beam	Cruisers	Steel	Glass fibre	Aluminium
Venetian Marine (Nantwich) Ltd	Cholmondeston, Nantwich, Cheshire CW56DD	01270 528251	-	Yes	Yes	-	-	Yes	-	-
Warble Narrowboats	Warble Wharf, Broadway, Hyde, Nr Stockport, Cheshire SK14 4QF	0161 367 9205	-	Yes	Yes		-	Yes	-	-
Warwickshire Fly Boat Co	Stop Lock Cottage, Stockton, Southam, Warwickshire CV41 8LD	01926 812093	Yes	Yes	Yes	-	-	Yes	-	-
Warwickshire Narrowboats	Fosseway, Stretton-under-Fosse, Rugby, Warks CV23 0PU	01788 832449	-	Yes	Yes	-	-	Yes	-	-
Weltonfield Narrowboats Ltd	Welton Hythe, Daventry, Northants NN11 5LG	01327 842282	-	Yes	Yes	Yes	-	Yes	-	-
Wessex Narrowboats	Wessex Wharf, Hilperton Marina, Trowbridge, Wilts BA14 8RS	01225 769847	Yes	Yes	Yes	Yes	-	Yes	-	-
John White Boatbuilders	Unit 17A, Weaver Industrial Estate, Blackburn Street, Liverpool L19 8JA	0151 427 7282	Yes	Yes	Yes	Yes	Yes	Yes	-	-
Whixall Marina Shropshire Ltd	Alders Lane, Whixall, Shropshire SY13 2QP	01948 880420	-	Yes	Yes	-	Yes	-	-	-
Wilderness Boats	Corsham, Wilts SN13 9AA	01249 712231	-	Yes	-	-	Yes	-	Yes	-
Wilson Boatbuilders	South Parade, Thorne, Doncaster, South Yorkshire DN8 5BY	01405 812500/ 814443	Yes	Yes	Yes	Yes	-	Yes	-	-
Keith Wood Narrowboats	The Old Wharf, Old Great North Road, Stibbington, Peterborough PE8 6LR	01780 784110	-	Yes	Yes	-	Yes	Yes	-	-
Worcestershire Steel Boatbuilders	13 Battens Close, Redditch, Worcestershire B98 7HY	01527 522703	Yes	Yes	Yes	Yes	Yes	Yes	-	-
Wyvern Shipping Co	Rothschild Road, Linslade, Leighton Buzzard, Beds LU7 7TF	01525 372355	-	Yes	Yes	-	-	Yes	-	-

APPENDIX 2

ENGINES

FOUR-STROKE OUTBOARD ENGINES

Model	Hp/rpm	CC/cyl	Weight (lbs)	Charge (Std/opt amps)	Prop size (ins – where given)	Start (Man or elec)

PETROL

**The following models are a representative selection from the manufacturer's ranges up to 80hp.
In some cases, other sizes or variants are available between the models shown.**

EVINRUDE
OMC (UK) Ltd, Moulton Park Business Centre, Redhouse Road, Moulton Park, Northampton NN13 1AQ
Tel: 01604 497641

Model	Hp/rpm	CC/cyl	Weight	Charge	Prop size	Start
6R4	6/6,000	128/1	70	–	Optional	M
8R4	8/5,500	211/2	81	–	Optional	M
10EL4	9.9/5,500	305/2	96	6/12	Optional	M&E
15EL4	15/5,500	305/2	103	6/12	Optional	M&E
40PL4	39.5/5,500	815/3	236	13/–	Optional	M&E
70PL4	70/5,500	1,298/4	328	17/–	Optional	M&E

HONDA
4 Power Road, Chiswick, London W4 5YT
Tel: 020 8746 9757

Model	Hp/rpm	CC/cyl	Weight	Charge	Prop size	Start
BF5	5/5,000	127/1	60	3/–	7.9 x 7.5	M
BF8	8/5,500	197/2	77	5/–	9.5 x 8.6/9.5 x 9.5	M
BF9.9	9.9/5,500	280/2	101	6/10	9.5 x 8.6/9.5 x 9.5	M&E
BF15	15/6,200	280/2	101	6/10	9.5 x 8.6/9.5 x 9.5	M&E
BF25	25/5,500	499/3	146	6/10	9.3 x 12/9.8 x 9.9	E
BF40	40/5,500	808/3	194	10/–	11.3 x 13/11.5 x14.5	E
BF75	75/5,500	1,590/4	347	16/–	Optional	E

MARINER
E P Barrus Ltd, Launton Road, Bicester, Oxon OX6 0UR   Tel: 01869 363636

Mariner produces a range identical to the Mercury models below

MERCURY
Sowester, Stinsford Road, Nuffield, Poole, Dorset BH17 7SW
Tel: 01202 667700

Model	Hp/rpm	CC/cyl	Weight	Charge	Prop size	Start
4	4/5,000	123/1	55	–/5	Optional	M
5	4.9/5,000	123/1	55	–/5	Optional	M
6	6/5,000	123/1	55	–/5	Optional	M
9.9	9.9/5,000	323/2	110	6/10	Optional	M&E
15	15/5,000	323/2	110	6/10	Optional	M&E
25	25/5,500	498/2	176	6/15	Optional	M&E
30	30/5,500	747/3	204	6/15	Optional	M&E
50	49.9/5,500	935/4	224	10/–	Optional	M&E
75	75/5,500	1,596/4	385	20/–	Optional	M&E

Mercury also produces a range of 5 electric outboards ranging from 10 to 22 kg of thrust

SUZUKI
Suzuki GB plc, 46-62 Gatwick Road, Crawley, West Sussex RH10 2XF
Tel: 01293 766000

Model	Hp/rpm	CC/cyl	Weight	Charge	Prop size	Start
DF9.9	9.9/4,500	302/2	101	6.7/–	7ins to 11ins pitch	M&E
DF15	15/5,400	302/2	101	6.7/–	7ins to 11ins pitch	M&E
DF30	30/5,500	597/3	211	15/–	10ins to 14ins pitch	M&E
DF50	50/5,000	814/3	237	18/–	9ins to 16ins pitch	M&E
DF70	70/5,000	1,298/4	341	25/–	15ins to 21ins pitch	M&E

TOHATSU
Tohatsu Marine, Portmore, Lymington, Hants SO41 5RF
Tel: 01590 670787

4	4/5,000	123/1	57	–/5	Optional	M
6	6/5,000	123/1	55	–/5	Optional	M&E
9.9	9.9/5,500	328/2	114	11/–	Optional	M&E
15	15/5,500	328/2	114	11/–	Optional	M&E

YAMAHA
Miitsui Machinery Sales (UK) Ltd, Sopwith Drive, Brooklands, Weybridge, Surrey KT13 0UZ
Tel: 01932 358000

F4A	3.8/4,500	112/1	50	–	3 from 6.5 x 8	M
F6A	5.9/4,500	197/2	82.5	–	5 from 5 x 8.5	M
F8C	7.9/5,500	197/2	82.5	6/–	5 from 5 x 8.5	M
F9.9C	9.8/5,000	323/2	105	6/–	8 from 6.5 x 12	M&E
F15A	14.7/5,000	323/2	105	6/10	8 from 6.5 x 12	M&E
F20/25A	24.5/5,500	498/2	149	6/15	9 from 8 x 14	M&E
F30A	29.5/5,500	747/3	193	6/15	19 from 9 x 17	M&E
F40B	39.4/5,500	747/3	193	6/15	19 from 9 x 17	M&E
F50A	49.6/5,500	935/4	238	10/–	19 from 9 x 17	M&E
F80A	78.8/5,500	1,596/4	368	20/–	23 from 11 x 28	M&E

Yamaha also produces a range of 4 electric outboards ranging from 13.6 to 22.7 kg of thrust

DIESEL

RUGGERINI
Ron Davis Marine, Castletown, Portland, Dorset DT5 1BD
Tel: 01305 821175

| F15 (air cool) | 16/3,600 | 654/2 | 178 | 15 | 9.5 x 8/- | E |
| F25 | 23/3,800 | 851/2 | 176 | 15 | 9.5 x 10/- | E |

YANMAR
E P Barrus Ltd, Launton Road, Bicester, Oxon OX6 0UR
Tel: 01869 363636

| D27 | 27/4,500 | 808/3 | 207 | 10/20 | 10.5 x 9/10.5 x 13 | E |
| D36 | 36/4,500 | 1,109/3 | 256 | 10/20 | 11.5 x 9/11.5 x 15 | E |

INBOARD DIESEL ENGINES

orsepower figures are given but, as noted in Chapter 10, torque is more important for narrowboat engines. Watch out for misleading torque quotes – sometimes companies quote figures aft of the gearbox which, with a typical 2:1 reduction, doubles the representative figure. These are corrected in this table.

Weights include gearbox. While companies were asked to recommend gearboxes, almost all will offer alternative types and ratios.

Propeller sizes depend on the gearbox ratio, the weight of the boat and the type of use so have not been included. Suppliers can compute exact sizes for your application.

Prices have also been omitted because manufacturers, almost without exception, offer discounts off their list prices. The amount of the discount depends on factors like the size of the manufacturer and how good his sales figures were last month.

Engines are being offered increasingly with two alternators as standard. Where two figures are shown, the smaller size is normally intended for the starter battery and the larger, for the domestic batteries.

Beta Marine, Merretts Mills, Bath Road, South Woodchester, Stroud, Gloucs GL5 5EU 01453 835282

Bukh (TW Marine), The Marina, Station Road, Furness Vale, High Peak SK23 7QA 01663 745757

Calcutt Boats Ltd (CB Marine), Calcutt Top Lock, Stockton, Nr Rugby, Warwickshire CV23 8HX 01926 813757

Club Line Swan Lane Wharf, Stoke Heath, Coventry, CV2 4QN 0024 7625 8864

Kingfisher (Darglow Engineering), Upton Cross, Poole, Dorset BH16 5PH 01202 624450

L Gardner and Sons, Patricroft, Eccles, Manchester, M30 7WA 0161 789 2201

MODEL	Power Hp @ rpm.	Torque ft lbs @ rpm.	Tickover Rpm	Cubic cap./ cylinders	Weight in lbs	Recommended gearbox	Alternator size - amps	Base engine
BZ 482	13.5 @ 3,600	21 @ 2,400	900	478 / 2	196	TMC 40	40	Kubota
BD 722	20 @ 3,600	36 @ 2,600	900	719 / 3	233	TMC 40	40	Kubota
BD 1005	28 @ 3,600	45 @ 2,400	850	1,001 / 3	330	PRM 120	45 + 70	Kubota
BV 1205	32 @ 3,600	53 @ 2,400	850	1,198 / 4	374	PRM 120	45 + 70	Kubota
BV 1305	35 @ 3,600	60 @ 2,400	850	1,335 / 4	374	PRM 120	45 + 70	Kubota
BV 1505	37.5 @ 3,000	74 @ 2,200	850	1,498 / 4	374	PRM 150	45 + 70	Kubota
BV 1903	43 @ 2,800	97 @ 1,500	800	1,857 / 4	535	PRM 150	45 + 95	Kubota
BV 2203	50 @ 2,800	115 @ 1,500	800	2,197 / 4	587	PRM 260	45 + 95	Kubota
BF 2803	62 @ 2,800	140 @ 1,400	800	2,764 / 5	770	PRM 260	45 + 95	Kubota
BV 3300	75 @ 2,600	180 @ 1,500	750	3,318 / 4	858	PRM 260	45 + 95	Kubota
JD 3 Tug	35 @ 1,400	157 @ 1,400	400	2,900 / 3	1078	PRM 260	70	John Deere
DV 24 MEC	22 @ 3,000	42 @ 1,800	750	964 / 2	463	ZF/ISA BW7	50	Bukh
DV 36 MEC	34 @ 3,000	66 @ 1,800	750	1447 / 3	628	ZF/ISA BW7	50	Bukh
BMC 1.8	36 @ 3,000	80 @ 2,400	700	1,800 / 4	585	PRM 150	55	BMC 1.8
Matador	32 @ 2,900	82 @ 2,300	500	1,800 / 4	592	PRM 150	55	Hanomag (Merc)
D3 152	42 @ 2,000	110 @ 1,600	400	2,500 / 3	680	PRM 260	55	Perkins D3
Ford XLD	58 @ 4,800	108 @ 2,200	950	1,750 / 4	315	PRM150	70	Ford
Cadet	6 @ 2,000	12.5 @ 1,800	600	330 / 1	280	C3 Manual	8	Coventry
Captain	14 @ 2,000	40 @ 1,750	500	707 / 2	480	MA 100	55	Coventry
Tugmaster	26.4 @ 1,800	70 @ 1,750	450	1,630 / 2	946	MA 100	55	Ruston
Tugmaster Sup.	26.4 @ 1,800	123 @ 1,650	400	2,445 / 3	1250	MA 125	55	Ruston
2LW	28 @ 1,300	115 @ 1,000	400	2,800 / 2	1040	PRM 260	50	Gardner

Lancing Marine, 51 Victoria Road, Portslade, Sussex BN41 1XY   01273 410025

Model	Power	Torque		cc / cyl	Weight	Gearbox		Engine
XLD LP	40 @ 2,600	80 @ 2,600	850	1,753 / 4	405	PRM 120	55	Ford XLD
XLD MP	50 @ 3,400	80 @ 2,600	850	1,753 / 4	405	PRM 120	55	Ford XLD
FSD LP	51 @ 2,500	125 @ 2,000	800	2,496 / 4	578	PRM 150	55	Ford FSD
FSD MP	61 @ 3,000	125 @ 2,000	800	2,496 / 4	578	PRM 150	55	Ford FSD
NHD 450L	85 @ 2,000	248 @ 1,500	725	5,000 / 4	955	PRM 500	45	New Holland
NHD 450	105 @ 2,500	248 @ 1,500	725	5,000 / 4	959	PRM 500	45	New Holland
2725 EL	110 @ 2,000	285 @ 2,000	700	6,200 / 6	1027	PRM 500	45	Ford

Lister Marine Diesels, Long Street, Dursley, Gloucs GL11 4HS   01453 544141

Model	Power	Torque		cc / cyl	Weight	Gearbox		Engine
LPA2	15 @ 3,000	29 @ 2,000	850	726 / 2	319	Hurth HBW 50	45	Lister Petter
LPA3	23 @ 3,000	43 @ 2,000	850	1,089 / 3	374	Hurth HBW 100	45	Lister Petter
Canal Star 18	18 @ 2,600	39 @ 1,800	800	930 / 2	330	PRM150	45	Lister Petter
Canal Star 27	27 @ 2,600	59 @ 1,800	800	1,395 / 3	396	PRM 150	45	Lister Petter
Canal Star 36	36 @ 2,600	78 @ 1,800	800	1,860 / 4	462	PRM 150	45	Lister Petter
TS2	23 @ 2,600	49 @ 1,800	900	1,266 / 2	682	Hurth HBW 100	55	Lister Petter
TS3	34 @ 2,600	74 @ 1,800	900	1,900 / 3	770	Hurth HBW 125	55	Lister Petter

Lombardini (Sowester), Stinsford Road, Nuffield Industrial Estate, Poole, Dorset BH17 0SW   01202 667700

Model	Power	Torque		cc / cyl	Weight	Gearbox		Engine
LDW 502 M	11 @ 3,600	15.5 @ 2,000	850	505 / 2	167	Hurth HBW 40	30	Lombardini
LDW 602 M	17 @ 3,600	24 @ 2,000	850	611 / 2	213	Hurth HBW 40	45	Lombardini
LDW 903 M	27 @ 3,600	41 @ 2,000	850	916 / 3	242	Hurth HSW 125	45	Lombardini
LDW 1204 M	33 @ 3,600	54.5 @ 1,800	850	1,222 / 4	297	Hurth HSW 125	45	Lombardini
LDW 1503 M	37 @ 3,000	71.5 @ 1,900	850	1,551 / 3	396	Hurth HSW 125	65	Lombardini
LDW 2004 M	48.5 @ 3,000	92 @ 1,900	850	2,068 / 4	506	Hurth HSW 125	65	Lombardini
LDW 2004 MT	82 @ 3,000	144 @ 2,200	850	2,068 / 4	567	Hurth HSW 250	65	Lombardini

Marine Engine Services, Uxbridge Wharf, Waterloo Road, Uxbridge, Middlesex UB8 2QX   01895 270422

Model	Power	Torque		cc / cyl	Weight	Gearbox		Engine
PM 12	16 @ 1,500	55	475	1,560 / 2	594	Hurth/PRM	45 or 55	Rigas
PM 24	24 @ 1,800	66	525	1,560 / 2	616	Hurth/PRM	45 or 55	Rigas
PM 32	32 @ 1,500	110	475	3,120 / 4	858	Hurth/PRM	45 or 55	Rigas
PM 45	45 @ 1,800	138	525	3,120 / 4	858	Hurth/PRM	45 or 55	Rigas
PM60T	60 @ 1,800	176	525	3,120 / 4	946	Hurth/PRM	45 or 55	Rigas

Mermaid Marine Engines, 70 - 72 Cobham Road, Ferndown Industrial Estate, Ferndown, Dorset BH21 7RN   01202 895882

Model	Power	Torque		cc / cyl	Weight	Gearbox		Engine
Meteor 2	56 @ 4,000	82 / 2,400	650	1,753 / 4	378	PRM 150	70	Ford XLD

Nannidiesel (A R Peachment), Riverside Estate, Brundall, Norwich NR13 5PL   01603 714077

2.50 KC	14 @ 3,600	20.5 @ 3,600	900	479 / 2	202	60	Hurth	Kubota
3.75 KC	21 @ 3,600	30.5 @ 3,600	900	719 / 3	231	60	Hurth	Kubota
3.100 KC	29 @ 3,600	42.5@ 3,600	900	1001 / 3	286	60	Hurth/TMC	Kubota
4.150 KC	37.5 @ 3000	65.5 @ 3,000	800	1498 / 4	320	60	PRM 150	Kubota
4.200 KC	43 @ 2,800	80.5 @ 2,800	800	2197 / 4	495	60	PRM150or260	Kubota
4.220 KC	50 @ 2,800	93.5 @ 2,800	800	2197 / 4	495	60	PRM 260	Kubota
5.280 KC	62 @ 2,800	116 @ 2,800	800	2746 / 5	620	60	PRM 260	Kubota

Ruggerini (Ron Davis Marine), Castletown, Portland, Dorset DT5 1BD   01305 821175

RM 90	9.9 @ 3,000	18.5 @ 2,500	700	477 / 1	175	33	TMC 40	Ruggerini
MM 150	14 @ 3.000	22.8 @ 2,800	800	654 / 2	187	33	TMC 40	Ruggerini
MM 190	20 @ 3,000	33 @ 2,600	800	851 / 2	191	33	TMC 40	Ruggerini
RM 270	27 @ 2,800	50 @ 2,300	600	1205 / 2	356	58	TMC 60	Ruggerini
MM 351	43 @ 3,600	62.5 @ 2,500	800	1566 / 3	375	58	TMC 60	Ruggerini
RoDa FNM 450	48 @ 4,500	59 @ 3,000	800	1366 / 4	341	58	TMC 60	Ruggerini

Russell Newbery* (R W Davis & Sons) 01453 511621, (The RN Engine Co) 01384 294131

DM1	10 @ 1,200	47 @ 1,000	350	1,314 / 1	1008	70	Hurth 150	RN
DM2	21 @ 1,200	95 @ 1,000	350	2,628 / 2	1456	70	PRM 260	RN
DM3	31 @ 1,200	145 @ 1,000	350	3,942 / 3	1848	70	PRM 260	RN

SABB UK, Wixenford Farm, Plymstock, Plymouth PL9 8AA   01752 402286

GG	10 @ 1,800	29 @ 1,600	350	760 / 1	440	75	SABB	SABB

Sabre Engines, 22 Cobham Road, Ferndown Industrial Estate, Wimborne, Dorset BH21 7PW.   01603 71@170

Phoenix 42	42 @ 2,800	98 @ 1,700	900	1,995 / 4	482	70	PRM 150	Perkins
3 HD 46	46 @ 2,250	110 / 1,600	500	2,500 / 3	915	55	PRM 260	Perkins

Thornycroft Engines, PO Box 860, New Longton, Preston, Lancs PR4 1GT   01772 611144

Type 33	16.5 @ 3,600	23 @ 2,500	750	635 / 2	236	40	TMC 40	Mitsubishi L
Type 55	21 @ 3,000	37.6 @ 2,000	750	900 /3	343	40	TMC 40	Mitsubishi K
Type 65	29 @ 3,600	46 @ 2,400	750	1,125 / 3	348	70	PRM 120	Mitsubishi SL
Type 75	31 @ 3,600	53 @ 2,200	750	1,318 / 3	348	70	PRM 120	Mitsubishi SL
Type 90	40 @ 4,000	58 @ 1,800	570	1,489 / 4	524	70	PRM 120	BMC 1.5
Type 95	39 @ 3,600	62.5 @ 2,000	750	1,500 / 4	420	70	PRM 150	Mitsubishi SL
Type 105	42.5 @ 3,600	73.5 @ 2,000	750	1,758 / 4	420	70	PRM 150	Mitsubishi SL
Type 108	50 @ 4,000	78 @ 2,400	570	1,799 / 4	547	70	PRM 150	BMC 1.8
Type 145	60 @ 3,600	99 @ 2,000	750	2,311 / 4	600	70	PRM 260	Mitsubishi SQ
Type 155	67 @ 3,600	107 @ 1,900	750	2,505 / 4	600	70	PRM 260	Mitsubishi SQ

Vetus Den Ouden, 39 South Hants Industrial Park, Totton, Southampton SO40 3SA   023 8086 1033

M 2.04	11 @ 3,600	850	464 / 2	TMC 40	216	40	Mitsubishi
M 2.06	15 @ 3,600	850	635 / 2	TMC 40	216	40	Mitsubishi
M 3.10	22 @ 3,600	850	979 / 3	HSW 125 H	340	50	Mitsubishi
M 4.14	33 @ 3,600	850	1415 / 4	HSW 125 H	408	50	Mitsubishi
P 4.17	42 @ 3,000	875	1769 / 4	HSW 125 H	408	90	Peugeot
P 4.19	52 @ 3,600	875	1905 / 4	HSW 125 H	408	90	Peugeot
D 4.29	65 @ 3,000	875	2910 / 4	HSW 250 A	649	90	Deutz oil cooled

Yanmar (E P Barrus), Launton Road, Bicester, Oxon OX6 0UR   01869 363636

Shire 800	20 @ 3,600	850	800 / 2	PRM80	213	50	Yanmar 3TNE68
Shire 1000	25 @ 3,600	850	1,000 / 3	PRM80	266	50	Yanmar 3TNE74
Shire 1200	30 @ 3,600	850	1,200 / 3	PRM 80	316	50	Yanmar 3TNE 78
Shire 1550	30 @ 2,400	850	1,550 / 3	PRM 120	330	65	Yanmar 3TNE88
Shire 1650	35 @ 3,600	850	1,650/3	PRM 150	350	40 + 65	Yanmar 3TNE88
Shire 2000	45 @ 2,600	850	2,000 / 4	PRM 150	400	40 + 80	Yanmar 4TNE84
Shire 2200	45 @ 2,600	850	2,200 / 4	PRM 150	400	40 + 80	Yanmar 4TNE88

* At the time of writing, these engines are not in production but it is hoped that they will be during the life of this book.

For the latest information, ring the numbers given.

APPENDIX 3

PRODUCTS AND EQUIPMENT

GLASS-FIBRE CANAL CRUISERS

Viking: Unit 11, Ongar Road Trading Estate, Great Dunmow, Essex CM6 1EU. Tel: 01371 875214.

Shetland : James Reinman Marine Ltd. O'Brien Grove Industrial Estate, Stanton, Bury St Edmunds, Suffolk IP31 2AR. Tel: 01359 251200.

Wilderness Boats, Stokes Road, Corsham, Wilts SN13 9AA. Tel: 01249 712231.

ENGINE MARINISING KITS

Calcutt Boats, Calcutt Top Lock, Stockton, Rugby CV23 8HX. Tel: 01926 813757.

Lancing Marine, 51 Victoria Road, Portslade, East Sussex BN4 1XP. Tel: 01273 411765 (Publishes an invaluable guide/brochure).

Marine Mart, Faversham House, Seymour Road, Nuneaton, Warks CV11 4JD. Tel: 024 7632 2112.

GEARBOXES

PRM: Newage Transmissions Ltd, Barlow Road, Coventry CV2 2LD. Tel: 024 7661 7141.

Borg Warner Marine, Kenfig Industrial Estate, Margam, Port Talbot, West Glamorgan SA13 2PG. Tel: 01656 741001.

ZF Great Britain Ltd, Abbeyfield Road, Lenton, Nottingham NG7 2SX. Tel: 0115 986 9211.

Technodrive: Ron Davis Marine, Castletown, Portland, Dorset DT5 1DB. Tel: 01305 821175.

Marine Mart, Faversham House, Seymour Road, Nuneaton, Warks CV11 4JD. Tel: 024 7632 2112.

PROPELLERS, STERN TUBES & SEALS

Crowther Marine, Eden Works, Honeywell Lane, Oldham OL8 2JP. Tel: 0161 652 4234.

Calcutt Boats, Calcutt Top Lock, Stockton, Rugby CV23 8HX. Tel: 01926 813757.

Five Towns Boatbuilding, 1 Whitebridge Lane, Stone, Staffs ST15 8LQ. Tel: 01785 817506.

Halyard (M&I),Whaddon Business Park, Southampton Road, Waddon, Salisbury SP 3HF. Tel: 01722 710922.

Midland Chandlers, Teddesley Road, Penkridge, Staffs ST19 5RH. Tel: 01785 712437.

Sea Otter Workboats Ltd, Unit 24, M1 Commerce Park, Markham Lane, Duckmanton, Chesterfield S44 5HS. Tel: 01246 825750.

Teignbridge Propellers, Great Western Way, Forde Road, Newton Abbot, Devon TQ12 4AW. Tel: 01626 333377.

Vetus den Ouden, 38 South Hants Industrial Park, Totton, Southampton. Tel: 023 8086 1033.

FLEXIBLE DRIVE SYSTEMS

Angled cardan shafts:
Wilson Drive Shafts, Unit 1, Bennerley Court, Blenheim Industrial Estate, Bulwell, Nottingham NG6 8UT. Tel: 0115 976 1202.

Aquadrive:
TW Marine, The Marina, Station Road, Furness Vale, Stockport SK12 7QA. Tel: 01663 741891.

Hydraulic drive:
ARS Marine, 1 Langley Road, Chadgrave, Norfolk NR14 6BN. Tel: 01508 520555.

OUTDRIVES

Enfield: Bob Knowles Plant Services, 9 Vulcan Road, Leicester LE5 3EF. Tel: 0116 253 8685.

Sonic/Transadrive: Sillette, 182 Church Hill Road, North Cheam, Sutton, Surrey SM3 8NF. Tel: 020 8715 0100.

ELECTRIC PROPULSION

Brimblow Engineering, The Old Mill, The Street, Catfield, Great Yarmouth, Norfolk NR29 5DH. Tel: 01692 582707.

Electric Boat Association, 150 Wayside Green, Woodcote, Reading, Berks RG8 0QJ. Tel: 01491 681449.

HFL Marine International, Lockfield Avenue, Enfield, Middlesex EN3 7PX. Tel: 020 8805 9088. (diesel-electric)

STEAM

Historic Steam, c/o Kew Bridge Steam Museum, Green Dragon Lane, Brentford, Middx TW8 0EN. Tel: 020 8568 4757.

The Steam Boat Association of Great Britain, 54 Park Road, Chilwell, Notts NG9 4DD. Tel: 0115 922 7654.

ENGINE SOUND INSULATION

TW Marine, The Marina, Station Road, Furness Vale, Stockport SK12 7QA. Tel: 01663 741891.

VINTAGE ENGINES & PARTS

Specialists in vintage engines tend to concentrate on a particular make although they may deal in others from time to time. A number of specialists are included below together with the makes they are normally associated with. As well as supplying original and rebuilt engines, they will also repair, service and supply spares for installed vintage engines.

Paul Aldridge, Giggetty Wharf, Wombourne, Wolverhampton WV5 8EA. Tel: 01902 892242.
Lister

Brian Chisholm, Marine Engine Room. 23 The Spring, Long Eaton, Nottingham NG10 1PJ. Tel: 0115 972 4311 (evenings).

Lister, Ruston & Hornsby
R W Davis, Junction Dry Dock, Saul, Gloucestershire GL2 7LA. Tel: 01452 740701.
Kelvin, Russell Newbery, Dorman

Tony Redshaw, The Locks, Hillmorton, Rugby, Warks CV21 4PP. Tel: 01788 553417.
Gardner

Seaward Engineering, 974 Pollokshaws Road, Glasgow G42 2HA. Tel: 0141 632 4910.
Kelvin, Gardner

Danny Williamson, Beechtree Bungalow, Roydmoor Lane, Hemsworth, West Yorkshire WF9 5LR. Tel: 01977 610329.
Gardner

The Russell Newbery Register was originally formed to enable owners to exchange information about RNs. The RN Diesel Engine Co Ltd has now been set up to sell spares, remanufactured engines and new engines. The register can be contacted on 01327 311724 and the engine company on 01384 294131.

CANAL CRUISER PARTS
Dawncraft: Wilsons Trimmers, 98 White Hill, Kinver, Staffs DY7 6AU. Tel: 01384 872983.

Plastic fender strip: Wilks (Rubber Plastics), Woodrolfe Road, Tollesbury, Maldon, Essex CM9 8RY. Tel: 01621 869609.

MAJOR CHANDLERS
Midland Chandlers, Teddesley Road, Penkridge, Staffs ST19 5RH. Tel: 01785 712437.
Also at Junction Wharf, London Road, Braunston, Northants NN11 7HB. Tel: 01788 891401.
And at Venetian Marine Cholmondeston, Nantwich, Cheshire CW5 6DD. Tel: 01270 528030.

Calcutt Boats, Calcutt Top Lock, Stockton, Rugby CV23 8HX. Tel: 01926 813757.

Nantwich Canal Centre, Nantwich Marina, Chester Road, Nantwich, Cheshire CW5 6JD. Tel: 01270 625122.

David Piper Boatbuilders, Red Bull Basin, Church Lawton, Cheshire ST7 3AJ. Tel: 01782 510610.

Rose Narrowboats, Stretton under Fosse, near Rugby, Warks CV23 0PU. Tel: 01788 832449.

Severn Valley Boat Centre, Mart Lane, Stourport-on-Severn, Worcs DY13 9ER. Tel: 01299 871165.

Stone Boat Building Co, Newcastle Road, Stone, Staffs. Tel: 01785 812688.

Uxbridge Boat Centre, Uxbridge Wharf, Waterloo Road, Uxbridge, Middx UB8 2QX. Tel: 01895 252019.

WINDOWS
Caldwell & Son, 1 Hartley Avenue, off Darlington Street, Wigan WN1 3BW. Tel: 01942 826406.

Channelglaze, 21A Rushey Lane, Tyseley, Birmingham B11 2BL. Tel: 0121 706 5777.

Stainless steel framed: M G Fabrications, Unit 2 Old Station Goods Yard, Long Buckby, Northants NN6 7QA. Tel: 01604 708177.

Brass portholes: Boatmans Cabin Co Ltd, The Boatyard, Mansion Lane, Iver, Bucks SL0 9RG. Tel: 01753 651496.

Opening brass portholes : Brenmarl Engineering Tel: 0121 503 0545. (Order via chandlers)

SACRIFICIAL ANODES
M G Duff, Unit 2 West, 68 Bognor Road, Chichester, West Sussex PO19 2NS. Tel: 01243 533336.

ELECTRIC SYSTEMS & APPLIANCES
Acorn Engineering, 5 Turner Street, Denton, Manchester M34 3EG. Tel: 0161 320 8023.

British Marine Electronics Association, Meadlake Place, Thorpe Lea Road, Egham, Surrey TW20 8HE. Tel: 01784 473377.

Mastervolt, Unit D 5, The Premier Centre, Abbey Park, Romsey, Hampshire SO51 9AQ. Tel: 01794 516443.

Electronic Alternator Controllers and Battery Management Systems:

Acorn Engineering, 5 Turner Street, Denton, Manchester M34 3EG. Tel: 0161 320 8023.

Adverc BM, 245 Trysull Road, Merry Hill, Wolverhampton WV3 7LG. Tel: 01902 380494.

Driftgate 2000 Ltd, Little End Road, Eaton Socon, Cambs PE19 3JH. Tel: 01480 470400.

TWC: Aqua Marine, 216 Fair Oak Road, Bishopsgate, Eastleigh, Hants S05 6NJ. Tel: 023 8069 4949.

Sterling Marine Power, Gregory's Mill Street, Worcester WR3 8BS. Tel: 01905 26166.

Inverters/chargers:
Heart Interface: Los Angeles & Huddersfield Power Systems , Warble Wharf, Broadway, Hyde, Cheshire SK14 4QF. Tel: 0161 368 2888.

Mastervolt Unit D 5, The Premier Centre, Abbey Park, Romsey, Hampshire SO51 9AQ. Tel: 01794 516443.

Victron Products, Kuranda Marine, Kuranda House, Forge Road, Whaley Bridge, High Peak, Derbyshire SK23 7HY. Tel: 01663 734800.

GENERATORS
Honda Power Products, 4 Power Road, Chiswick, London W4 5YT. Tel: 020 8746 9757.

Brownpower Engineering Ltd, The Wharf, Stetton under Fosse, Rugby, Warks CV23 0PR. Tel: 01788 833383.

Yanmar portable diesel generators: E P Barrus, Launton Road, Bicester, Oxon OX6 0UR. Tel: 01869 363636.

Beta Marine, Merretts Mills, Bath Road, South Woodchester, Stroud, Glos GL5 5EU. Tel: 01453 835282.

Fischer Panda, Building 6, 28 Blackmoor Road, Ebblake Estate, Verwood, Dorset BH31 6BB. Tel: 01202 820840.

Stephen Goldsbrough Boats, Knowle Hall Wharf, Kenilworth Road, Knowle, Solihull B93 0JJ. Tel: 01564 778210.

Lister-Petter Marine, Thrupp, Stroud, Glos GL5 2BW. Tel: 01453 544141.

SOLAR & WIND POWER
Wind & Sun, Humber Marsh, Stoke Prior, Leominster, Hereford HR6 0NE. Tel: 01568 760671.

Ampair, PO Box 416, Poole, Dorset BH12 3LZ. Tel: 01202 749994.

Marlec Engineering, Rutland House, Trevithick Road, Corby, Northants NN17 1XY. Tel: 01536 201588.

CENTRAL HEATING
Gas:
Alde International (UK), Sandfield Close, Moulton Park, Northampton NN3 1AB. Tel: 01604 494193.

Carver Technology, Coppice Side Industrial Estate, Brownhills, Walsall, WS8 7ES. Tel: 01543 452122.

Truma, Truma House, Hawkins Lane, Burton-upon-Trent, Staffordshire DE14 1PT. Tel: 01283 511092.

CAK Tanks, Aqua House, Princes Drive, Kenilworth, Warwickshire CV8 2FD. Tel: 01926 854271.

Diesel, natural draught:
Harworth Heating Ltd, Blyth Road, Harworth, Doncaster DN11 8NE. Tel: 01302 742520.

Kuranda Marine, Kuranda House, Forge Road, Whaley Bridge, High Peak, Derbyshire SK23 7HY. Tel: 01663 734800.

Lockgate Marine Stoves, Barratt Lane, Attenborough, Nottingham NG9 6AG. Tel: 0115 925 7526.

Diesel, forced combustion:
Eberspacher (UK) Headlands Business Park, Salisbury Road, Ringwood, Hants BH24 3PB. Tel: 01425 480151.

Mikuni Heating UK, Unit 5, Second Avenue Business Park, Millbrook, Southampton SO15 0LP. Tel: 023 8052 8777.

Webasto: Water Travel, Oxley Moor Road, Wolverhampton. Tel: 01902 782371.

CABIN APPLIANCES
Narrowboat chandlers are the best place to compare cabin appliances – cookers, fridges, showers, washbasins, wcs, solid fuel stoves, lighting, etc. Caravan accessory shops are useful for smaller items like compact cooker/sink units provided they are boat compliant. Domestic kitchen centres offer luxurious sinks with clever features but MFI and Texas are where most narrowboaters buy their sink.

Sanitary equipment
Lee Sanitation, Wharf Road, Fenny Compton, Warwickshire CV33 0XE. Tel: 01295 770000.

Gasless cooking
Blakes Lavac Taylor, 13 Harvey Crescent, Warsash, Southampton SO31 9TA. Tel: 01489 580580.

Kuranda Marine, Kuranda House, Forge Road, Whaley Bridge, High Peak, Derbyshire SK23 7HY. Tel: 01663 734800.

Esse oil and solid fuel ranges, Ouzledale Foundry Co, Long Ing, Barnoldswick, Colne, Lancashire BB8 6BN. Tel: 01282 813235.

Gas Cookers
Stoves, Stoney Lane, Prescot, Merseyside L35 2XW. Tel: 0151 426 6551.

Fridges
Electrolux Leisure Appliances, Oakley Road, Luton, Bedfordshire LU4 9QQ. Tel: 01582 494111.

Ranger Refrigeration, (Manufacturers of the Inlander range) 272a Long Lane, Halesowen, West Mids B62 9JY. Tel: 0121 422 9707.

Shoreline Refrigeration, Unit C4, Modern Moulds Business Centre, Harwoods Road, Littlehampton, West Sussex BN17 7AU. Tel: 01903 733877.

Lec Refrigeration, Bognor Regis, Sussex PO22 9NQ. Tel: 01243 863161.

Aqua Marine, (Engel sole importer) 216 Fair Oak Road, Bishopstoke, Eastleigh, Hants SO50 8NJ. Tel: 023 8069 4949.

Weaco International, (Coolmatic) Unit D1 Roman Hill Trading Estate, Broadmayne, Dorset DT2 8LY. Tel: 01305 854000.

Sowester, (Isotherm sole importer) Stinsford Road, Nuffield Industrial Estate, Poole, Dorset BH17 0SW. Tel: 01202 667700.

BRASSWARE & PORTHOLES
Boatmans Cabin Company, The Boatyard, Mansion Lane, Iver, Bucks SL0 9RG. Tel: 01753 651496.

Brenmarl Engineering Tel: 0121 503 0545. (Order via chandlers).

Fenda Products, Unit 14, Hinckley Business Park, Brindley Road, Hinckley, Leicestershire LE10 3BY. Tel: 01455 890333.

Light Alloys (L D Brown), Unit 64 Boughton Industrial Estate, New Ollerton, Newark, Notts NG22 9LD.

Puffer Parts, Excelsior Works, Hall Terrace, Riddlesden, Keighley, West Yorkshire BD20 5AU. Tel: 01535 605703.

PAINTS & SCUMBLE

Blakes Marine Paints, Centurion Industrial Park, Southampton, Hampshire SO18 1UB. Tel: 023 8063 6373.

Bradite Paints, Ogwen Valley, Bethesda, Gwynedd, North Wales LL57 4YP. Tel: 01248 600315.

International Paints, 24/30 Canute Road, Southampton. Tel: 023 8022 6722.

Jotun-Henry Clark, 142 Minories, London, EC3N 1LS. Tel: 020 7481 2741.

The Indestructible Paint Company (Rylard) Haden Street, Birmingham B12 9DB. Tel: 0121 702 2485.

Joseph Mason Paints, Nottingham Road, Derby DE21 6AR. Tel: 01332 295959.

Tekaloid, Croda Paints, Bankside, Hull HU5 1SQ. Tel: 01482 41441.

Wales Dove, (Hull Paints), Mainline Building Products, South Sefton Business Centre, Canal Street, Bootle, Merseyside L20 8AH. Tel: 0151 933 8446.

Wrights of Lymm, (Scumble, combs and rubbers) Wright House, Millers Lane, Lymm, Cheshire WA13 9RG. Tel: 01925 752226.

J H Ratcliffe & Co, (Scumble) 135a Linaker Street, Southport PR8 5DF. Tel: 01704 537999.

Combs and knotting rubbers also from major chandlers and specialists.

CANOPIES

Wilsons, 98 White Hill, Kinver, Staffs DY7 6AU. Tel: 01384 872983.

J&H Trimmers, Ashwood Marina, Greensforge, Kingswinford, West Midlands DY6 0AQ. Tel: 01384 279527.

Coverit Canopies, 98 Bolton Road, Atherton, Lancs. Tel: 01942 883310.

Non-fitted tarpaulins: Bradshaws Tarpaulins, Nicolson Link, Clifton Moor, York YO1 1SS. Tel: 01904 691169.

FENDERS

J Langford, L&F Boat Fenders, 21 Aintree Way, Dudley, West Midlands DY1 2SL. Tel: 01384 241804.

The Fender Shop, Lower Cape, Warwick CV34 5DP. Tel: 01926 410588.

The Fender Maker (Eric Johns), The Old Wharf, Appletree Lane, near Cropredy, Banbury, Oxon OX17 1PZ. Tel: 01295 758734.

Tradline Fenders, The Old Blacksmith's Forge, Braunston Marina, near Daventry, Northants NN11 7JH. Tel: 01788 891761.

FURNITURE & UPHOLSTERY

M B Bailey, Dobson's Boatyard, The Wharf, Shardlow, Derbys DE7 2GJ. Tel: 01332 792922.

Calliope Covers & Curtains, Unit 7 Barns Heath Farm, Snarestone Road, Appleby Magna, Swadlincote DE12 7AJ. Tel: 01827 830253.

The Cut Covers Company, The Toll House, Sutton Stop, Longford, Coventry, CV6 6DF. Tel: 024 7636 4521.

Foam for Comfort, 401 Otley Old Road, Cookridge, Leeds LS16 7DF. Tel: 01532 678281.

Galloway Upholstery, 25 Browning Street, Stafford ST16 3AX. Tel: 01785 259645.

Wilsons Trimmers, 98 White Hill, Kinver, Staffs DY7 6AU. Tel: 01384 872983.

APPENDIX 4

SERVICES

GENERAL REFERENCES

British Waterways, Willow Grange, Church Road, Watford, Herts WD1 3QA. Tel: 01923 226422. Boat Safety Enquiries: 01923 201278.

British Marine Industries Federation, Meadlake Place, Thorpe Lea Road, Egham, Surrey TW20 8BE. Tel: 01784 473377.

Canal Boatbuilders' Association, via BMIF or: Parkland House, Audley Avenue, Newport, Shropshire TF10 7BX. Tel: 01952 813572.

CORGI, 1 Elmwood, Chinham Business Park, Crockford Lane, Basingstoke RG24 8WG. Tel: 01256 372200.

Inland Waterways Association, P O Box 114, Rickmansworth WD3 1ZY. Tel: 01923 711114.

National Association of Boat Owners, 111 Maas Road, Northfield, Birmingham B31 2PP.

Residential Boat Owners Association, PO Box 46, Grays RM18 8DZ. Tel: 0370 785869.

Royal Yachting Association, RYA House, Romsey Road, Eastleigh, Hants, SO50 9YA. Tel: 023 8062 7400.

Yacht Designers & Surveyors Association, Wheel House, Petersfield Road, Whitehill, Bordon, Hants GU35 9BU. Tel: 01420 473862.

Drawings for DIY shell construction:

M&TBS, Hunters Park, Hernstone Lane, Peak Forest, Buxton, Derbyshire, SK17 8EJ. Tel: 0161 320 8023.

SURVEYORS

The following is a selection of surveyors who can carry out all types of surveys and are authorised to issue Boat Safety Certificates.

Acorn Engineering (Peter Hopley), 5 Turner Street, Denton, Manchester M34 3EG. Tel: 0161 320 8023.

Anglo-European Marine Surveys (Balliol Fowden), Burleigh House, 273 Hillmorton Road, Rugby CV22 5BH. Tel: 01788 541020.

J T G Bowen, Tecardy (Marine Services), Half Acre, Brentford. Tel: 020 8568 3693.

Malcolm Braine, The Wharf, Saltworks Lane, Weston, Staffs ST18 0JE. Tel: 01889 270172.

I R Burgoyne, 61 St Clements, Oxford OX1AH. Tel: 01865 792266.

Derrick Davison, Houseboat *Hirondelle*, Trent Lock, Nottingham. Tel: 0115 972 7764.

Allan McGregor, Farquharson-McGregor Services Ltd, Orchard House, Shocklach, Chester SY14 7BJ. Tel: 01829 250508.

D S Fford, Highcroft, Church Place, Stroud GL5 3NF. Tel: 01453 752598.

Foxton Boat Services (Tony Matts), Bottom Lock, Foxton, Market Harborough, Leics. Tel: 0116 279 2285.

David Fuller, The Survey Office, Woodedge Lane, Marchington, Staffordshire ST14 8LY. Tel: 01283 820228.

Jeff Greatwood, 105 Main Street, Alrewas, Burton-on-Trent, Staffs DE13 7ED. Tel: 01283 790611.

Captain Derek A Hansing, 'Katoomba', 15 Astorville Park Road, Chellaston, Derby DE73 1XW. Tel: 01332 705242.

Dr R Lorenz, 26 Worsley Road, Worsley, Manchester M28 4GQ. Tel: 0161 794 1441.

Ian Marsh, 131 Planks Lane, Wombourne, Wolverhampton WV5 8EA. Tel: 07802 177505.

MacDonald Marine (James MacDonald), Cassio Wharf, Watford, Herts WD1 8SL. Tel: 01923 248145.

Philip Mitchell, The Lawn, 31 Wilne Lane, Shardlow, Derby. Tel: 01332 792271.

Barrie Morse, 11 Silver Street, Charcombe, Banbury, Oxfordshire. Tel: 01295 711941.

Captain J A Polley, 36 Arragon Road, London E6 1QP. Tel: 020 8471 5252.

Roger Preen, Calcutt Boats Ltd, Stockton, Rugby CV23 8HX. Tel: 01926 813757.

Raine & Associates, Easegill, Coalpit Lane, Whittington, Oswestry, Shropshire SY11 4BS. Tel: 01691 662459.

Brian G Taylor, 12 Overton Close, Middlewich, Cheshire CW10 0PZ. Tel: 01606 836689.

Tucker Designs, 15 Renfield, Boxmoor, Hemel Hempstead, Herts HP1 1RN. Tel: 01442 253775.

H Wallace-Sims, Moorhall Road, Harefield, UB9 6PD. Tel: 01304 612655.

Trevor Whitling, 1 Ashworth Close, Crick, Northants NN3 9DA. Tel: 01788 824191.

ARBITRATORS

MacDonald Marine, Cassio Wharf, Watford, Herts WD1 8SL. Tel: 01923 248145.

Dr R Lorenz, 26 Worsley Road, Worsley, Manchester M28 4GQ. Tel: 0161 794 1441.

INSURERS

Aquacraft, K.Drewe Insurance, The Post House, 14 Load Street, Bewdley, Worcestershire DY12 2AE. Tel: 01299 401663.

Collidge & Partners, 16 Hawley Square, Margate, Kent CT9 1PF. Tel: 01843 295925.

GJW Direct, Silkhouse Court, Tithebarn Street, Liverpool L2 2QW. Tel: 0151 473 8050.

Haven Knox-Johnson, 10 Kingshill Avenue, Kingshill, West Malling, Kent ME19 4QZ. Tel: 020 7377 9777.

Hill House Hammond, Chamberlain's House, 41 West Street, Marlow, Bucks SL7 2LS. Tel: 01628 890888.

Navigators and General Insurance, PO Box 848, Brighton BN1 4PR. Tel: 01273 863400.

Newton Crum. Droxford House, Charles Road, St Leonards, East Sussex TN38 0JU. Tel: 01424 718800.

Select Direct, Plaza Tower, East Kilbride G74 1LW. Tel: 0345 125911.

Severn City Marine, 40 Foregate Street, Worcester, Worcs. Tel: 01905 25181.

Michael Stimpson, 6 Norfolk Road, Rickmansworth, Herts WD3 1QE. Tel: 01923 770425.

St Margarets Insurances, 153 – 155 High Street, Penge, London SE20 7DL. Tel: 020 8778 6161.

NARROWBOAT BROKERS

Alvechurch Boat Centres, Scarfield Wharf, Alvechurch, Birmingham B48 7SQ. Tel: 0121 445 2909.

Alvechurch Boat Centres, Gayton Marina, Blisworth Arm, Northants NN7 3EP. Tel: 01604 858685.

Alvechurch Boat Centres, Anderton Marina, Uplands Road, Anderton, Nr Northwich, Cheshire CW9 6AQ. Tel: 01606 79642.

Andy Burnett Narrowboat Brokerage, Crick Wharf, West Haddon Road, Northants NN6 7XT. Tel: 01788 822115.

Braunston Brokerage, Braunston Marina Ltd, The Wharf, Braunston, Nr Daventry, Northants NN11 7JH. Tel: 01788 891373.

Calcutt Boats, Calcutt Top Lock, Stockton, Southam, Warks CV47 8HX. Tel: 01926 813757.

Canal Craft Brokerage, Cornhill Lane, Bugbrooke, Northants NN7 3ZB. Tel: 01604 832889.

Canal Craft Brokerage, Hanbury Wharf, Droitwich, Worcs WR9 7DU. Tel: 01905 771018.

Canal Craft Brokerage, Nantwich Canal Centre, Chester Road, Nantwich, Cheshire CW5 8LB. Tel: 01270 627155.

Canal Craft Brokerage, Wharf Street, Shipley, West Yorkshire BD17 7DW. Tel: 01274 595914.

Chertsey Meads Marine, The Meads, Chertsey, Surrey KT16 8LN. Tel: 01932 564699.

Cowroast Marinas, Fenny Marina, Fenny Compton, Warks CV47 2XD. Tel: 01295 770461.

Cowroast Marinas, Cowroast Marina, Tring, Herts HP23 5RE. Tel: 01442 823222.

Devizes Marina, Horton Avenue, Devizes, Wiltshire SN10 2RH. Tel: 01380 725300.

Harefield Marina Boat Sales. Harefield Marina, Middlesex UB9 6PD. Tel: 01895 822036.

Harral Brokerage Services Ltd, Wincham Wharf, 220 Manchester Road, Northwich, Cheshire CW9 7NT. Tel: 01606 47078/46348.

High Line Yachting Ltd. Mansion Lane, Iver, Bucks SL0 9RG. Tel: 01753 651496.

Jannel Cruisers, Shobnall Marina, Shobnall Road, Burton-on-Trent, Staffs DE14 2AU. Tel: 01283 542718.

Longport Brokerage, Longport Wharf, Longport, Stoke-on-Trent ST6 4NA. Tel: 01782 813831.

Lower Park Marina, Kelbrook Road, Barnoldswick, Lancs BB18 5TB. Tel: 01282 815883.

Maestermyn Marine, Ellesmere Road, Whittington, Oswestry, Salop SY11 4NU. Tel: 01691 662424.

Marine Services, Chirk Marina, Chirk, Wrexham LL14 5AD. Tel: 01691 774558.

Marine Services, Festival Park, Etruria, Stoke-on-Trent ST1 5PS. Tel: 01782 201981.

MCC Stenson Boat Sales, Stenson Marina, Stenson, Derby DE73 1HL, Tel: 01283 701933.

Narrowcraft Ltd, The Boatyard, Robeys Lane, Alvecote, Nr Tamworth, Staffs B78 1AS. Tel: 01827 898585.

Northern Narrowboats, Bluewater Marina Ltd, South End, Thorne, South Yorks DN8 5QR. Tel: 01405 813165.

Norton Canes Boat Sales, Norton Canes Docks, Lime Lane, Pelsall, Walsall, West Midlands WS3 5AP. Tel: 01543 374888.

Nottingham Castle Marina, Marina Road, Castle Marina Park, Nottingham NG7 1TN. Tel: 0115 941 2672.

Nu-Way Acorn, Lundsfield, Carnforth LA5 9NB. Tel: 01524 734457.

Otherton Boat Haven, Otherton, Penkridge, Stafford ST19 5NX. Tel: 01785 712515.

Preston Brook Marina, Marina Lane, Runcorn, Cheshire WA7 3AF. Tel: 01928 719081.

Pyrford Marina Narrowboat Brokerage, Lock Lane, Pyrford, Surrey GU22 8XL. Tel: 01932 340739.

Reading Marine, Aldermaston Wharf, Padworth, Reading, Berks RG7 4JS. Tel: 0118 971 3666.

Sawley Marina, Sawley Lane, Long Eaton, Nottingham NG10 3AE. Tel: 0115 973 4278.

Severn Valley Boat Centre, Boat Shop, Mart Lane, Stourport-on-Severn, Worcs DY13 9ER. Tel: 01299 871165.

Shardlow Marina, London Road, Shardlow, Derby DE72 2GL. Tel: 01332 792832.

Shepley Bridge Marina, Huddersfield Road, Mirfield, W Yorks WF14 9HR. Tel: 01924 491872.

Shire Cruisers, The Wharf, Sowerby Bridge, W Yorks HX6 2AG. Tel: 01422 832712.

Sileby Mill Boatyard, Mill Lane, Sileby, Loughborough, Leics LE12 7NP. Tel: 01509 813583.

Streethay Wharf, Streethay, Lichfield, Staffs WS13 8RJ. Tel: 01543 414808.

Thorne Marina, Hatfield Road, Thorne, Nr Doncaster DN8 5RA. Tel: 01405 814443.

Tovil Bridge Boatyard, Tovil Bridge, Maidstone, Kent ME15 6RU. Tel: 01622 868341.

Venetian Marine (Nantwich) Ltd, Cholmondeston, Nantwich, Cheshire CW5 6DD. Tel: 01270 528251.

Virginia Currer Marine, PO Box 402, Windsor, Berkshire SL4 2YB. Tel: 01753 832312 Mobile: 0860 480079.

Warwickshire Fly Boat Co, Shop Lock Cottage, Stockton, Nr Rugby, Warks. Tel: 01926 812093.

Weltonfield Narrowboats Ltd, Welton Hythe, Daventry, Northants NN11 5LG. Tel: 01327 842282.

Whilton Marina, Whilton Locks, Nr Daventry, Northants NN11 5NH, Tel: 01327 842577.

White Bear Marina, Park Road, Adlington, Chorley, Lancashire PR7 4HZ. Tel: 01257 481054.

York Marine Services, Ferry Lane, Bishopthorpe, York YO2 1SB, Tel: 01904 704442.

NARROWBOAT ROAD TRANSPORT
R&J Dempster, 142 Church Street, Stone, Staffordshire ST15 8BW. Tel: 01785 814175.

Streethay Wharf, Streethay, Lichfield, Staffs WS13 8RJ. Tel: 01543 414808.

A B Tuckey, Glebe Farm, Stockton, Southam, Warwickshire CV47 8JG. Tel: 01926 812134.

Wincham Wharf Boatbuilders, 220 Manchester Road, Lostock Gralam, Cheshire CW9 7NT. Tel: 01606 44672.

SPRAYED FOAM INSULATION
ELF Urethane Ltd, 292 Whalley Road, Clayton le Moors, Accrington, Lancs BB5 5QX. Tel: 01254 237066.

Insulair, 26 Wolversdene Road, Andover, Hants. Tel: 01264 337777.

Warmways, Hurst House, Hurst Close, Crowthorne Road, Bracknell RG12 4EJ. Tel: 01344 868489.

Websters Insulation Ltd, Crow Tree Farm, Thorne Levels, Doncaster, South Yorkshire DN8 5BR. Tel: 0800 581247.

GRIT BLASTING
B J Wood & Sons (with dry dock), Lion Wharf, off Richmond Road, Old Isleworth, Isleworth, TW7 7BW. Tel: 020 8560 4848.

Mercian Shot Blasting. Brookhall, Suckley, Worcester WR6 5DJ. Tel: 01886 884591.

Middlewich Narrowboats, 9 Canal Terrace, Middlewich, Cheshire CW10 9BD. Tel: 01606 832460.

Tom Bryan, Wharf View, Wharf Road, Gnosall, Stafford ST20 0DA. Tel: 01785 823318.

Phil Jones, Marine Mechanical & Welding Services, 105 Griffiths Drive, Wolverhampton WV11 2JW. Tel: 01902 710799.

Limekiln Narrowboats, r/o 4 Bridgnorth Rd, Compton, Wolverhampton, West Midlands WV6 8AA. Tel: 01902 751147.

OUTBOARD SERVICE
Fred Bull, Lincolnshire Marine Services, Morton Boats, Eagle Road, Morton, Swinderby, Lincs LN6 9HT. Tel: 01522 868107. (especially useful for difficult and obsolete parts).

Rose Narrowboats, Stretton under Fosse, near Rugby, Warks CV23 0PU. Tel: 01788 832449.

DIESEL ENGINEERS
Engineers are prolific on the canals (except when you need one). The following sample was chosen partly for geographic spread:

Andy Clarke, The Upside Down House, 15 Worton Road, Middle Barton, Chipping Norton, Oxon OX7 7EE. Tel: 01869 340001.

AP Boats (Peter Borshik). Bottom Lock, Braunston, Daventry, Northants NN11 7HL. Tel: 01788 891886.

Bob Knowles Plant Services, 9 Vulcan Road, Leicester LE5 3EF. Tel: 0116 253 8685.
Brian Chisholm, 23 The Spring, Long Eaton, Nottingham NG10 1PJ. Tel: 0115 972 4311.

C T & P Fox, (Boatbuilders), 10 Marina Drive, March, Cambs PE15 0AU. Tel: 01354 52770.

East Midlands Boat Services, Willow Moorings, London Road, Kegworth, Derbys. Tel: 01509 672385.

Guy Taylor, 14 White Hill, Kinver, Staffs. Tel: 01384 877773.

Jannel Cruisers, Shobnall Marina, Shobnall Road, Burton-upon-Trent, Staffs DE14 2AU. Tel: 01283 542718.

Jon Pattle, 27 Wellfield, Hazelmere, Bucks. Tel: 01494 812991.

Middlesex & Herts Boat Services, Winkwell Dock, Bourne End, Hemel Hempstead, Herts HP1 2RZ. Tel: 01442 872985.

Lorenz Canal Services (Paul Lorenz), Bedford Basin, Henry Street, Leigh, Lancs WN7 2PG. Tel: 01942 679690.

Mark Paris, n/b *Helen of Troy* (Oxfordshire). Tel: 0860 711003.

Middlewich Narrowboats, 9 Canal Terrace, Middlewich, Cheshire CW10 9BD. Tel: 01606 832460.

Mick Sivewright, Kings Lock Boatyard, Booth Lane, Middlewich, Cheshire CW10 0JJ. Tel: 01606 737564.

Peter Thompson, Marine Engine Services, Uxbridge Wharf, Waterloo Road, Uxbridge, Middlesex UB8 2QX. Tel: 01895 270422.

Peter Jordan (The Boat Doctor), 97A The Circle, Old Sinfin, Derby DE24 9HR. Tel: 01332 771622.

Roger Drennen, Cotswold Diesel Services (Gloucestershire). Taitshill Industrial Estate, Taitshill, Dursley, Gloucester GL11 6BL. Tel: 01453 545261.

Shire Cruisers, The Wharf, Sowerby Bridge, West Yorks HX6 2AG. Tel: 01422 832712.

Snaygill Boats, Skipton Road, Bradley, Yorks BD20 9HA. Tel: 01756 795150.

Tim Leech, 3 Tunnel End, Dutton, Warrington, Cheshire WA4 4LA. Tel: 01928 716701.

Tony Redshaw, Little Heath Piece, Desford Road, Newbold Verdon, Leics LE9 9LG. Tel: 01455 822853.

TW Marine, The Marina, Station Road, Furness Vale, Stockport SK12 7QA. Tel: 01663 745757.

Warwickshire Fly Boat Co, Shop Lock Cottage, Stockton, near Rugby. Tel: 01926 812093 (specialises in vintage engines).
The Canalboat Builders Association runs a national breakdown service called C-BASS. If you have a problem while cruising, a phone call to the help line will connect you to the member of the scheme nearest to you. He will offer advice and, if necessary come out to your boat to repair it. The first 3 hours are at standard rates throughout the country after which regional variations (the North/South divide) apply. Tel: 01384 215859.

ELECTRICIANS
Acorn Engineering, 5 Turner Street, Denton, Manchester M34 3EG. Tel: 0161 320 8023.

Ampower Services, Fosse Way, Stretton-under-Fosse, Rugby, Warks CV23 0PU. Tel: 01788 832449.

Evesham Boat Care, Common Road, Evesham, Worcs. Tel: 01386 765081.

Matrix Controls, 26 Station Road, Holmes Chapel, Cheshire CW4 7AY. Tel: 01477 535801.

J D Boat Services, The Wharf, Gailey, Staffs ST19 5PR. Tel: 01902 790612.

Guy Taylor, 14 White Hill, Kinver, Staffs. Tel: 01384 877773.

SIGNWRITERS
Ron Hough, 31 The Green, Braunston, Northants. Tel: 01788 890910.

J W Mombrun, 9 Victoria Road, Bicester, Oxon. Tel: 01869 253959.

Dave Moore, 20 Victoria Street, Brierley Hill, West Midlands DY5 1RD. Tel: 01384 571204.

D J Moseley, 14 Old Acre, Brocton, Stafford ST17 0TW. Tel: 01785 661726.

Steve Radford, 15 Northern Road, Heanor, Derbys DE75 7EP. Tel: 01773 762408.

Andy Russell, 37 Barnaby Road, Poynton, Cheshire SK12 1LR. Tel: 01625 850853.

Philip Speight, Wordsley Dock, Dadford Wharf, Mill Street, Wordsley, Stourbridge, West Midlands DY8 5SX. Tel: 01384 482238.

Tony Stephenson, 1 The Garth, Elslack, near Skipton, North Yorks. Tel: 01282 843907.

John West, 103 Abbotswood Close, Winyates Green, Redditch, Worcs B98 0QF. Tel: 01527 516771.

APPENDIX 5

INLAND DIRECTORY

Modern inland boating does not involve a whole new language of nautical terms but the following is a list of some technical terms and acronyms that may need explanation.

A

abutment The supporting or retaining wall of a brick, concrete or masonry structure, particularly where it joins the item (eg bridge girder or arch) which it supports.

aegre Tidal **bore** or wave which is set up by the first of a flood tide as it runs up the river Trent. Sometimes spelt 'Aegir'.

air draught The overall height of a vessel measured from the water line to the highest fixed part of the **superstructure.**

ait An island (small) on the Thames.

animal A boatman's name for a donkey. Pronounced '*Hanimal*'. A pair of animals took the place of a towing horse.

anode (sacrificial) Lumps of metal (usually magnesium in fresh water boating), fitted to the underwater part of steel hulls to corode instead of the steel plate.

antifouling Paint applied underwater to inhibit weed growth on the hull. Usually applied to river and canal cruisers rather than narrowboats (the hulls of which are invariably coated with bitumen paint, which has some antifouling characteristics).

APCO The Association of Pleasure Craft Operators – body representing the interests of the narrowboat hire industry . A subsidiary organisation of BMIF (qv) – not to be confused with ACPO, the Association of Chief Police Officers.

aqueduct A bridge across which a waterway/watercourse is carried. Any engineering structure for the conveyance of water.

AWCC Association of Waterways Cruising Clubs – umbrella body for the numerous boat clubs of Britain's inland waterways.

B

BACAT *B*arge *A*board *Cat*amaran. A system of carrying special inland **barges** from the Humber between Hull and the Continent aboard an ocean going mother ship, killed off by opposition from dock workers.

balance beam Beam projecting from a **lock gate**, to counterbalance the weight of the gate and give leverage for its movement.

ballast Non-structural material added to increase a boat's **displacement**, and thus its stability.

barge Particularly not a **narrowboat** – the owners of which may be upset if you call their craft 'barges'. Barges are generally wider commercial inland boats – or leisure boats based on the bluff shape of the commercial type. However, some barge styles (like the Dutch luxemotor) have been copied in narrow-width versions for narrow canals. In Ireland, now used for narrowboats-style craft of over 7ft (2.1m) beam.

bascule bridge An opening bridge which has its deck pivoting at one end about a horizontal axis. It may be counterbalanced by overhead arms or weights beneath the road surface.

basin A section of water which is partly enclosed and is placed off a **navigation** channel and usually consists of **wharves** and moorings.

beam The overall width of a boat.

berth 1. The bunk or bed in a boat. 2. The space occupied by a vessel when moored.

bight A loose loop in a rope; also used to describe the outside of a pronounced bend in a river. See also **ness**

bilge The lowest internal part of a boat's hull. Also the lowest curved section of hull between side and bottom in a round **chined** vessel.

bilge pump A pump for removing water that has collected in the **bilge**.

Billy Boy Yorkshire coasting sailing **barge,** related to the **Humber keel** and **sloop**. Was able to go up the inland **navigations** but also to cross to the Continent, as it was fitted with **bulwarks.**

blade(s) Narrowboater's term for propeller. Curiously, the propeller is often said to be fitted with several 'bats' rather than blades.

blow Colloquial term for a warning signal, given when the view is restricted and there is danger of a collision. Boatmen of old either cracked a whip or blew a polished brass mouth horn.

BMIF British Marine Industries Federation – organisation that represents the interests of the entire UK boat industry. A number of specialist trade representative bodies are under its umbrella (see APCO, CBA, NYHA). Also owns National Boat Shows Ltd, which organises many major UK shows – including London and Southampton.

boat hook A light **shaft** usually made of wood with a metal hook at one end.

boatman's cabin Originally the 8ft (2.4m) long after cabin of a working **narrowboat,** where the crew lived. Often recreated in modern **traditional-style** narrowboats – as an annexe to the main cabin accommodation.

bobbins Hollow wooden rollers used to prevent the traces chafing against the flanks of the horse when towing a boat.

Bolinder Swedish engine manufacturer, well known for single cylinder slow running 'semi-diesels' used in **narrowboats** and **barges**. Engine has a characteristic irregular beat. The company is now part of Volvo Penta.

bollard Metal, concrete or wooden post for tying up or slowing the movement of a boat.

boot topping Band of paint just above the waterline. Neatens the edge of **antifouling** paint, hides waterline scum.

bore Tidal wave on the river Severn caused by the incoming tide being 'funnelled' by the shape of the estuary (wide and deep to narrow and shallow), causing a wall of water to build up and move at approx 10 mph (16kph). Happens on highest of tides particularly at the autumn equinox. A similar **aegre** occurs on the Trent.

bow The foremost part of a vessel's hull.

bow hauling Boat being hauled by man instead of horse. Also 'Bow Yanking'. Term derived from the loop often made in the end of the line used and not from the term **bow** above, for the front of the vessel.

bow wave A wave made at the **bow** of a boat as the hull passes through the water.

breach Burst or collapse of a canal bank or dyke, allowing water to escape, perhaps causing flooding etc.

breast/mitre post Vertical post of a **gate** farthest from its hanging; where the gates are in pairs, the two breasts are usually mitred to bed against each other when shut.

bridge guards Curved steel rails fastened between the forward outer edge of the cabin roof and the **foredeck** of a canal boat to protect the **superstructure** from damage.

bridge hole The narrow channel beneath a bridge.

broad The East Anglian term for lake.

BSS Boat Safety Scheme – British Waterways' version of an MoT certificate; this indicates that a boat meets minimum safety standards, but should not be taken as a reflection of overall quality. Safety standards are harmonised with the Environment Agency and the Broads Authority. A Boat Safety Certificate is mandatory for all hire boats, house boats and private craft except those built after 16 June 1998 which are covered under the **RCD** (qv) for the first 4 years.

bulkhead Vertical panels separating a boat into compartments.

bulls-eye Small (up to 6in (15cm) diameter) circular **porthole** set in the cabin top, fitted with convex glass.

bulwarks Solid upward extensions of a vessel's sides around the deck to reduce the danger of people or equipment being washed overboard at sea.

buoy A marker which is in a fixed position and floats on the surface of the water. They are often used for mooring purposes or to delineate the **navigation** channel.

butty boat An unpowered **narrowboat** that is towed by a powered boat.

BW British Waterways – navigation authority for most of Britain's inland waterways and, particularly, the narrow-beam canals. Has so far (at 2000) resisted efforts to become unified with other waterways navigation authorities, like **EA** (qv).

by-wash A weir stream (open or culverted), situated by a canal **lock** and passing excess water from the upper to the lower **pound**.

bye trader An independent carrier not in the ownership of the **navigation** authority along whose waterway he trades.

C

cadger Alternative name for **kedger** or **kedge** anchor. Term used on the river Trent.

campshedding The protection of a canal or river bank using a covering of timber or interlocking steel trench sheets.

Canalmanac Regular publication by *Waterways World* Ltd, listing addresses and phone numbers of all organisations connected to Britain's waterways.

cants Rails or strip plinths that edge the **foredeck** and aft deck of **traditional-style** narrowboats. Now usually made of steel and entirely decorative, but originally applied as a timber edging to take wear.

capstan Rotating drum for hauling ropes which may be used for opening **lock gates,** raising anchors etc.

cardan shaft A long intermediate hollow shaft in the drive line between gearbox and propeller. Has universal joints at either end. Often used where the engine is installed forward of **boatman's cabin** because it is relatively light and is tolerant of engine misalignment.

carvel-built Wooden boat construction when the planks of the hull are butted together and sealed by some kind of **caulking**.

caulking The sealing of joints in wooden boats by hammering in **oakum** (or, in light craft, cotton).

cavitation Loss of efficiency caused by air being drawn into the propeller.

cavitation plate In a **narrowboat,** the horizontal plate approximately at waterline level, that sits over the propeller. The plate helps to direct the propeller's thrust aft, and reduces opportunities for **cavitation**. In other craft, or on **outboard motor** legs, any plate that performs a similar function.

CBA Canal Boatbuilders' Association – body representing the interests of narrowboat builders. A subsidiary organisation of BMIF (qv) but relatively young. It was, at first, treated with suspicion by some of the more independently minded builders but many are now joining to benefit from advice on RCD (qv) procedures.

chalico Used in wooden boats to fill a space or crevice. Contains tar, cow hair and horse dung and is used hot.

channel The deepest area of a navigable waterway.

chine Where hull bottom and hull sides are flat surfaces (rather than curving gradually from one to the other as in '**round bilge**') the chine is the sharp edge where they meet.

cill See **sill.**

cleat T-shaped fitting used for tying-off ropes.

clinker-built Wooden boat construction in which the planks of the hull overlap each other.

clough (pronounced *clow*) A **lock paddle** or **sluice.** Particularly on northern English waterways.

coaming The raised edging around a well or **hatch.**

cock boat See **cog boat.**

cockpit Open area, usually set lower than surrounding side-decks; used for sitting-out and for utility storage.

cog or coggie boat A dinghy used to **tender** dredgers, **keels** or **sloops.** Used on the north east waterways. Known as cock boat on the river Mersey.

compartment boat Rectangular boat used on the Aire & Calder Navigation, worked in trains along with similar boats. Known as **Tom Puddings** or pans.

composite The construction of a vessel's hull when two different materials are used, eg iron sides and wooden bottom. In sea going craft may refer to wooden construction on iron framing.

contour canal An artificial channel that follows as near as possible to the land contours.

counter The round or elliptical (looking from above) **stern** of a **narrowboat.**

cratch Optional assembly over the forward **cockpit** of a **narrowboat**. Based on a triangular **deckboard** or 'cratch-board' which is supported from the cabin top by a 'top plank'. The assembly is completed by a fitted soft cover, usually of vinyl, sometimes of proofed canvas. The result greatly extends the usability of the cockpit. Either side of the cover can be rolled up to allow access, or is fitted with a zipped door panel. Cratches are descended from covers over the fodder stores of horse-drawn narrowboats, and the term derives from the word 'creche'.

cross bed Transverse bed across the centre corridor of a traditional **boatman's cabin**. Flap across the corridor folds up to make a cupboard door, behind which bedding can be stored. Original cross beds in 8ft (2.4m) long boatman's cabins were decidedly narrow for a double berth. Modern cross beds are often 4ft (1.2m) wide, in a 9ft (2.7m) long cabin.

cross straps Tow ropes crossed at the bow of tow, securing tight to the tug, which allows a pair of narrowboats to operate as a single articulated unit. Only used when craft are running empty.

cruiser stern/style A style of pleasure craft based on the lines of former working boats but adapted to provide a large open deck space under which accommodation there may be an engine compartment.

crumb drawer Drawer under the **table cupboard** in a traditional **boatman's cabin**. Originally used for cutlery storage, but light-heartedly tagged 'crumb drawer' because any food remnants on the table could fall in.

cut Alternative name for canal or any artificial channel.

cut & fill Used to obtain a level bed by excavating cuttings and using the excess soil for the construction of embankments.

cutlass bearing Aft bearing for the propeller shaft (where it emerges through the hull), made of neoprene to allow angular flexibility. Most prop shafts on inland boats are fitted with metal bearings, however, as being more resistant to water-borne grit and fishing line.

cut water A point formed at the foot of the pier of a river bridge to separate the flow of water through arches either side.

D

davit Small crane, sometimes in pairs used to hoist aboard or launch a **tender** or life boat.

day boats Working boats without cabins or sleeping accommodation, used for short distance traffic.

deckboard The triangular board at the after edge of a **narrowboat** foredeck which forms the forward **bulkhead** of the **cratch**.

deckhead Cabin ceiling. In strict nautical terms, it is the underside of a deck, but ceiling is also applied to the floor of the hold of **barges.**

dinette A table with a bench seat either side, which, in conjunction with the seat, can also be lowered to form a bed.

dinghy A small open boat, often used as **tender** to a cruiser. Also a small sailing boat.

displacement Water displaced equivalent to weight of a boat. In marine practice, various equations are used to calculate theoretical displacements, but only actual weight is relevant on inland waterways.

dolly An upright cylindrical metal deck fitting to which ropes may be secured. See also **T-Stud.**

dolphin A staging for mooring or protection of a masonry bridge or lock structure not always connected to the bank or shore, but supported on massive timber or metal piles.

door A Fen term for **gate**; in the Fens, lock gates are called sluice doors.

double-chine Where a flat hull bottom transforms into flat hull sides via a flat intermediate surface, two hard edges (or chines) are formed. A feature of some early leisure **narrowboat** styles (like the Harborough and Fernie hulls), more often used now on wider steel boats.

draught The maximum underwater depth of a vessel's hull.

draw 1. To draw (eg a **paddle**), means to open so as to allow water to pass through. Reverse is to 'lower', 'drop' or 'shut in'. 2. The amount of water a vessel draws is her **draught.**

dredge To clean the bottom of a waterway and also to deepen it.

drive To drift a boat stern first with the tide dragging an anchor or mud weight on the bottom to give steerage.

drugging Thames term for **drive.**

E

EA Environment Agency – incorporates the old National Rivers Authority. Responsible for monitoring the condition of Britain's natural waterways (even some coastal parts), whether navigable or not. Also the navigation authority for the river Thames (and some other south-eastern rivers), and for Anglian waterways (excluding the Norfolk Broads). As such, it is jointly involved with BW (qv) in harmonising boat safety standards.

ebb The period during a tidal cycle when sea level is falling.

'ellum Traditional term for the rudder of a **narrowboat**.

entrance The forward part of the hull below the waterline.

eyot An island (small) on the Thames.

F

fairlead Deck fitting to guide ropes and reduce wear.

fend off To push a boat clear of another boat or object, either by hand or with the **boat hook** or portable **fender** etc; similarly to push an object away from the boat.

fender Traditionally rope or, nowadays sometimes, plastic object to protect the sides, **bows** and **sterns** of boats.

fettling Tidying up a boat, making minor repairs and touching up paint.

fiddle A raised lip or rail around the edge of a horizontal surface to prevent objects from sliding off.

flash An inland lake caused by subsidence of the ground through mining. Also small inland lakes forming part of the Basingstoke Canal.

flash or flush A body of accumulated water suddenly released to move grounded **barges** etc. Movement of water along a normally still canal caused by emptying of a **lock.**

flash lock An early means of controlling water levels on a river using a **weir** and single **navigation** opening, closeable with **paddles** or a **gate.**

flat A type of **barge** on the river Mersey which conducted the bulk of the traffic on that river and neighbouring **navigations.**

flight A series of **locks** built close together.

flood/flow (as **ebb** but . . . rising).

flood lock A **lock** at the upstream end of a section of canal on a river **navigation** used only during flood conditions.

fly boat Originally a **horse boat** using relays of horses which travelled day and night. The term now applies to any type of boat so travelling, so the boatman is said to be 'working fly'.

foredeck The deck area in the bow of a vessel.

fore-well A well in the bows of a vessel, immediately astern of the **foredeck.**

frame Vertical and longitudinal steel sections inside the shell of a vessel. Frames provide some reinforcing effect, and are used for attaching the cabin's internal timberwork.

freeboard Height of deck above water, particularly the height any waves would have to reach to enter the boat. So freeboard might be to large **cockpit** drainholes, or to engine compartment ventilation grilles in hull sides.

G

gabbart Type of small sailing **barge.**

gang A number of Fen **lighters** chained together to carry cargo. There are usually five in a gang.

gang plank A means of getting from the boat to the bank (see also **running planks**).

gate The moveable wooden or steel device for keeping water in a **lock.**

gate paddle A **sluice** on a **gate** to allow water to enter or leave a **lock.**

gongoozler A term of unknown origin for someone who idly stands and stares at anything unusual, particularly boats.

grab rail A rail, usually fixed to the cabin roof, to give a secure handhold when moving along the deck or **gunwale.**

ground paddle A **sluice** provided to allow water to enter or leave a **lock** by way of a culvert through the masonry structure.

guard **Rubbing strake** of a hull. Used particularly in connection with the raised top rubbing strip round the bow of a **traditional-style narrowboat.**

guillotine gate A form of **lock gate** which is raised vertically in a frame. When it is lowered, it makes a seal with the bottom and sides of the chamber to keep the water in.

gunnel See **gunwale.**

gunwale The top edge of a vessel's side.

H

haling way A Fen term for a **towing path.**

handspike A length of wood used as a lever. On some **locks** on the Calder & Hebble Navigation a handspike is still needed for working lock **paddle gear** instead of a windlass. It is also used for working the anchor chain **capstan** or **bilge pump** on river **barges.**

hatch A horizontal opening with a moveable cover in the deck or **superstructure** of a vessel.

hauling bank/path Another name for **towing path.**

head (of a lock) The portion immediately above the top **gates,** the portion below the bottom **gates** being the **tail.**

heel post The vertical post of a **lock gate** which rests against the **hollow quoin** of the lock side.

helm Steering wheel, not the **tiller** – although the tiller/ rudder of working boats was colloquially referred to as the **'ellum.**

hold in/hold out Used by boatmen as directions for steering, in reference to the position of the **towing path.** 'Hold in' means hold the boat in to the towing path side of the canal and vice versa.

hollow quoin The rounded recess in which the **heel post** of

a **lock gate** is fitted, and in which it partially revolves when being opened and closed.

horse boat A small open boat that ferried the horses from one side of the **navigation** to the other when the **towpath** changed side but there was no bridge. Also loosely used to describe a horse drawn **narrowboat.**

horse marine A man who contracted for the haulage of vessels by horse on the canals of Yorkshire.

Hotchkiss cones Small internal paddlewheel system sometimes used for powering former **butties** or horse-drawn **narrowboats.**

Humber keel **Barge,** based on Yorkshire waterways, originally sailing with a square rig. Hold was 7ft 6in (2.3m) deep. Different sizes traded onto different waterways radiating from the Humber Estuary. Eg Sheffield **keels** are 61ft 6in x 15ft 6in (18.8m x 4.8m); Calder & Hebble keels known as **West Country keels** were limited to 57ft 6in x 14ft 2in (17.6m x 4.3m).

Humber sloop A fore-and-aft rigged sailing **barge** based on the Humber waterways, similar to **Humber keel** except in rig.

hydraulic drive Drive transmitted from engine to propeller hydraulically instead of via a conventional gear-box.

I

ice plates Thin iron or steel sheeting nailed to a wooden hull at both loaded and empty water lines to protect from the cutting action of broken ice.

inboard motor An engine mounted within a vessel's hull.

inclined plane A device on wheels which lifts boats from one level to another without using **locks,** either afloat in a tank or in a dry cradle on a slope fitted with rails.

ing Water meadow (particularly Yorkshire).

invert An inverted arch of brickwork or masonry, used chiefly in canal work to form the bottom of **locks,** bridges and tunnels in cases where lateral or upward pressure has to be resisted.

IWA Inland Waterways Association – a voluntary body set up in 1946 to rescue Britain's waterways from threatened dereliction. Represents the interests of all waterways users – not just boaters. Its fund campaigning includes several rallies, of which the best known is the National Waterways Festival, held every August.

IWAAC Inland Waterways Amenity Advisory Council. An advisory body (or QANGO) set up in 1968 to advise British Waterways (qv) and the Government on use and management of waterways under BW's jurisdiction.

J

jack clough A wooden **ground paddle** operated by a lever which pivots to open or close the culvert.

joey Term for a **day boat** or boatman working short haul traffic, particularly in the Birmingham area. The boatmen lived ashore and their craft had only minimal cabin accommodation, if any.

Josher Colloquial name for a working boat belonging to carrying company Fellows Morton & Clayton Limited – derived from Joshua Fellows.

K

keb A rake made from iron which is used for fishing up coal or other articles from the bottom of canals.

kedge anchor Anchor used for **warping**. Also called **kedger** or **cadger**. Also used trailed behind a boat moving **stern** first with the tide to slow the boat down and give steerage. Called **drugging** on the Thames.

kedger Alternative name for **kedge anchor** or **cadger**.

keel 1. One or more parallel longitudinal fins on the underside of the hull, strong enough for a boat to sit on when not afloat. Main function is to improve directional stability through water. Not needed in conventional square-sectioned **narrowboats** because the flat hull sides grip water. 2. Square rigged sailing **barge.**

keelson As **keel**, but inside the boat, for structural reinforcement.

ketch Square-rigged sailing **barge** used on the river Trent.

knee Bracing piece or frame fixed part the way up the side and across the bottom of the boat, so holding the vessel in shape. A wooden knee is usually made out of timber which has grown with a suitable natural curve. **Composite** craft and **narrowboats** may have wrought iron or steel knees made with a corrugated section to provide rigidity.

knot Unit of speed. One nautical mile per hour; one nautical mile is 1.152 statute miles, seven knots = 8mph). Inland boaters prefer the conventional statute mile, and miles per hour.

L

land water Drainage water entering a navigation from the land.

LASH *Lighter Aboard Ship*. A system of carrying special **barges** from the European inland waterways aboard a mother ship to the USA. Introduced in 1971.

lay Direction in which the strands of a rope are twisted (right or left handed). A laid rope is one in which the strands are twisted together, as distinct from being woven or plaited.

lee-board Large pear-shaped wooden board on each side of certain flat bottomed sailing **barges** (eg **keels, sloops, ketches**). That on the **leeward** side is lowered into the water when running against the wind to prevent the vessel being simply pushed downwind. Owing to the need for shallow draught, such vessels could not have conventional fixed **keels.**

leeward In the direction away from the wind (downwind).

left bank An often confusing term referring to the left bank of a river *when travelling downstream*

legging Method used to propel unpowered boats through tunnels with no **towing path**. Involved the boatman lying on his back and using his feet to walk along the side or top of arch.

lengthsman A canal company's employee responsible for routine maintenance of a certain piece or length of waterway.

let go To drop anchor.

let off A **sluice** that enables the discharge of water from the canal in rainy weather so it does not overflow its banks. Also used to empty a canal for maintenance.

level A long **pound** in an artificial waterway, sometimes given a distinguishing name, eg Birmingham Level.

lift bridge A movable bridge, the deck of which is either hinged or moves vertically upwards.

lighter A type of usually unpowered **barge** (with **swim** ends, in the Thames area). Often limited to dock and harbour work handling cargo between local **wharves** and ships. Others were used to relieve larger craft of part of their cargoes, lightening the larger vessel, with the consequent reduction in **draught** allowing access to their discharging berth.

list When looking end-on, the angle which a boat sits from vertical.

lock A means of raising or lowering a boat between water levels, comprising a chamber with lock **gate**(s) and **paddle**(s) at each end.

lock, to To work a vessel through a **lock**.

lock key See **windlass**.

lockwheel, to To prepare or 'set' a **lock** ahead of a vessel.

long boat River Severn area term for **narrowboat** – which in that area were deeper and bluffer than many and carried up to 40 tons.

lutchet A socket into which a sailing or towing mast can be stepped.

M

mast step The recess into which the mast is located within the bottom of a boat.

mitre gate One of two **lock gates** closing together to form a shallow v-shape – see **breast post**.

monkey boat Old term for **narrowboat** in the London and Thames area. Thought to originate with an early narrowboat carrier named Monk.

mud weight Weight, usually of iron, used as an anchor where bottom conditions do not provide a good holding for a conventional anchor, eg a silty riverbed.

N

nab Point of land, often between two confluent rivers.

NABO National Association of Boat Owners – relatively young voluntary body set up by boat owners, who consider that IWA (qv) does not fully represent their interests.

narrowboat Measuring approximately 70ft to 72ft (21.3m to 21.9m) long by 6ft 10in to 7ft (2.1m) beam. Used extensively throughout the Midland canal system. Also known as a **monkey boat** or **long boat**.

navigation A navigable river or canal.

navvy Originally a canal construction worker. An abbreviation of Navigator. Later applied to steam excavators.

neap tides The tides having least range in a tidal cycle – that is, lowest high water and highest low water – caused by the gravitational pull of sun and moon being at right angles to one another.

ness The shallow inside of the bend of a river. See **bight**.

noddy boat Derogatory term for a small boat or cruiser.

noggin Timber frame attached to the steel frame of a steel shell. Makes it easier to fit the internal ply/timber lining panels in place, and reduces transfer of cold from steel shell to linings.

NRA National Rivers Authority, now incorporated in Environment Agency (**EA**).

number one Applied to the boat or its owner when it was owned by the actual boatman that was working it, instead of a firm or company.

NYHA: National Yacht Harbours Association – body

representing many marina operators. A subsidiary organisation of BMIF (qv).

O

oakum Hemp or hessian treated with linseed and twisted into a sort of loose rope used to **caulk** boats.

outboard motor Portable engine for dinghies or larger boats, usually mounted on the **transom** or **counter**, sometimes over one side or in a **well** aft. Generally can be tilted forward to raise the propeller in shallow water.

outdrive Where an inboard motor drives a propeller unit mounted outboard on a vessel's **transom** through a system of shafts and bevel gears; also called a 'Z-Drive', 'Sterndrive', or an 'Inboard-Outboard' drive.

overflow A **weir** set in the bank of a canal to take away excess water and prevent flooding. Also called storm **weir**.

P

paddle The sliding cover of a **sluice,** the opening (or **drawing**) of which allows passage of water.

paddle gear An inclusive term for the mechanism by which a **paddle** is operated.

painter Line used to secure or tow a small boat.

pawl Catch which engages in **paddle gear** to prevent it dropping.

pen A Fen and north eastern term for a **lock** chamber. To pen means **to lock** a vessel.

pigeon box Ventilator on cabin top of a **traditional-style narrowboat**. Box-shaped with opening top panels – which are often pitched like a house roof, and usually fitted with tiny **portholes**. Traditionally made of timber; now usually of steel.

piling Long heavy sections of metal, reinforced concrete, or timber, driven vertically into the bed of a waterway or unstable ground to support a structure or protect the banks from wave action.

pintle The cast iron or steel pin fitted to the foot of a wooden **gate heel post** which acts as a bearing in a cup built into the bed of the **lock** chamber.

pipe cot A **berth** made up of canvas slung between a tubular frame.

pitch As applied to a propeller, the theoretical forward distance through which it would travel during one revolution, assuming no slip.

pointing door A Fenland term for a **mitre gate** of a **lock** or drainage **sluice.**

port Left side of boat when looking forward.

portage A term for lifting craft around **locks** and **sluices**. This means that light craft can use a derelict waterway even though the locks are out of order.

porthole Circular window in cabin, or hull, side.

pound The level stretch of water on a canal between two **locks**.

pound lock Sometimes applied to the ordinary **lock** with two sets of **gates** in distinction to the term **flash lock**, or a **staunch** or navigation weir, which has only one set of gates.

powerhead The engine of an outboard motor.

pram canopy Vinyl pram-type canopy fitted on hinged frames. Used with a windscreen to provide weatherproof shelter for the helmsman in the aft **cockpit** of a cruiser. Equally useful for **narrowboats** but not so popular, because it does not suit narrowboat appearance.

puddle Clay worked up with water and spread in layers on the bottom and sides of a canal or reservoir, to make it watertight.

pulpit Guard rail around extreme **bow** of boat, high enough to lean against when standing on the **foredeck.**

push (tug) A tug designed to push, rather than pull, boats. Push 'towing' is the standard on the Continent and in America.

pushpit Guard rail around the extreme **stern** of a boat, high enough to lean against when standing on the **counter** or **transom**. Could also be called a **taffrail** although a boat might have a taffrail inside a pushpit.

push tow An assembly of **push tug** and unpowered **barge(s).**

Q

quant A Norfolk Broads term for a pole or **shaft**, usually with a flat end to enable it to be thrust into the mud, used to propel sailing boats when there is no wind.

quant, to To propel a vessel by means of a **quant**.

R

rack 1. **Reach** of a river – especially the Trent. 2. An Irish term for **gate paddle** – a land rack is a **ground paddle.**

ram's head A Z-shaped piece made from steel which is attached to the upper end of a **narrowboat's** rudder stock, and to which the **tiller** is fitted.

ranter Term for **gate paddle**.

RBOA Residential Boat Owners Association – represents the interests of live-aboard boaters, and provides information for would-be's.

RCD Recreational Craft Directive – Europe's first major impact on UK waterways has been mandatory standards for the construction of new boats and for builders to maintain supporting technical documentation. This was optional from June 1996 and mandatory from June 1998. The initial certificate lasts for 4 years, after which boats must be examined to ensure that they have not been altered or that they comply with the BSS (qv). The requirement to create a library of documentation had a bad reception from an industry not used to producing paperwork. Some builders struggled with the first boat but found subsequent ones easier while others employ a surveyor to handle the documentation.

reach A straight stretch of a river – especially the Thames.

reefing To reduce sail area by rolling or tying up part of the sail, used in times of strong wind.

registration Inland waterway vessels which were used as a dwelling had to be registered with a local authority under the terms of the Canal Boats Act 1877 & 1884. The local authority was responsible for the education of children living aboard and for sanitary inspection of the cabins. The name of the authority, their number and any identifying mark had to be clearly displayed on the boat. This had nothing to do with the possibility that any boats trading inland were Registered British Ships. This latter is normally a requirement for vessels trading internationally on tidal waters or to prevent fraud in the case of craft which have been mortgaged. The name & port of registry is permanently marked on the stern and the official number is cut into one of the vessel's frames.

right bank An often confusing term referring to right bank of a river *when travelling downstream.*

rimers The posts in the removable portions of **flash locks** or **weirs** on the Upper Thames against which the weir **paddles** are placed.

riser Another name for **staircase locks**.

Rodney boatman Derogatory term for a boatman who did not keep his boat smart.

rond anchor Stockless anchor with a single fluke used when tying up to an unprotected bank.

round-bilge When the hull bottom transforms gradually to hull sides through a curve, the hull shape is described as 'round-bilged'.

roving bridge A bridge that enables horses to change **towpaths** without having to be detached from the rope when crossing the bridge.

rubbing strake A reinforcing strip attached to the hull of a boat to lessen damage to the sides.

running planks Planks set up over a **narrowboat**'s hold to allow access to the **foredeck**. Also known as planks or gang planks. Serve to support the top cloth covering the cargo.

RYA Royal Yachting Association, mainly concerned with coastal cruising, but offers much advice on inland boating abroad.

S

scour Bank of silt caused by a flow of water.

scumble Painted graining on cabin woodwork – interior or exterior.

scuppers Holes through **bulwarks** for draining decks.

Seffle Engine manufacturer known for single cylinder **semi-diesels** similar to **Bolinder** introduced for **narrowboat** propulsion by Willow Wren Canal Carrying Co in the early 1950s. Unlike Bolinders, Seffle engines are fitted with a reverse gear box and have a steady beat.

semi-diesel A compression ignition internal combustion engine which requires a special 'bulb' on the cylinder head to be preheated, usually with a blowlamp, before starting.

semi-trad stern/style A style of pleasure **narrowboat** based on the lines of former working boats but with a larger deck behind the accommodation which is surrounded with high side plates that continue the line of the cabin.

set, to To set a **staunch** is to close it so that the water may accumulate. To set a **lock** is to make it ready for boat to pass through.

shaft Canal term for a **boat hook** with a long wooden pole. **Narrowboats** also carried a cabin shaft – less than 8ft (2.5m) in length and easily kept to hand on the back cabin roof.

shaft, to To propel a boat between **locks** or moorings or through a tunnel with a long **shaft** as an alternative to **bow hauling** or **legging**.

sheer When looking sideways at a boat, the curve upwards to bow or stern. As in the gentle curve upwards of the aft 8ft (2.5m) or so of a **traditional-style** cabin.

shell The empty structure of a glass-fibre or steel boat.

shoal Shallow water.

Shroppie Affectionate term for the Shropshire Union Canal.

shutts False floor in the bottom of the hold.

side paddle The **paddle** situated in the culvert connecting a **lock** chamber and a **side pond**.

side pond A brick or masonry lined reservoir alongside a **lock** chamber used for the temporary storage of water which would otherwise run to waste as the **lock** is worked.

sill (of a lock) The bar of masonry often faced with a timber sealing piece below water against which the bottom of the **lock gates** rest when closed.

single lever control A hand lever combining the functions of both gear operation and throttle control.

skeg A short piece of metal running fore-and-aft beneath the propeller, for which it provides some protection; also functions as a housing and bearing for the lower end of the rudder stock.

slack water 1. A period when no tidal movement occurs. 2. The relatively still water outside the main current in a river.

slacker Fenland term for **paddle**.

slide Sliding **hatch** over a cabin door in a **narrowboat**.

slip(way) Paved incline from land into water, used for launching or recovering boats on trailers or trollies.

sloop Fore-and-aft-rigged sister to the **keel**.

sluice A device to control volume or flow of water.

snubber Heavy towing rope, about 70ft in length, used by powered **narrowboats** to tow their **butties** on longer **pounds**.

sponson Buoyancy pontoon fitted alongside another vessel to increase stability – often used in conjunction with narrow beam dredgers.

Springer Type of pleasure **narrowboat** formerly constructed by Springer Engineering of Market Harborough. The first builders to 'manufacture' narrowboats on a production line.

springs When lying alongside a pier, quay or another boat, spring lines are required in addition to **bow** and **stern** lines to prevent the boat from moving forward or aft, and to keep it parallel, regardless of the effects of wind and tidal stream or current. A fore spring is secured at the **bow** and extends aft to the mooring whilst a **stern** spring extends forwards from the aftermost **cleat.**

spring tides Tides of greatest range (ie greatest height at high water with least height at low water) occurring twice in a lunar month when the gravitational pull of sun and moon are in the same direction.

spritsail A fore and aft sail supported and extended by a sprit, which is a boom set diagonally across a sail from the mast up to the peak.

staircase locks A series of two or more **lock** chambers each of which leads directly into the next without a **pound**/stretch of water between two locks. The bottom **gates** of one lock thus form the top gates of the one below.

staith(e) A coal loading **wharf**, on the Humber, Trent, and Ouse.

stands The immediate support for the **running planks** of a **narrowboat**.

stank A temporary water-tight dam constructed of **piling** from within which the water can be pumped to enable below water repairs to be carried out.

starboard Right side of boat when looking forward.

staunch An appliance for overcoming changes of level on

a navigable river. Also known as a 'navigation weir' or a **flash lock**.

stem Bow of boat. Also the practice of using the bow to push against an object – as in pushing open **lock gates** (frowned upon), or holding bow against bank when turning boat round, or holding a boat under engine power against a flow of water ("stemming the tide").

stem head The top of the foremost timber or steel member forming the **bow** of a boat, taken above **foredeck** level and rounded to prevent the bow jamming under projections.

stemmed up A boatman's term for running aground on a mud-bank. To **stem** an object, such as a bridge, is to collide with it head on.

stem post Vertical bar forming extreme **bow** of boat.

stern The back of a boat.

stern drive See **outdrive**.

stern gland An arrangement – usually by means of greased packing in a stuffing box – whereby water is prevented from entering a vessel at the point where the propeller shaft passes through the hull.

stern post Vertical edge of hull or fin, through which prop shaft emerges.

stern rail An enclosed safety rail around the **stern** of a vessel.

stern tube Casing which contains the prop shaft's aft bearing (where it emerges through **stern post**). Also contains a waterproof seal at forward end of bearing.

stop gate(s) Made in the form of **lock gates**, but always kept open except when needed. On long **pounds** of canals and embankments it is usual for stop gates to be fitted at intervals, in case of a leak or burst so that the escape of water can be confined to that portion of the canal between the two gates.

stop grooves Vertical grooves, usually provided at the **head** and **tail** of a **lock** and in other situations where underwater repairs may have to be carried out, into which **stop planks** can be inserted to form a temporary dam or **stank**.

stop or stop lock A **lock** with a small rise in level sited at the junction of two canals, originally constructed to prevent loss of water from one canal to another.

stoppage A temporary closure of a waterway while it is repaired. **stop planks** Wooden boards used to seal off section of canal.

strake Line of planks, running the length of a vessel's sides. Garboard strake is the one next to the keel on a V-bottomed boat or to the **chine** angle on a flat bottomed craft, whilst top strake receives the **gunwale**. Raised rubbing strip along hull side.

strap Term used for specific rope used in navigation – usually short and strong and often placed around a **bollard** ashore to slow the vessel's movement, but see **cross strap.**

stud The T-headed pin fitted on **bow** and **stern** of a **narrowboat** to which mooring lines are attached.

stuffing box Traditional type of seal at forward end of the aft prop shaft bearing (see **stern tube**). Uses combination of special rope packing and grease to prevent water entering the hull.

summit level The highest **pound** in a section of canal.

superstructure The upper works of a vessel above **gunwale** level.

swan's neck Evocatively named curved steel bar that connects the top of the rudder to the **tiller.**

sweep A long oar with a narrow flat blade.

swim The tapers at forward and aft end of a **narrowboat's** hull sides – from full hull width to **stem post** or to **stern post.**

swim ended (headed) A vessel's **bow** or **stern**, usually rectangular in plan, with an outward taper from the water-line. eg Thames **lighter.**

swim, to A boat light in **draught** and which answers readily to the **helm** is described by boatmen as 'a good swimmer', or may be said to 'swim well'.

swing bridge A movable bridge which pivots horizontally on some form of turntable.

T

table cupboard Distinctive table in traditional **boatman's cabin**. Hinged along bottom edge so that it folds up to become door to cupboard. Sometimes also used as a feature in main cabins of modern **narrowboats.**

T-stud A metal T-shaped deck fitting, to which ropes may be secured.

tachometer Gauge for measuring engine speed (in revolutions per minute).

tackle 1. Boatman's name for the harness of a boat horse. 2. Seaman's name for a system of ropes and pulleys used to hoist or move heavy objects eg cargo, sails or anchors.

taff rail Rail around aft **cockpit,** usually high enough and wide enough to sit on.

tail The portion immediately below the bottom **gates** of a **lock**; the portion above the top gates being the head.

tender A small boat or **dinghy** used to transport the boat crew to and from the boat on a midstream mooring. Usually towed astern or carried ready for use in **davits.**

ticket drawer Small drawer just inside the aft door of a traditional **boatman's cabin.**

tiller Lever against which the steerer pushes to steer a **narrowboat**. Often removable.

timber heads Posts formed from extended upper ends of hull framing to which mooring lines could be tied.

toll The charge payable by a trader for the use of a canal.

Tom Pudding Coal-carrying compartment boat used in 'trains' of up to 19 in the North East until the 1980s. Designed by Bartholomew, engineer of the Aire & Calder Navigation Co.

tonneau Fitted vinyl or canvas storage cover stretched over **cockpit.**

top planks See **running planks.**

towing path A path by the side of the canal used by horses towing boats.

towpath see **towing path.**

traditional-style/trad stern A style of pleasure craft based on the lines of former working **narrowboats** in which the **stern** deck extends only up to 3ft (0.9m) astern of the accommodation and the tiller is arranged so that the steerer (or helmsman) stands within the aft doors of the cabin.

transom The flat **stern** member of a square sterned vessel.

trim Angle at which a boat sits relative to the water, looking from the side. Level trim, with sidedeck parallel to the waterline, is said to be ideal for narrowboats, although invariably sidedecks rise gradually towards the **bow.**

trow (rhymes with *crow*). Sailing **barge** used on the river Severn. There were two types of trow: large, working on Severn Estuary and Bristol Channel; small, not working below Gloucester but going up river when depth allowed.

tub boats Small box boats carrying from 3 to 5 tons – especially used on the isolated Shropshire Canal system.

tumblehome Angle at which the cabin side of a **narrowboat** leans in, when seen end-on. Most narrowboat hull sides also tumble home – with slight lean-in from top **rubbing strake** to the sidedeck; and from the top rubbing strake down to the **chine.** So 'slab-sided' narrowboats are not actually vertical at any point along their sides.

turf-sided locks Pound **lock**s, usually on river **navigations,** where the only masonry provided is immediately in support of the **gates.** The chamber sides are simple earth banks sloping outwards.

turnbridge See **swing bridge.**

turned round A **lock** either emptied or filled for traffic in the opposite direction.

turns A system adopted at a **flight** of canal **locks** in dry weather in order to make the most use of the water. Each boat has to wait for a boat to come the opposite way, so as to make sure that the maximum amount of traffic passes for the minimum water consumed.

U

underpropped Having a propeller too small or too finely pitched to efficiently drive the boat.

W

wake The disturbed water astern of a moving boat.

warp A mooring rope. A towing rope. The rope cable attached to an anchor.

warping To carry a **kedge** anchor ahead of a **barge** in a **cog boat** to a fresh anchoring position, drop overboard, then winch the barge to that new position.

wash Waves along the bank created by a vessel's movement through the water.

Waterways World The Number One inland waterway magazine.

weed hatch A watertight compartment with a removable lid, in the **stern** of the boat, which provides access to the propeller from deck level, used mostly for the purpose of removing rubbish.

weir An overspill dam placed across a river for regulating the depth and flow of a river.

well deck The floor of a well or **cockpit.**

West Country The name for the flat-bottomed **swim headed barges** that traded upon the Upper Thames. Bargemen working "beyond the flux of the tide" were said to be travelling "West Country". Also used in reference to the Calder & Hebble Navigation in Yorkshire.

wharf Structure built of brick, concrete, masonry or timber, for cargo loading or discharge. In some places also known as a **staith.**

wherry A decked sailing vessel of very shallow **draught** used for the transport of small quantities of freight on the Norfolk Broads. On the Thames it refers to a rowed passenger boat, used as a water taxi.

wide boat A boat over 7ft (2.1m), but usually under 14ft

(4.3m), beam in use on canals with wide **locks.**

wind To turn a boat around. Pronounced with short 'i' as in win. Originates from use of wind or breeze to facilitate turning unpowered craft.

wind dodger Vinyl curtain stretched around a **taff rail** to provide shelter, and to prevent infants from falling overboard from the **cockpit.**

winding hole A bay in one bank of a canal to provide sufficient room for craft longer than the canal's width to turn around.

windlass 1. L-shaped handle for operating **paddles.** Has a square socket at one end to fit on the spindle operating the **paddle gear.** Also known as a crank in some districts. Sometimes termed 'lock key' today. 2. Drum winch with cranked handles or removable hand spikes used for raising an anchor.

wings Flat pieces of board rigged to lie on for the purpose of **legging** in tunnels when the tunnels are too wide for the leggers to reach the side walls with their feet from the boat's deck.

WRG Waterway Recovery Group – radical arm of IWA (qv). While the IWA campaigns, WRG takes direct action to recover waterways with shovels, JCBs and concrete mixers.

Y

YDSA Yacht Designers & Surveyors Association – the professional oganisation for narrowboat and cruiser surveyors. Sets qualitative and experience standards for entry.

Z

Z-drive See **outdrive.**

APPENDIX 6

DATING THE PLATE

British Waterways introduced registration plates for boats on its territory in 1981. These are useful for identifying the date of first registration. However a boat may be older than its registration for several reasons. For example, the system lumps all craft built before plating began as '1980/81'. Similarly craft that began life on other authorities' waterways can only be dated to their first year of registration with BW.

From	To	Issue Date
UNPOWERED		
00001 –	00618	1987
00619 –	01117	1988
01118 –	01541	1989
01542 –	01979	1990
01980 –	02303	1991
02304 –	02401	1992
02402 –	02404	1995
14501		1989
PLASTIC		
30000 –	31125	1990
31126 –	31839	1991
31840 –	32054	1992
32055 –	39999	Written off
RED (TRADE PLATES)		
40000 –	40499	Undated
METAL		
45001 – 45505	1988	
45506 –	47299	1989
47300 –	49586	1990
49587 –	51320	1991
51321 –	52606	1992
52607 –	53554	1993
53555 –	54394	1994
54395 –	55000	1995
CRAFT ON BRIDGEWATER CANAL		
55001 –	55070	1987
55071 –	55166	1988
55167 –	55184	1989
55185 –	55194	1990
55195 –	55215	1991
55216 –	55229	1992
55230 –	55242	1993
55243 –	55275	1994
55276 –	55287	1995
55288 –	55302	1996
55303 –	55314	1997
55315 –	56322	1998
55323 –	55343	1999
55344 –		2000
METAL		
60000 –	60002	1988
60003 –	60008	1990
60009		1989
60010		1987
60011 –	70561	1980/1*

From	To	Issue Date
70562 –	71580	1984
71581 –	72567	1985
72568 –	72599	1986
72600 –	72999	1987
73000 –	73099	1983
73100 –	73800	1986
73801 –	74856	1987
74857 –	74999	1988
75000 –	75399	1983
75400 –	75999	1988
76000 –	77499	1982
77500 –	77599	1980/1*
77600 –	77699	1982
77700 –	79999	1980/1*
PLASTIC		
80000 –	80699	1988
80700 –	80999	1989
81000 –	81875	1984
81876 –	82886	1985
82887 –	83869	1986
83870 –	84860	1987
84861 –	84900	1988
84901 –	84999	1982
85000 –	86709	1980/1*
86710 –	87823	1982
87824 –	88687	1983
88688 –	89949	1984
89950 –	99999	1980/1*
PLASTIC		
100000 –	100024	BW use
100025 –	100888	1992
100889 –	101819	1993
101820 –	102947	1994
102948 –	104053	1995
100011 –	100024	1995
104054 –	105127	1996
105128 –	105899	1997
105900 –	106668	1998
106669 –	107357	1999
107358 –		2000
METAL		
500010 –	500398	1995
500399 –	501364	1996
501365 –	502357	1997
502358 –	503369	1998
503370 –	504424	1999
504425 –		2000

*Plates issued in 1980/1 include craft built before then.

Plastic plates were originally issued to craft under 20ft long.

Thanks to Chris Port of BW for compiling this list.

1